THE BOOK OF

PHOBIAS

&

MANIAS

Also by Kate Summerscale

The Queen of Whale Cay
The Suspicions of Mr Whicher
Mrs Robinson's Disgrace
The Wicked Boy
The Haunting of Alma Fielding

THE BOOK OF
PHOBIAS
&
MANIAS

A HISTORY OF OBSESSION

KATE SUMMERSCALE

PENGUIN BOOKS

PENGUIN BOOKS
An imprint of Penguin Random House LLC
penguinrandomhouse.com

Lines from "Counter-Attack" © Siegfried Sassoon and
reproduced by kind permission of the Estate of George Sassoon

Library of Congress record available at https://lccn.loc.gov/2022943198

ISBN 9780593489758 (hardcover)
ISBN 9780593489765 (ebook)

Printed in the United States of America
1st Printing

For Sam Randall

CONTENTS

INTRODUCTION 1

HOW TO USE THIS BOOK 7

A–Z OF PHOBIAS AND MANIAS

INTRODUCTION

We are all driven by our fears and desires, and sometimes we are in thrall to them. Benjamin Rush, a Founding Father of the United States, kicked off the craze for naming such fixations in 1786. Until then, the word 'phobia' (which is derived from Phobos, the Greek god of panic and terror) had been applied only to symptoms of physical disease, and the word 'mania' (from the Greek for 'madness') to social fashions. Rush recast both as psychological phenomena. 'I shall define phobia to be a fear of an imaginary evil,' he wrote, 'or an undue fear of a real one.' He listed eighteen phobias, among them terrors of dirt, ghosts, doctors and rats, and twenty-six new manias, including 'gaming-mania', 'military-mania' and 'liberty-mania'. Rush adopted a lightly comic tone – 'home phobia', he said, afflicted gentlemen who felt compelled to stop off at the tavern after work – but over the next century psychiatrists developed a more complex understanding of these traits. They came to see phobias and manias as lurid traces of our evolutionary and personal histories, manifestations both of submerged animal instincts and of desires that we had repressed.

A string of manias was added to Rush's list in the early part of the nineteenth century, and a great flurry of phobias and manias at the century's close. The phobias included irrational fears of public spaces, small spaces, blushing and being buried alive (agoraphobia, claustrophobia, erythrophobia, taphephobia). The manias included compulsions to dance, to wander, to count and to pluck hair (choreomania, dromomania, arithmomania, trichotillomania). And we have continued to discover new anxieties: nomophobia (a fear of being without a mobile phone), bambakomallophobia (a dread of cotton wool), coulrophobia (a horror of clowns), trypophobia (an aversion to clusters of holes). Many have been given more than one name – a fear of flying, for instance, appears in this book as aerophobia, but is also known as aviophobia, pteromerhanophobia and, more straightforwardly, flying phobia.

All phobias and manias are cultural creations: the moment at which each was identified – or invented – marked a change in how we thought about ourselves. A few of those described here are not psychiatric diagnoses at all, being words coined to name prejudice (homophobia, xenophobia), to mock fads or fashions (Beatlemania, tulipomania) or to make a joke (aibohphobia, hippopotomonstrosesquipediophobia, the supposed fears of palindromes and long words). But most of the entries in this volume describe real and sometimes tormenting conditions. Phobias and manias reveal our inner landscapes – what we recoil from or lurch towards, what we can't get out of our heads. Collectively, they are the most common anxiety disorders of our time.

'Phobia particularises anxiety,' observes the literary scholar David Trotter, 'to the point at which it can be felt and known *in its particularity*, and thus counteracted or got around.' A mania, too, can condense a host of fears and desires. These private obsessions are the madnesses of the sane; perhaps the madnesses that keep us sane by crystallising our frights and fancies, and allowing us to proceed as if everything else makes sense.

To be diagnosed as a phobia, according to the American Psychiatric Association's *Diagnostic and Statistical Manual 5* (2013), a fear must be excessive, unreasonable and have lasted for six months or more; and it must have driven the individual to avoid the feared situation or object in a way that interferes with normal functioning. The *DSM-5* distinguishes social phobias, which are overwhelming fears of social situations, from specific phobias, which can be divided into five types: animal phobias; natural environment phobias (fears of heights, for instance, or of water); blood, injection and injury phobias; situational phobias (such as entrapment in closed spaces); and other extreme fears, such as a dread of vomiting, choking or noise.

Though specific phobias can be more responsive to treatment than any other anxious conditions, most people don't report them, choosing instead to avoid the objects that they fear – it is thought that only one in eight people with such a phobia seeks help. This makes it difficult to measure their prevalence. But a review in *The Lancet Psychiatry* in 2018, which synthesised twenty-five surveys carried out between 1984 and 2014, found that 7.2 per cent of us are likely to experience a specific phobia at some point in our lives, and a survey carried out by the World Health Organization in 2017, using data from twenty-two countries, came to very similar conclusions. These studies also indicated that specific phobias are much more common in children than adults, that the rates halve among the elderly, and that women are twice as phobic as men. This means that, on average, one woman in ten experiences a specific phobia, and one man in twenty. National surveys suggest that a further 7 per cent of Americans and 12 per cent of Britons have social phobias.

These figures are for phobic disorders, which interfere with everyday life. Many more of us have milder aversions or dreads that we sometimes refer to as phobias: a strong dislike of public speaking or of visiting the dentist, of the sound of thunder, or the sight of spiders. In the US, more than 70 per cent of people say they have an unreasonable fear. When I began researching this book, I did not think of myself as having any particular phobias – apart, perhaps, from my teenage dread of blushing and an enduring anxiety about flying – but by the time I'd finished I had talked myself into almost every one. Some terrors are no sooner imagined than felt.

The causes of these conditions are much disputed. Phobias of specific objects, words or numbers can seem like ancient superstitions, vestiges of pagan beliefs. The American psychologist Granville Stanley Hall, who catalogued 132 phobias in an essay of 1914, observed that some children developed an obsessive fear after having a fright. Shock, he wrote, was 'a fertile mother of phobias'. Sigmund Freud, who analysed phobic symptoms in two famous studies of 1909, proposed that a phobia was a suppressed fear displaced onto an external object: both an expression of anxiety and a defence against it. 'Fleeing from an internal danger is a difficult enterprise,' he explained. 'One can save oneself from an external danger by flight.'

Evolutionary psychologists argue that many phobias are adaptive: our fears of heights and snakes are hardwired in our brains to prevent us from falling from heights or being bitten by snakes; our disgust at rats and slugs protects us from disease. Phobias of this kind may be part of our evolutionary inheritance, 'biologically prepared' fears designed to shield us from external threats. A phobic reaction does feel like an instinctive reflex. On detecting a threatening object or situation, our primitive brains release chemicals to help us fight or flee, and our physical responses – a shudder or a flinch, a wave of heat or nausea – seem to take us over.

Evolution may help to explain why women are disproportionately phobic, especially in the years in which they are able to bear children: their heightened caution protects their offspring as well as themselves. But phobias may also seem more common in women because the social environment is more hostile to them – they have more reasons to be afraid – or because their fears are more often dismissed as irrational. Evolutionary accounts of phobia are based on post hoc reasoning, and they don't account for all phobias, nor why some individuals are phobic and others are not. In 1919 the American behavioural psychologists James Broadus Watson and Rosalie Rayner devised an experiment to show that a phobia could be induced by conditioning. In the 1960s, Albert Bandura demonstrated that a phobia could also be learnt by direct exposure to the anxieties and irrational fears of someone else, such as a parent. Families pass on fear as much by example as by genes. Even if we are predisposed to certain anxieties, they need to be triggered by experience or education.

If a phobia is a compulsion to avoid something, a mania is usually a compulsion to do something. The great French psychiatrist Jean-Étienne Esquirol invented the concept of monomania, or specific mania, early in the nineteenth century, while his countryman Pierre Janet wrote tender and attentive case studies of the men and women he treated for such conditions at the turn of the twentieth century. Most of the manias in this book are obsessive behaviours, centred on an object, action or idea – hair-plucking, for example, or hoarding. Their prevalence is hard to assess, partly because modern medicine has subsumed many into categories such as addiction, obsessive-compulsive disorder, body-focused repetitive disorder, impulse-control disorder and borderline personality disorder. Like phobias, they are sometimes ascribed to chemical imbalances in the brain and sometimes to difficult or forbidden feelings. Often they magnify ordinary desires – the wishes to laugh, shout, buy things, steal things, tell a lie, light a fire, have sex, get high, pick at a scab, surrender to misery, be adored.

Along with the private urges, this book includes several communal manias, in which people have danced, giggled, trembled or screamed together. In the 1860s, for instance, a bout of demonomania seized the Alpine town of Morzine, and in the 1960s wild laughing broke out by a lake in Tanzania. These shared convulsions can seem like rebellions, in which unacknowledged feelings surge into view, and they can occasionally force us to reconsider what is rational. When we decide that a particular behaviour is manic or phobic, we mark out our cultural as well as our psychological boundaries: we indicate the beliefs on which our social world is constructed. These borders shift over time, and in a moment of collective crisis – a war, a pandemic – they can change fast.

A phobia or a mania acts like a spell, endowing an object or an action with mysterious meaning and giving it the power to possess and transform us. These conditions may be oppressive, but they also enchant the world around us, making it as scary and vivid as a fairy tale. They exert a physical hold, like magic, and in doing so reveal our own strangeness.

HOW TO USE
THIS BOOK

The phobias and manias in this book are arranged alphabetically but can be grouped into themes like these:

A fear of **ANIMALS** in general is known as **zoophobia**, while our aversions to particular types of creature include **acarophobia** (a horror of mites), **ailurophobia** (cats), **arachnophobia** (spiders), **batrachophobia** (frogs and toads), **cynophobia** (dogs), **entomophobia** (insects), **hippophobia** (horses), **musophobia** (rats and mice), **ophidiophobia** (snakes) and **ornithophobia** (birds).

Among the **TEXTURES** that disturb us are cotton wool (an aversion known as **bambakomallophobia**), fur (**doraphobia**), feathers (**pteronophobia**) and clusters of holes (**trypophobia**).

The **COMMUNAL CRAZES** that have gripped us over the centuries include **bibliomania**, an obsession with books, **Beatlemania**, a passion for the Beatles, **demonomania**, a belief that one is demonically possessed, **laughing mania**, which broke out among Tanzanian schoolgirls in the 1960s, **Plutomania**, a fetish for money and later an enthusiasm for a planet, and **syllogomania**, an obsession with gathering objects. The seventeenth-century Dutch frenzy for tulips became known as **tulipomania** and the bursts of compulsive dancing in medieval Europe as **choreomania**.

The **MASS PANICS** that have seized us include **kayak phobia,** which affected Inuit seal-hunters in Greenland in the late nineteenth century, and **coulrophobia**, a fear of clowns that emerged in America a hundred years later.

Disgust or fear about our **BODIES** can manifest as a terror of blood or needles (**blood-injection-injury phobia**) or dentists (**odontophobia**), as a dread of vomiting (**emetophobia**), ageing (**gerascophobia**) or of giving birth (**tokophobia**). Some of us develop an aversion to smells (**osmophobia**) and some can't bear to use public lavatories (**public urination phobia**).

The **INANIMATE OBJECTS** that most often become a focus of fear include balloons (**globophobia**), buttons (**koumpounophobia**) and dolls (**pediophobia**). The compulsive hoarding of objects is known as **syllogomania**, while compulsive shopping is **oniomania** and stealing is **kleptomania**.

Ideas about the **EVOLUTIONARY PURPOSE** of phobias and manias appear throughout this book. There is the mystery of why the sight of blood should make some of us faint (**blood-injection-injury phobia**), and the puzzle of **arachnophobia,** the fear of spiders, which is one of the most common and extensively investigated of all our fears. Our fear of heights (**acrophobia**) seems more obviously self-protective, as do our fears of water (**aquaphobia, hydrophobia, thalassophobia**), thunder (**brontophobia**), small spaces (**claustrophobia**), forests (**xylophobia**), open spaces (**agoraphobia**) and darkness (**nyctophobia**). An impulse to shield ourselves from harm probably also lies behind disgust-related phobias such as **pogonophobia** (an aversion to beards), **mysophobia** (fear of germs), **entomophobia** (fear of insects) and **trypophobia** (an aversion to clusters of holes). The same feelings may inform compulsive behaviours such as hair-plucking (**trichotillomania**), nail-pulling (**onychotillomania**), skin-picking (**dermatillomania**) and hoarding (**syllogomania**). Even our fears of the dentist (**odontophobia**) and of blushing (**erythrophobia**) can be traced to our species' earliest history. Evolutionary psychologists remind us that a lack of fear (**hypophobia**) can be fatal, and some argue that our fear of snakes (**ophidiophobia**) explains how we became capable of anxiety, language and imagination in the first place.

Worry about **NEW TECHNOLOGIES** has given rise to **aerophobia** (a fear of plane travel), **siderodromophobia** (a fear of travelling on trains) and **telephonophobia** (anxiety about making or taking phone calls).

Aversions to **FOOD and DRINK** can emerge in **ovophobia** (disgust at eggs) and **popcorn phobia**, while people with **emetophobia** (a fear of vomiting) or **pnigophobia** (a fear of choking) may avoid all sorts of consumption. An overpowering desire to drink alcohol used to be known as **dipsomania**.

The compulsive desire to **TOUCH** is **haphemania**, while an aversion to being touched is **haphephobia**. An obsession with **HAIR** can take the form of **trichomania** (a love of hair), **pogonophobia** (a loathing of beards) or **trichotillomania** (compulsive hair-plucking). A fear of **WASHING** is known as **ablutophobia**, and a compulsion to wash often stems from **mysophobia**, the dread of dirt or germs.

Fears of **ISOLATION** and abandonment emerge in **claustrophobia**, **hypnophobia** (a fear of falling asleep), **lypemania** (compulsive sadness), **monophobia** (a dread of being alone), **nomophobia** (a fear of being without a phone), **nyctophobia** (fear of darkness), **sedatephobia** (fear of silence) and **taphephobia** (a terror of being buried alive).

Our anxiety about **OTHER PEOPLE**, or social phobia, can take the form of **agoraphobia**, **erythrophobia** (the fear of blushing), **gelotophobia** (the fear of being laughed at), **glossophobia** (the fear of public speaking) and **public urination phobia**. A fear and loathing of specific groups of people is described by terms such as

homophobia (an aversion to homosexuality) and **xenophobia** (a prejudice against people of a different nation or race).

The many **COMPULSIVE MANIAS** include **aboulomania** (compulsive indecision), **arithmomania** (counting), **dromomania** (walking or wandering), **graphomania** (writing), **homicidal monomania** (murder), **klazomania** (shouting), **kleptomania** (stealing), **mythomania** (lying), **nymphomania** (sex), **oniomania** (shopping) and **pyromania** (fire-setting).

Some phobias and manias were **NAMED IN FUN**, as satire or wordplay rather than to describe real conditions – **aibohphobia** is supposedly a fear of palindromes, **ergophobia** is an aversion to work, **giftomania** is excessive generosity and **hippopotomonstrosesquipediophobia** a terror of long words.

The most common treatments for phobias and manias are **COGNITIVE AND BEHAVIOURAL THERAPIES**, as described in the entries on **acrophobia** (the fear of heights), **ailurophobia** (cats), **arachnophobia** (spiders), **aerophobia** (flying), **batrachophobia** (frogs and toads), **blood-injection-injury phobia**, **brontophobia** (thunder), **cynophobia** (dogs), **glossophobia** (public speaking), **kleptomania** (stealing), **mysophobia** (germs), **nyctophobia** (darkness), **onychotillomania** (the picking and pulling of toenails and fingernails), **pediophobia** (dolls), **phonophobia** (noises) and **pnigophobia** (choking). A behaviourist attempt to induce a phobia features in the entry on **doraphobia** (the fear of fur).

Our obsessions with **NUMBERS** include **arithmomania** (a compulsion to count), **triskaidekaphobia** (fear of the number thirteen) and **tetraphobia** (fear of the number four).

Our obsessions with **WORDS** include **onomatomania** (a fixation on a single word), **hippopotomonstrosesquipediophobia** (an aversion to long words), **aibohphobia** (a loathing of palindromes), **bibliomania** (a longing for books) and **graphomania** (a compulsion to write).

PSYCHOANALYTIC IDEAS about manias and phobias appear in the entries on **agoraphobia** (open spaces), **arachnophobia** (spiders), **arithmomania** (counting), **claustrophobia** (confined spaces), **doraphobia** (fur), **erythrophobia** (blushing), **fykiaphobia** (seaweed), **hippophobia** (horses), **kleptomania** (stealing), **musophobia** (rats), **mysophobia** (germs), **mythomania** (lying), **nyctophobia** (darkness), **oniomania** (shopping), **ornithophobia** (birds), **pediophobia** (dolls), **pyromania** (fire), **siderodromophobia** (trains) and **xenophobia** (people of a different nationality, colour or creed).

Among our fears of **NOISE** are **brontophobia** (thunder), **globophobia** (balloons), **telephonophobia** (telephones) and **phonophobia** (sounds in general), while **sedatephobia** is a fear of silence.

Phobias and manias that verge on **DELUSION** include **acarophobia** (being infested with tiny insects), **demonomania** (demonic possession), **egomania** (an obsession with oneself), **erotomania** (the false belief that one is desired), **hydrophobia** (a terror of the sound, sight or touch of water), **megalomania** (grandiose delusions), **micromania** (a belief that a part of the body is very small) and **mysophobia** (an obsessive fear of dirt and germs). **Pantophobia** is the fear of everything.

A

ABLUTOPHOBIA

A fear of washing – or ablutophobia, from the Latin *abluere*, to wash, and the Greek *phobia*, or fear – especially affects children. It is often a temporary terror, experienced in infancy, though in some cases it can last for years. A seventeen-year-old girl once told the American psychologist Granville Stanley Hall that until the age of eleven she used to scream in horror if bathed. Another teenager informed him: 'To be washed always made me stiffen out, my eyes bulge, and I was almost convulsed with fear.'

The fear of washing was common in France in the early nineteenth century, when many believed that dirt was a shield against disease and the stink of sweat was proof of health and sexual vigour. As the historian Steven Zdatny explains, thorough washing was in any case difficult in a society that considered nudity shameful. A woman in a rural French hospital was outraged by the suggestion that she take a bath. 'I am sixty-eight,' she said indignantly, 'and *never* have I washed *there*!' The upper classes were similarly fastidious. 'No one in my family ever took a bath!' recalled the comtesse de Pange. 'The idea of plunging into water up to our necks seemed pagan.' In the second half of the century, as scientists established a link between dirt and the spread of disease, teachers tried to teach modern hygiene practices to children who had never used a sponge or immersed themselves in water. The French army, too, tried to instil cleaner habits in its recruits, and in 1902 published a *Manuel d'hygiène* that instructed soldiers to brush their teeth, scrub their bodies and wear underclothes. In Douai, northern France, a military commander ordered his men to forcibly clean a young artilleryman who claimed to be afraid of bathing. The soldiers dragged their dirty comrade into the bath-house and held him under a shower. According to Zdatny, the artilleryman's death eight days later was attributed to his shock and horror at the sensation of water on his skin. His fear, it seemed, had killed him.

☞ *See also: aquaphobia, hydrophobia, mysophobia, thalassophobia*

ABOULOMANIA

In 1916 the American psychoanalyst Ralph W. Reed treated a pathologically indecisive bank clerk of twenty-two who was 'continually doubting the validity or correctness of anything he has done in the course of his daily duties'. Each time he added up a column of figures, the clerk felt compelled to check it, and then check it again. He made the same agonised return to every calculation, however trivial. Reed noted that this kind of mental paralysis often coincided with paranoid delusions: both were disabling doubts about what had happened or what might take place. He diagnosed the clerk with aboulomania.

The term aboulomania – from the Greek *a* (without), *boulē* (will) and *mania* (madness) – was coined by the neurologist William Alexander Hammond in 1883. Aboulomania, explained Hammond, was 'a form of insanity characterised by an inertness, torpor, or paralysis of the will'. He described one patient, a Massachusetts man, who was seized by indecision when dressing or undressing himself. As soon as he started to take off one shoe, he would wonder whether he should take the other off first. He would switch helplessly between the shoes for several minutes, before deciding to walk around the room to deliberate on the matter. Then he might catch sight of himself in the mirror, and, noticing his necktie, think, 'Ah, of course that is the thing to take off first.' But when he tried to remove the tie, he would again hesitate and become powerless. 'And so it went on, if he was left to himself,' wrote Hammond, 'till it has frequently happened that daylight would find him still with every stitch of clothing on his body.'

In 1921 the French psychiatrist Pierre Janet described the feeling of 'incompleteness' that affected such individuals, rendering them continually unsatisfied, as if something was missing. They 'watch themselves', he wrote, 'and by dint of observations, through anxiety about themselves, they fall into a sort of perpetual auto-analysis. They become psychologists; which is in its way a disease of the mind.' Aboulomania is an obsession that springs from self-consciousness, Janet suggested, a disorder made possible by our tendency to reflect on our own thoughts.

It seems odd to categorise a state of chronic uncertainty as a compulsion: an inability to make choices looks more like a fear of error than a passion for indecision. But by identifying pathological doubt as a mania, Hammond reminded us that it is not just an absence of conviction. Rather, it is a powerful emotional state, a turbulent and painful condition in which all possibilities are still available; several futures are jostling and nothing has been closed off.

☛ *See also: arithmomania, mysophobia, syllogomania*

ACAROPHOBIA

Acarophobia (from the Greek *akari*, or mite) is an extreme fear of tiny insects, first identified by the French dermatologist Georges Thibierge in 1894, which can develop into a belief that minuscule creatures have invaded the body. The itchy feeling of 'formication' may be caused by the imagination alone, or by a physical condition such as shingles, tuberculosis, syphilis, skin cancer, the menopause or malnutrition. It can also be provoked by substances such as pesticides, methamphetamine and cocaine.

Since itchiness is very suggestive, acarophobic delusions are sometimes transmitted from person to person. The public health officer William G. Waldron investigated several reports of biting insects in Los Angeles workplaces in the 1960s. At a flight-booking centre that he visited, all the female employees were experiencing a tingling sensation and a slight 'pulling' on their nylon stockings, just above the ankle. Waldron could find no insects on the premises, but he speculated that the women might be picking up a static electric charge from an uncovered telephone cable beneath their desks. He noticed that morale among the 150 employees was low. Perhaps, he thought, the oppressive working conditions were contributing to their prickly unease – the workers sat at their desks for hours on end, making complex telephone bookings, while three bosses watched them constantly from a darkened booth at one end of the room. Waldron recommended that the airline company cover the phone cable and turn on the light in the supervision booth. After this, the women told him, the itching stopped.

In attempts to dislodge insects, some acarophobes gouge out the flesh of their faces, necks or arms, scalps, chests, armpits or groins. 'I found him stripped to the waist,' wrote Luis Buñuel after visiting the artist Salvador Dalí in a Parisian hotel in the 1920s, 'an enormous bandage on his back. Apparently he thought he'd felt a "flea" or some other strange beast and had attacked his back with a razor blade. Bleeding profusely, he got the hotel manager to call a doctor, only to discover that the "flea" was in reality a pimple.' Buñuel's film *Un Chien Andalou*, on which Dalí collaborated in 1928, opens with a razor blade slicing into an eyeball, releasing a swell of jelly, and goes on to show a swarm of ants teeming from a man's palm, the flesh erupting with alien life.

☞ *See also: arachnophobia, dermatillomania, entomophobia, zoophobia*

ACROPHOBIA

Andrea Verga, the Italian physician who invented the term acrophobia in 1887, himself suffered from a morbid fear of heights. An acrophobe, he explained, 'has palpitations on mounting a step-ladder, finds it unpleasant to ride on the top of a coach or to look out of even a first-storey window'. Verga derived his term from the Greek *acron*, meaning peak, and described its chief symptom as the dizzy, spinning sensation known as vertigo.

Almost 20 per cent of us have a fear of heights, and for about 5 per cent of us it is a terror. The condition is sometimes attributed to traumatic experience – the detective in Alfred Hitchcock's *Vertigo* (1958) develops a horror of heights after seeing a fellow policeman fall to his death – but only about one in seven acrophobes can recall an incident of this kind. In fact, in 2002 a study of eleven- and eighteen-year-olds with acrophobia found that both groups had unusually little experience of heights. If anything, it seemed that their phobia had been caused or exacerbated by a lack of familiarity with high places.

In 1897, Granville Stanley Hall analysed eighty-three accounts of acrophobia and other 'gravity-related' fears, from which he deduced that the phobia was rooted in a primordial anxiety, an 'instinct-feeling' that was 'incalculably more ancient than the intellect'. Many of Hall's subjects said that when they found themselves in high places they experienced a 'sudden giddiness, nausea, tremor, gasping, or sense of smothering'. In response, they 'grew rigid, livid, clenched their hands and teeth'. But, oddly, he noticed that many acrophobes seemed to fear not an accidental fall but their own 'jumping-off instinct'. 'Very common is the impulse,' he wrote, 'usually very sudden, to hurl oneself down from towers, windows, roofs, bridges, high galleries in church or theatre, precipices, etc.' Some acrophobes clung to railings or bystanders in order to stop themselves from plunging over a precipice and 'ending it all'. One man admitted that he was tempted by 'the exquisite pleasure of dropping'. Others were drawn to the 'beautiful sensation' of leaping into the air, wrote Hall, imagining that they might be 'upborne by their clothes, a parasol, flapping hands or arms like wings'.

Hall suggested that to be afraid of heights was to be afraid not only of a deathly plunge but also of one's own primitive impulses, which might include a longing to jump or to fly. 'What man really most fears is himself,' he wrote, 'because his inner primal nature is that which he knows least and which might seize and control most completely his body and soul.' Hall, who was fascinated by both Charles Darwin and Sigmund Freud, was edging towards a new understanding of phobias, in which fear was forged not only by the adaptations of evolution, but also by conflicts in an individual's psyche. The whirl of vertigo could seem like the giddiness of yearning.

'What is vertigo?' asks the novelist Milan Kundera in *The Book of Laughter and Forgetting* (1980). 'Fear of falling? No. Vertigo is something other than fear of falling. It is the voice of the emptiness below us which tempts and lures us, it is the desire to fall, against which, terrified, we defend ourselves.'

Some psychologists believe that acrophobia affects individuals who overattend to and dramatically misinterpret their bodily sensations. In exposure treatments, acrophobes are encouraged to climb to a height and wait until their terror recedes – at first, their hearts race, adrenaline courses through them, their breathing quickens; but after ten to fifteen minutes, the heart rate will usually subside, adrenaline levels will drop, and breathing will slow. By waiting for the symptoms of fear to pass, they can learn to associate heights with normal feelings.

In 2018 a hundred acrophobes were recruited by Oxford University for a randomised experiment. After they had filled out a questionnaire to measure their fear of heights, half were assigned to receive immersive virtual-reality therapy and half to a control group. At six thirty-minute sessions, over about two weeks, the virtual-reality group wore headsets that enabled them to undertake different activities while they navigated ascending floors of a simulated ten-storey office block. They might rescue a cat from a tree on one floor, play a xylophone near the edge of the next floor, throw balls out of the window on another. In this way, they acquired memories of being secure while high up.

When they answered a questionnaire at the end of the trial, the virtual-reality group reported a reduction in acrophobic symptoms of almost 70 per cent, while the control group's fear had reduced by less than 4 per cent. When they filled out the questionnaire again two weeks later, more than two-thirds of the people in the virtual-reality group fell below the trial's fear-of-heights entry criteria: they were no longer acrophobic. 'The treatment effects produced,' concluded the study's authors, 'were at least as good as – and most likely better – than the best psychological intervention delivered face-to-face with a therapist.'

☞ *See also: aerophobia, agoraphobia*

AEROPHOBIA

Aerophobia (from the Greek *aer*, or air) originally described a terror of breezes that was common in rabies victims; but it is now often used to describe a fear of flying. Many of us experience this fear, and for an estimated 2.5 per cent of the population it is a phobia. The Boeing corporation estimated in 1982 that the US airline industry would be making an extra $1.6 billion a year if everyone conquered their fear of flying, and in 2002, the year after the 9/11 terrorist attacks, aerophobia had a tangible effect on mortality rates, too: so many Americans chose to travel by car rather than plane that an extra 1,595 people died in road accidents.

The risks of air travel are very low. A study by Harvard University in 2006 found that the odds of an individual dying in a plane crash were 1 in 11 million – compared to a 1 in 5,000 chance of dying in a road accident. But recent psychological research has shown that we notice rare events more than we do common ones. And Aaron T. Beck, who pioneered cognitive behavioural therapy in the 1970s, pointed out that anxiety is based not only on the chances of a feared event taking place, but also on our perception of how devastating and inescapable the event would be. Those of us with a fear of flying aren't alarmed by the probability that our plane will crash, after all: what terrifies us is the barely imaginable horror that we would undergo if it were to do so.

A character in Julian Barnes's novel *Staring at the Sun* (1986) articulates the tormenting thoughts that air travel can inspire. A plane crash, thinks Gregory, would be the worst way to die. Strapped into your seat on a plummeting aircraft, amid the screaming of the other passengers, you would know that your death was imminent, and that it would be both violent and tawdry. 'You died with a headrest and an antimacassar,' reflects Gregory. 'You died with a little plastic fold-down table whose surface bore a circular indentation so that your coffee cup would be held safely. You died with overhead luggage racks and little plastic blinds to pull down over the mean windows.' As the plane hit the earth, smashing these tinny tokens of civilisation, your life would be rendered meaningless. 'You died domestically,' thinks Gregory, 'yet not in your own home, in someone else's, someone whom you never met before and who had invited a load of strangers round. How, in such circumstances, could you see your own extinction as something tragic, or even important, or even relevant? It would be a death which mocked you.'

Aerophobes hate the surrender of personal agency that flight entails. Some fear that the pilot will lose control of a malfunctioning aircraft, while others fear that they will experience a panic attack in which they themselves lose control. The phobia can be fuelled by the memory of an alarming flight, by news stories about crashes and hijackings, by disaster movies. Some aerophobes are physiologically vulnerable to the effects of air travel. They may, for instance, suffer from a dysfunction of the inner ear that leads to vertigo or to spatial disorientation during a flight; or from an undetected hypoxia (a lack of oxygen) that creates panicky feelings. Among those aerophobes who do fly, a fifth say that they use alcohol or sedatives to blunt their anxiety.

As a condition with behavioural, physiological and cognitive components, aerophobia is often treated with cognitive behavioural therapy (CBT). Typically, the phobic individual is encouraged to analyse the distortions in his or her automatic thoughts about flight – for instance a tendency to catastrophise (a process of negative overgeneralisation) or to polarise (all-or-nothing thinking) or to attend too much to distressing perceptions and internal sensations. The therapist provides information about air travel: how a plane works, the causes of turbulence, the chances of a crash, and so on. The patient then draws up a hierarchy of flight-related fears, from packing a suitcase to takeoff to landing, and is taught to use relaxation techniques while imagining each stressful situation in turn. The treatment often culminates with the aerophobe taking a flight, real or simulated.

Some aerophobes feel a superstitious attachment to their phobia, in case it is their fear that has so far protected them from disaster. As the plane takes off at the beginning of Erica Jong's novel *Fear of Flying* (1973), Isadora Wing's fingers and toes and nipples turn to ice, her stomach leaps, her heart screams in concert with the aircraft's engines. She maintains a fierce focus while the plane climbs. 'I happen to know that only my own concentration ... keeps this bird aloft,' she explains. 'I congratulate myself on every successful takeoff, but not too enthusiastically because it's also part of my personal religion that the minute you grow over-confident and really *relax* about the flight, the plane crashes instantly.' By the end of the book, Wing has achieved liberation – creative, sexual, emotional – and she has shed her delusion that only her anxiety keeps a plane in the air.

☛ *See also: acrophobia, agoraphobia, claustrophobia, emetophobia, siderodromophobia*

AGORAPHOBIA

The word agoraphobia was coined in 1871 by Carl Otto Westphal, a Berlin psychiatrist who found himself treating several men with a terror of traversing the city. One patient, a thirty-two-year-old travelling salesman, had a dread of certain neighbourhoods, especially if the streets were deserted and the shops shut. At the edge of the city, where the houses ran out, his nerve would fail him entirely. He was disturbed by busy spaces, too, and experienced palpitations when boarding an omnibus or entering a theatre.

Another patient, an engineer aged twenty-six, said that when he encountered an open space he felt as if something grabbed his heart. 'He becomes red and hot in the face,' wrote Westphal; 'his fear becomes more intense and can become a real fear of death, there is a feeling of insecurity in him, as he can no longer walk with certainty, and it also seems to him that the cobblestones are melting into each other.' The engineer compared his fear of crossing a city square to the feeling of swimming out of a narrow channel into a lake. He lost his bearings, and if he succeeded in reaching the other side would barely be able to remember having done so: the crossing was hazy, like a dream.

Westphal's patients told him that they were less frightened if they had a companion on their walks through town, or could keep close to the buildings in a square, or follow a carriage through the streets. One felt consoled by the sight of the red lanterns outside the taverns on his route home. Using a cane could relieve anxiety a little, as could the consumption of beer or wine. Westphal heard of a priest in the town of Driburg who would cover himself with an umbrella when he stepped outside, as if to carry with him the vaulted roof of his church.

Agoraphobia – from the Greek *agora*, or marketplace – is a wide-ranging term that can mean fear of social contact, of leaving one's home, of crowded spaces or empty spaces, even a fear of being afraid. As David Trotter explains in *The Uses of Phobia*, the condition was associated from the start with the stresses of modern life. In 1889 the Viennese architect Camillo Sitte ascribed agoraphobia to the rapid changes in the cities of Europe, where winding alleys and wonky buildings were being razed to make way for wide boulevards and blank monumental blocks. A city square could seem an abyss; an avenue a chasm.

The psychiatrist Henri Legrand du Saulle was consulted by Parisians whose '*peur des espaces*' made them hesitate at a boundary, whether the edge of a city square, the kerb of a pavement, the ledge of a window or the rise of a bridge. His patient 'Madame B' could not cross a boulevard or square alone. She was scared of empty restaurants and of climbing the wide staircase to her apartment. Once indoors, she was unable to look out of the window. Another of Legrand du Saulle's patients was an infantry officer who could cross open spaces when wearing a uniform but not in civilian clothes. 'Here,' writes Trotter, 'it is not companionship but performance that saves an agoraphobe from his anxiety. Putting on a show, one accompanies oneself across the empty space.' A third patient, who had to be escorted everywhere by his wife, would stop at the entrance to a square, frozen with fear, and mutter to himself: 'Mama, Rata, *bibi, bitaquo*, I'm going to die.'

Legrand du Saulle argued that spatial phobias had multiplied in Paris after the German siege of the city in 1871. 'In Legrand's terms,' writes the architectural historian Anthony Vidler, 'the successive closing and sudden opening of the city, its passage so to speak from claustrophobia to agoraphobia, had the effect of fostering the veritable cause of spatial fear.'

In the years after Westphal and Legrand du Saulle published their findings, other agoraphobes came forward to detail their symptoms. 'I stop,' wrote Dr J. Headley Neale in *The Lancet* in 1898; 'the earth seems seized in an iron grip. I feel as though I were going down into the earth and the earth were coming up to meet me. There is no semblance of giddiness or faintness in these attacks, it is more a feeling of collapse as though one were being shut up like a crush hat or a Chinese lantern.' Some argued that the condition was a sign of hereditary degeneracy, but Sigmund Freud disagreed: 'The more frequent cause of agoraphobia as well as of most other phobias lies not in heredity,' he wrote in 1892, 'but in abnormalities of sexual life.' Freud proposed that agoraphobes, fearing that they might succumb to the sexual temptations of the street, converted their dread into a fear of the street itself. 'The phobia,' he said, 'is thrown before the anxiety like a fortress on the frontier.'

Agoraphobia can manifest as a terror of open country and wide skies. David Trotter describes how the novelist Ford Madox Ford kept panic at bay while walking in the fields of southern

England by sucking on lozenges and choosing paths that were punctuated by benches. Like Westphal's city dwellers, he tackled his horror of vacancy by focusing on small, particular objects and actions. When his friend Olive Garnett took a walk with him on Salisbury Plain in the summer of 1904, Ford was seized by fear, she wrote, '& said that if I didn't take his arm he would fall down. I held on in all the blaze for miles it seemed to me, but the town reached, he walked off briskly to get tobacco and a shave.' In 1990, the novelist John Lanchester recalled once climbing a misty mountain in the Lake District and upon reaching the suddenly clear skies at the summit being overwhelmed by the 'terrifying extensiveness' of the panorama that opened up before him. He succumbed to a 'full-scale panic attack – a gasping, palpitating, trembling panic attack' – before finding his way down the slope to safety.

The attention of others can trigger the same symptoms. The actor Macaulay Culkin developed agoraphobia after becoming famous as the child star of *Home Alone* (1990). 'There was always photographers in the bushes and things like that,' he told the television host Larry King in 2004, 'and there was a lot of things out there that were trying to consume me.' He became terrified of leaving the house because the world seemed so hungry for him. 'It felt like the buildings were going to eat me.' The reclusive poet Emily Dickinson used similar language to describe an encounter with a group of neighbours outside a local church one Sunday in 1853: 'Several soared around me,' she wrote to her sister-in-law, 'and, sought to devour me.'

For much of the twentieth century, agoraphobia was attributed to psychological problems such as separation anxiety, dependency and displaced sexual and aggressive feelings, but since the 1970s it has often been treated as a physiological condition. The psychologist David Clark, for instance, argues that agoraphobes may misunderstand their bodily sensations, responding with panic to minor internal changes. In the first stage of this vicious circle, he says, they selectively attend to fluctuations in their bodies, finding significance in a slight rise in heart rate, a dizzy spell, some shortness of breath. They respond to the fear by producing adrenaline, which causes further physiological changes (a racing heart, fast, shallow breathing) that they dramatically misinterpret as signs that they are about to faint, suffocate or suffer a heart attack. In effect, agoraphobia is a panic disorder: a fear of fear.

But the American anthropologist Kathryn Milun warns against treating agoraphobia as purely physiological. She points out that this understanding of the condition has benefited pharmaceutical companies, which are able to sell benzodiazepines and other medications to a huge new constituency, but it erases the phobia's social, historical and cultural components; its relation to modernity. Milun laments the 'complete disappearance of a concern with the social space that originally gave rise to the psychological problem'.

Up to three times as many women as men are diagnosed with agoraphobia, a disparity that the feminist psychologist Maureen McHugh attributes, at least in part, to social history. In the past, women were often expected to act in ways that we now label as pathological. They were encouraged to stay at home, dissuaded from taking part in public life or venturing out alone. Even now, some cultures hold to these expectations, and women can feel vulnerable when outdoors. 'The phobic's anxiety is only unrealistic to the extent that the streets are objectively safe,' observes McHugh, 'and that public spaces are comfortable for women.' In *Women Who Marry Houses* (1983), Robert Seidenberg and Karen DeCrow describe an agoraphobic woman as 'a living and acting metaphor, making a statement, registering a protest, effecting a sit-in strike'. She unconsciously exaggerates her roles as a wife and mother and housekeeper, a person so defined by the home that she is unable to leave it.

During the Covid-19 pandemic, as governments told people to keep to their homes, many of us developed agoraphobic behaviours. To fear public spaces had become sensible, not phobic, and returning to them was difficult for some. Like the citizens of Paris after the German siege of 1871, we had become accustomed to confinement. In October 2020, *The New York Times* reported that parents were concerned about 'Generation Agoraphobia', the children who had developed an aversion to going out: 'This phenomenon is incredibly widespread,' said Nina Kaiser, a child psychologist in San Francisco, whose own four-year-old son had become frightened of leaving the house. The anxieties of many teenage and adult agoraphobes, meanwhile, had been reinforced by the new dangers in the outside world.

When Carl Westphal named agoraphobia in 1871 he identified perhaps the quintessential anxiety disorder: an indeterminate, existential dread in a world robbed of the old certainties. He was part of a generation of psychiatrists who, in the wake of Charles Darwin's *On the Origin of Species* (1859), were seeking scientific explanations for emotional experiences. Those experiences seemed to be changing, too. If people could no longer rely on God to guide them, they might reach more urgently for the arm of a companion as they stepped outside, or the handle of a cane.

☛ *See also: acrophobia, claustrophobia, kayak phobia, mysophobia, pantophobia*

AIBOHPHOBIA

This playful term for an excessive fear of palindromes – words that read the same backwards as forwards – seems to have been coined by the Liverpudlian folk singer and computer scientist Stan Kelly-Bootle in *The Devil's DP Dictionary* (1981). Aibohphobia is not a documented psychological disorder, but it is a palindrome.

☛ *See also: hippopotomonstrosesquipediophobia, onomatomania*

AILUROPHOBIA

An extreme fear of cats was one of the phobias identified by the American physician Benjamin Rush in 1786. 'I know several gentlemen of unquestionable courage,' wrote Rush, 'who have retreated a thousand times from the sight of a cat; and who have even discovered signs of fear and terror upon being confined in a room with a cat that was out of sight.'

In 1905, his countryman Silas Weir Mitchell conducted a study of ailurophobia, a word he derived from the Greek *ailouros*, or cat. Mitchell was especially interested in the uncanny sensitivity of some ailurophobes. He sent out questionnaires that began with the question: 'Have you any antipathy to cats?' and enquired whether the respondent could sense the presence of a cat 'when it is not in sight or known to be near'.

Many of the participants reported physical reactions. 'If a cat comes into a room where I am alone I feel as if cold water had been thrown over me,' wrote Frances A. Wakefield. 'My teeth shut tightly. I cannot even call out, in fact for a minute I can hardly prevent an utter collapse.' R. H. Wood, an attorney from Virginia, said that the touch of these 'sneaky, stealthy' creatures was like an electric shock.

Thirty-one of Mitchel's 159 respondents claimed to be able to detect a cat before seeing it. Mary, from Philadelphia, told of a cat-sensitive cousin with whom she had dined at a Montreal hotel. The cousin had turned 'ashy pale' on being led to their table, exclaiming: 'There is a cat in this room.' The room was long and gloomy, said Mary: only the table at which they were seated was lit. The waiter assured them that there was no cat, but Mary's cousin grew paler and paler. She started to tremble. There *is*, she repeated. 'There *is* a cat here.' The waiter scoured the room and eventually found the animal in a far, dark corner.

In 1914 Mitchell's colleague Granville Stanley Hall published his research on children with a cat phobia. They told him that they hated the way that cats could 'pop up on the outside of any window' and were 'quicker than lightning'. They walked so softly, and jumped so far. 'A cat can run up to you and stick its claws in your eyes and tear it out if it wants to,' said one child. 'Its eyes are so shiny and glistening at night,' said another, 'that you can see nothing but two glary balls of fire.' One of Hall's interviewees believed that a cat 'can chew up bone and bite through your finger and never let go', and one that cats were 'full of everything filthy'. These fears were not confined to children, said Hall. When the German kaiser visited his relatives at Buckingham Palace, an official searched every room in his suite for lurking felines.

Hall argued that our terror of domestic cats is rooted in primeval fears of sabre-toothed tigers. But even if the aversion is 'biologically prepared', it also has cultural components. In Christian societies, the cat has often been treated with suspicion – it was 'the Devil's favourite animal', said Pope Innocent VIII in 1484, 'and idol of all witches'. The ailurophobes who wrote to Silas Weir Mitchell about eerie invisible feline presences may have been influenced by tales of witches and their familiars.

At the Bethlem Royal Hospital in the suburbs of south London in 1959, Drs Hugh L. Freeman and Donald C. Kendrick tried a new type of behaviour therapy, devised by the South African psychiatrist Joseph Wolpe, on 'Mrs A', an ailurophobic woman of thirty-seven. She told the doctors that she had seen her father drown a kitten in a bucket when she was four. As a child, she was so scared of being touched by the family cat that she would sit at the kitchen table with her legs stretched straight out in front of her. The anxiety became worse when she was fourteen, and her parents – 'for some reason which is not clear', said the doctors – put a piece of fur inside her bed.

Her father had been strict and controlling, said Mrs A. He castigated her when she received poor school reports and he used to steam open her letters to monitor her private life. To get away from home, she joined the Women's Royal Naval Service during the Second World War (if sleeping on board a ship, she always chose a top bunk to keep clear of the cats). She became engaged to a sailor, and though her father opposed the marriage the wedding went ahead as soon as the war ended. In 1950 her father died of a heart attack.

Mrs A's husband was a mild, easy-going man who after the war became a schoolteacher. He was sympathetic about Mrs A's ailurophobia, as were their two children. When visiting friends, the family would check rooms for cats before she came in.

The phobia had worsened in the last couple of years, said Mrs A, because cats had colonised the overgrown garden of the abandoned house next door. She dreaded hanging out the laundry for fear that a cat would spring at her, and her anxiety had started to spread. 'She could not bear to touch any cat-like fur or wear fur gloves,' wrote Dr Freeman in the *British Medical Journal*, 'and felt uneasy sitting next to anyone wearing a fur coat on public transport. Pictures of cats in books, or on television or the cinema made her feel uneasy.' Recently, she had found that she could think of little but cats. She had horrible dreams about them. She became upset even if she unexpectedly saw her daughter's toy koala bear.

In accordance with Wolpe's 'systematic desensitisation' therapy, the doctors helped Mrs A draw up a hierarchy of her cat-related fears and then started to work through her list. The theory was that the gradual familiarisation would slowly defuse the phobia, reconditioning Mrs A to associate cat textures and images with safety instead of danger. First they offered her velvet, then pieces of increasingly soft fur, culminating in rabbit. Having accustomed herself to these, she was encouraged to move on to cat toys, cat pictures and, within a month, a live kitten. When the small animal was placed on her lap, she laughed and then cried with relief. This was 'one of the greatest days of my life', she said later. She took the kitten home with her, so that she would learn to feel easy with it as it grew bigger.

Ten weeks after beginning her treatment, Mrs A found that she was able to touch a fully grown cat, and she told the psychologists that her cat nightmares had been replaced with violent dreams about her father. In one, she was whacking him with a poker. She confessed that she had often had feelings of this sort when her father was alive but had never expressed them. The behavioural therapy, which had cured Mrs A of her phobia, seemed also to have freed her to voice the fear and anger that she had felt when her phobia was forged. The success of her treatment apparently proved the behaviourists' argument that a phobia could be eradicated without the patient gaining any insight into its origin; and yet the procedure seemed also to have unlocked something in

Mrs A, releasing a part of her that had been submerged a long time ago.

Three years later, Dr Kendrick checked up on Mrs A. Her ailurophobia had not returned, he found, and no other symptoms of anxiety had replaced it. She still had her cat – the kitten from the clinic – and often looked after another cat, too. It was as if she were 'two persons', she told Kendrick: 'the one with all the fear and the one now'.

☛ *See also: doraphobia, zoophobia*

AQUAPHOBIA

Aquaphobia is an intense fear of water, especially of drowning, which affects more than 2 per cent of the global population. Aquaphobes are not more likely than anyone else to have had a frightening encounter with water. On the contrary, it seems that those of us who are unafraid have been educated out of our natural fear by learning to swim. The psychologist Stanley J. Rachman proposed that some phobias were spontaneous: 'Rather than assume that a significant proportion of the population *acquires identical fears,*' he wrote in *Fear and Courage* (1978), 'we can entertain the view that the predisposition to develop the most common fears is innate and universal, or nearly so, and that what we learn is how to overcome our existing predispositions.' Though we are not aquaphobic at birth, the fear usually sets in when we are about six months old, the point at which we start to move independently and an awareness of physical danger becomes useful.

The fear of water has striking cultural variations. A paper in the *Journal of Black Studies* in 2011 reported that only a third of Black Americans were confident swimmers, compared to more than two-thirds of whites. In part, the authors argued, this stemmed from a perception of swimming as an expensive, 'country club' pursuit, itself a legacy of the racist early twentieth-century policy of banning Black citizens from municipal swimming pools.

Aquaphobia is a circular anxiety, which comes to justify itself: to a person who avoids water, water is genuinely dangerous. The Centers for Disease Control and Prevention estimated in 2016 that Black children in the United States were six to ten times more likely to die by drowning than their white peers.

☛ *See also: ablutophobia, hydrophobia, thalassophobia*

ARACHNOPHOBIA

'Ladies seem to be particularly subject to arachnophobia,' observed the English parson and natural historian the Reverend John George Wood in 1863. If a spider scuttled across his drawing-room carpet, he said, the ladies of the household would 'scream and jump upon chairs', then 'ring for the footman to crush the poor thing, and the housemaid to follow in his steps with dustpan and brush'. Wood himself was delighted by arachnids (from the Greek *arachnēs*, or spider). He loved to see the spiders in his garden grow fat on the crane flies that he fed them at dusk. They would rush down from their webs, he said, to snatch the spindly insects from his fingers.

As many as 4 per cent of us are terrified by spiders – in most surveys, they come second only to snakes as objects of phobia. For the author Jenny Diski, autumn was an 'annual festival of anxiety and horror', because it was the season in which spiders came indoors to nest. On seeing a spider in the house, she would grab a blowtorch and, in a state of 'desperate abandon', blast flames at the creature. She knew that she risked starting a fire, she said, 'but death was never a worse alternative to being in the same room as a spider. I suppose this sounds like a writer's hyperbole, but I'm writing with all the accuracy I can muster.'

Many arachnophobes are sure that their aversion is instinctive. The writer and producer Charlie Brooker insists that his fear of these 'mobile nightmare units' is a reflex, 'a residual evolutionary trait that some people have and some don't, just as some people can fold their tongues and others can't'. If he sees a spider, he says,

'I'm across the room before I know what's happened, like an animal running from an explosion.' Neurological research confirms that an arachnophobic reaction bypasses conscious thought: our primitive, emotional brain instantly processes the image of a spider – within milliseconds, the thalamus prompts the amygdala to release epinephrine, insulin and cortisol, increasing our pulse, blood pressure and rate of breathing in readiness for flight or a fight – while the prefrontal cortex more slowly assesses the risk and decides whether to cancel the amygdala's preparations or to act upon them.

But a reflex can be learnt, and there is no obvious evolutionary reason for reacting to a spider in this way. Only about 0.1 per cent of the 50,000 or so spider species in the world are dangerous. There are far deadlier creatures that excite less horror. Spiders arguably even protect us by weaving webs that snare potential pests such as earwigs and flies. In an attempt to make evolutionary sense of arachnophobia, the biologist Tim Flannery speculated that there might have been a very dangerous spider in the part of Africa in which *Homo sapiens* first emerged as a species, and he looked for an arachnid that fitted the bill. He found one: the six-eyed sand spider (*Sicarius hahnii*) is a leathery, crablike creature that hides just beneath the surface of the southern African desert, ambushes its prey and has a venomous bite that can kill children. Our fear of spiders, says Flannery, might be a vestige of the moment in our evolution at which this creature posed a fatal threat.

There is a further oddity about our aversion to spiders. Scans of brain activity indicate that not only the amygdala is activated when an arachnophobe sees a spider, but also the insula, the part of the brain that generates the disgust response. Our facial reactions to seeing spiders bear this out: arachnophobes often tense and raise their upper lips in disgust, as well as raising their brows in fear. Researchers were initially surprised by such findings, since the disgust response is usually provoked by creatures and substances that might contaminate or infect us, and the spider does neither.

One explanation for this response – cultural as well as biological – is that we have adopted our medieval ancestors' suspicion that spiders are carriers of disease. For hundreds of years, according to the psychologist Graham Davey, spiders were blamed for the plagues that afflicted Europe: it was not until the nineteenth century that rat-borne fleas were identified as the real agents of infection. Davey argued in a paper of 1994 that this myth of spiders as disease-carriers could explain the feelings of disgust that they provoke, since disgust responses are culturally conditioned as well as innate. Arachnophobia is common in countries populated by Europeans and their descendants, Davey notes, whereas in parts of Africa and the Caribbean spiders are not reviled as unclean but consumed as a delicacy.

When the Reverend Wood made his loving observations about the creatures in his garden in 1863, the image of the spider was undergoing a cultural transformation. In the eighteenth century, arachnids had been lauded for their industry, skill and creativity; their webs were hailed as wonders of the natural world. But in the Gothic fiction of the late nineteenth century, as Claire Charlotte McKechnie writes in the *Journal of Victorian Culture*, the spider became a sinister and sometimes racist trope: the hero of Bertram Mitford's *The Sign of the Spider* (1896) fights a giant, carnivorous African spider that has 'a head, as large as that of a man, black, hairy, bearing a strange resemblance to the most awful and cruel human face ever stamped with the devil's image – whose dull, goggle eyes, fixed on the appalled ones of its discoverer, seemed to glow and burn with a truly diabolical glare'. And in 1897 the naturalist Grant Allen made the wild claim that 'for sheer ferocity and lust of blood, perhaps no creature on earth can equal that uncanny brute, the common garden spider. He is small, but he is savage.' McKechnie argues that spiders came to express 'fears of invasion, concerns about the morality of colonialism, and suspicion about the alien other in the corners of empire'. Arachnophobia had become fused with xenophobia, and with anxiety about the repercussions of imperialism.

The spider's symbolic meanings have continued to change. In 1922, Freud's follower Karl Abraham proposed that the creature represented a voracious, ensnaring and castrating mother – 'the penis embedded in the female genitals'. In 2012 the environmental philosopher Mick Smith argued that we fear spiders as emissaries from an anarchic natural world – insistent reminders of wilderness in a Western culture that has distinguished itself 'precisely by its ability to separate itself from and culturally control nature'. These silent creatures slip into our civilised domestic spaces on invisible threads, says Smith, finding the fissures in walls, adorning their sticky webs with insect corpses. He quotes Paul Shepard, an ecologist and philosopher who suggested that spiders had become 'unconscious proxies for something else ... as though they were invented to remind us of something we want to forget, but cannot remember either'. They disturb us because they are found in 'the cracks that are the zones of separation, or under things, the surfaces between places'. They make us uncomfortable because they are creatures of the in-between.

In 2006 Jenny Diski tried to dispel her arachnophobia by enrolling on the Friendly Spider Programme at London Zoo. She and seventeen other arachnophobes discussed their feelings about spiders, listened to a talk on the subject, underwent a twenty-minute relaxation and hypnosis session ('Spiders are safe,' the hypnotist assured them) and then proceeded to the zoo's Invertebrate House. To her astonishment, Diski was able to let one spider scamper across her palm, and to stroke the soft, hairy leg of another. She was cured. But 'I have the strangest sense of loss,' she reflected. 'A person who is not afraid of spiders is almost a definition of someone who is not *me* ... Some way in which I knew myself has vanished.' If she rid herself of all her anxieties and nervous habits, she wondered if there would be anything of her left.

A great many therapies have been developed for arachnophobia. In the same year that Diski was cured by a combination of hypnosis, education and real-life exposure, a forty-four-year-old British businessman was accidentally relieved of the phobia when he had an operation to remove his amygdala in a Brighton hospital. A week after the procedure, which was intended to stop his epileptic seizures, he noticed that he was no longer afraid of spiders. His level of fear was otherwise unaffected: he was as unfazed by snakes as he had been before the operation, he reported – and as anxious as ever about public speaking.

In the US in 2017, Paul Siegel and Joel Weinberger carried out a 'very brief exposure' treatment for arachnophobia, whereby images of tarantulas were flashed up before phobic individuals (for .033 seconds) and followed at once with neutral, 'masking' pictures of flowers. The experimental subjects were unaware of having seen spiders, and yet they afterwards reported less fear of the creatures and were able to get closer than before to a live tarantula in an aquarium. The effect held even after a year. The brain's fear circuitry had been desensitised, even though the exposure was delivered unconsciously. When the same procedure was carried out with consciously registered spider images, the arachnophobes became distressed during the experiment, and showed no decrease in their spider-fear.

In 2015 two researchers at the University of Amsterdam tested another rapid cure for arachnophobia. Marieke Soeter and Merel Kindt exposed forty-five arachnophobes to a tarantula, for two minutes, and then gave half of the group a 40-milligram dose of propranolol, a beta-blocker that can be used to induce amnesia. They hoped that by activating and then erasing their subjects' spider memories, they might also erase their fear of spiders. Their experiment drew on the neurologist Joseph LeDoux's theory of memory reconsolidation, which proposed that memories retrieved via the amygdala are briefly malleable: a recollection could be altered or extinguished in the hours immediately after it is triggered.

The Dutch trial worked: the arachnophobes who had been given the amnesic drug were markedly less phobic than the control group, even a year later. A single, brief intervention, announced the researchers, had led to 'a sudden, substantial and lasting loss of fear'. They described their revolutionary new treatment as 'more like surgery than therapy'. They had not tempered arachnophobia, but excised it from the brain.

☛ *See also: entomophobia, ophidiophobia, zoophobia*

ARITHMOMANIA

Arithmomania, a condition first identified in France in the late nineteenth century, is a pathological desire to count or an unnatural preoccupation with the mathematical properties of objects and events – in Greek, *arithmos* means number. In 1894 the English psychiatrist Daniel Hack Tuke described an arithmomaniac female patient, referred to him by a Dr Strangman Grubb of Ealing, who 'came to preface every act of her life by counting'. She needed to count to a certain number before turning over in bed, before entering the breakfast room, or lifting a teapot. She frequently felt compelled to count the number of times that she breathed and each step that she took along a road. She sometimes wondered, she told Dr Tuke, if the counting might be a way of staving off a terrible thought. In Vienna in the same period, Sigmund Freud interpreted a young woman's obsessive counting of floorboards and stairs as an attempt to distract herself from erotic wishes. In Paris, Georges Gilles de la Tourette observed that arithmomania, like other forms of obsessive-compulsive disorder, was a common feature of the tic syndrome that he had identified in 1885.

For an obsessive-compulsive arithmomane, as Nikki Rayne Craig explained in a blog of 2016, number-worry leaks into everything. 'I can't look away from a digital clock until the numbers feel right,' she writes. 'The volume on my car radio and TV must be a multiple of nine to keep my hands from hurting. It's how many times I have to wash my hands before I feel clean, and how many times I have to check the faucet before I know it's off.' When faced with a disturbing number, she explains, 'The joints in your wrists and fingers ache, your skin feels too tight, you have to bite your lip or press your nails to mask the feeling for even a moment.' Though many people have a mild obsession with numbers, for the arithmomane the preoccupation interferes with daily life. 'Do you turn the music louder than you're comfortable with to satisfy an arithmetic standard?' asks Craig. 'This is arithmomania.'

The Serbian-American engineer Nikola Tesla, who invented the alternating-current induction motor in the 1880s, was so obsessed with the number three that he would count his steps to ensure that they reached a figure divisible by three and would walk three times round a building before entering. When staying at a hotel (always in a room with a number that could be divided by three) he would demand eighteen fresh towels each day and eighteen napkins at the dining table. In *Obsession: A History* (2008), Lennard J. Davis speculates that routines of this sort may – like other compulsive manias – be peculiarly modern phenomena, products of our era's reverence for mechanical processes. 'When an industrial culture evolves to emphasise and rely on a greater sense of precision, repetition, standardisation and mechanisation,' he writes, 'that same society will perhaps regard those attributes differently, and members of that society will mime, imitate, embody, internalise, and exaggerate those qualities.' People who perform obsessive rituals may have incorporated the focused, obsessive tics of a machine.

In 1972 the television series *Sesame Street* introduced its viewers to the arithmomaniac Count von Count, whose love of counting sometimes irritated his friends. In one episode in 1974 the Count took such pleasure in enumerating the rings of the telephone that he refused to let Ernie answer the call. In 1984 he was so set on counting all the way to the top of an elevator shaft that he forgot to let Kermit out at the right floor. By including the Count in its cast, *Sesame Street* made fun of its own compulsive repetitions of letters and numbers, the rhythmic invocations by which it educated as well as entertained its young audience.

Count von Count was modelled on Count Dracula because vampires were reputed to be compulsive counters. If waylaid by a heap of poppy, mustard or millet seeds, according to East European legend, a vampire would be unable to resist stopping to count them. In American folklore, witches were held to be similarly distractible: if you hung a sieve over your front door, a witch would become so absorbed in counting its holes that she would never get round to bringing her wickedness into your house.

☛ See also: *aboulomania, graphomania, mysophobia, tetraphobia, triskaidekaphobia*

BAMBAKOMALLOPHOBIA

Bambakomallophobia – from the Greek words *bambakion* (cotton) and *mallos* (wool) – is an aversion to cotton wool. This phobia arouses an intense discomfort of the sort that many of us feel at the rasp of nails on a blackboard, the shriek of a knife on a plate, or the lightly fuzzed skin of a peach. Some people are horrified by the way that a cotton ball squeezes down into a spongy substance, springs back puffily, squeaks when pulled apart. In the *Guardian*, Chris Hall recalls how the phobia haunted his childhood: he was afraid of the fluffy little clouds of cotton wool on a homemade Christmas card, and of the cotton-wool swabs that a nurse pressed on his arm after an injection, or that a dentist wedged against his gum. He was wary even of stuffed toys, with their mysterious squashy innards.

For bambakomallophobes, the thin creak of cotton wool can be worse than the wince-inducing squeal of polystyrene. 'The imagined squeak is horrible and I associate it with static,' writes the author Laurence Scott. 'I can give myself somatic symptoms (shivering, an electric crackle in the back molars) just by imagining it. And the idea is so unpleasant that I never do it, and so I never learn that pulling cotton wool apart might not really be like how I remember it, or that it's possible to pull it apart and not experience these "symptoms".'

Another sufferer, Crystal Ponti, agrees that the noise made by cotton balls is 'enough to unhinge my nervous system – it sounds like the way popcorn squeaks in your mouth when it slips from your tooth'. She says that when she first encountered the substance, at the age of six, it was 'as if my stomach was collapsing into itself. Sweat immediately formed on my palms and a sense of dread washed over me.' To touch cotton wool can bring on an *unheimlich* shiver of wrongness – like a brush with the uncanny, it exposes a weird disjunction between what is heard, felt and seen.

☛ *See also: koumpounophobia, popcorn phobia, trypophobia*

BATRACHOPHOBIA

Batrachophobes are horrified by a frog's gleaming eyes and slimy skin, the pulsing sac at its throat; its webbed, knobby feet, its perfect stillness and its sudden, vaulting leap. The word is derived from *batrachos*, Greek for 'frog', and is applied to those alarmed by frogs, toads and other amphibians.

To conquer batrachophobia, the philosopher John Locke recommended a form of exposure therapy that is still considered the most effective treatment for phobias of many kinds. 'If your child shrieks and runs away at the sight of a frog,' wrote Locke in his *Essay Concerning Human Understanding* (1690), 'let another catch it and lay it down at a good distance from him; at first accustom him to look upon it; when he can do that, to come nearer to it and see it leap without emotion; then to touch it lightly, when it is held fast in another's hand; and so on, until he can come to handle it as confidently as a butterfly or sparrow.' A phobia can be overcome, Locke believed, by systematically undoing the negative feelings that we associate with the object of our fear.

In 1983 psychologists at the University of Michigan used exposure therapy to cure a twenty-six-year-old woman of her severe phobia of frogs. The batrachophobia had developed while she was mowing her lawn eighteen months earlier, she told them. She had been pushing her mower through the thick grass near a riverbank when she suddenly saw bloody chunks of frog spewing from the machine, and live frogs springing away to either side of her to escape the blades. She had been unable to mow the lawn since; she had nightmares about frogs; she hated to hear them croaking by the river; and she had to leave the house if a lone frog found its way inside. Her visceral horror at seeing the pulped frog flesh seemed to have coalesced with a guilty dread that the creatures might seek revenge.

In 2019 shopkeepers in Porto, Portugal, were found to be using the Roma people's well-known fear of frogs to deter them from entering their premises. The merchants simply placed green ceramic frogs at the shop doors, a practice that did not fall foul of discrimination laws. Ten shopkeepers confessed to an Al Jazeera reporter that they used this technique, which they said was especially effective with older Roma, but only one grocer gave the journalist permission to name her. 'It's to scare away Gypsies, because they are afraid of frogs,' confirmed Helena Conceição, apparently unashamed of her xenophobic behaviour. 'No one likes to have Gypsies around.'

☞ *See also: xenophobia, zoophobia*

BEATLEMANIA

Towards the end of 1963, violence broke out in a queue to buy tickets to see the Beatles in Carlisle: 600 girls were caught up in the crush, and nine were taken to hospital. Similar scenes were reported in Bournemouth, Manchester, Newcastle-upon-Tyne, Belfast, Dublin. 'This is Beatlemania,' said the *Daily Mail*. 'Where will it all lead?'

The craze followed the Beatles to America the next year. Thousands of girls and young women awaited the band at Kennedy airport, hundreds more at the Plaza Hotel in Manhattan. Every night of the twenty-three-city tour, the Beatles' songs were drowned out by the screaming of the audience. Amid the sobbing and keening, the band would play on, seemingly impervious. Some of the fans swooned and fainted, as if in sexual or spiritual ecstasy. *The New York Times* compared them to the jitterbug enthusiasts of the 1940s, whom the German sociologist Theodor Adorno had described as 'rhythmic obedients', driven by an atavistic wish to merge as a crowd. Another commentator suggested that the 'Beatlemanes' might be anticipating motherhood, rehearsing the screams with which they would give birth to their babies.

In his oral history of Beatlemania, Garry Berman quotes a young woman who was overcome by seeing the Beatles on *The Ed Sullivan Show* that year. 'We were feeling the TV and touching it and screaming,' she said. 'I had to clean the TV after that ... I remember we were just lying on the floor and it was like, "Oh my God, what was that?"'

'I just screamed,' recalled another girl after a Beatles concert. 'I could not help it. It was like I had no control over myself whatsoever.' A fellow fan remembered 'ripping part of my hair out of my head, screaming, nonstop screaming – we couldn't talk after the concert we were screaming so bad'. Some girls were engulfed by relief or sadness. 'I cried,' one told Berman. 'I remember just sitting there crying. I didn't know why.' In *Vocal Tracks* (2008), Jacob Smith compares the screaming of the Beatles' fans to the primal scream therapy later practised by John Lennon and Yoko Ono: shrieks and wails could be ways of releasing a submerged, libidinal self.

Less sympathetically, Noël Coward recorded in his diary in 1965 that he had just watched 'four innocuous, rather silly-looking young men' perform in a stadium in Rome, while the audience indulged in a 'mass masturbation orgy'. 'Personally,' he added, 'I should have liked to take some of those squealing young maniacs and cracked their heads together.' Paul Johnson of the *New*

Statesman was similarly scornful: 'Those who flock round the Beatles, who scream themselves into hysteria, whose vacant faces flicker over the TV screen, are the least fortunate of their generation, the dull, the idle, the failures.'

Mass manias for pop stars have recurred since the 1960s, among them the 'Bieber Fever' inspired by the Canadian singer Justin Bieber in 2012. The author Dorian Lynskey points out that Beatlemania was prefigured by Lisztomania, a term coined by the German poet Heinrich Heine in 1844 to describe the 'true madness, unheard of in the annals of furore' that erupted at the concerts of the handsome and charismatic pianist Franz Liszt. His female admirers would shout, rhythmically stamp their feet, and emit involuntary screams of ecstasy. They collected locks of Liszt's hair, his piano strings, cigar butts and coffee grounds.

Yet Beatlemania, like Bieber Fever and Lisztomania, was essentially chaste: these were erotic passions that would not be consummated, shared obsessions that forged bonds between fans. And the Beatles were figures to emulate as well as to desire. 'It didn't feel sexual,' recalled a female fan in Lisa Lewis's *The Adoring Audience* (1992). 'It felt more about wanting freedom. I didn't want to grow up and be a wife and it seemed to me that the Beatles had the kind of freedom I wanted. No rules, they could spend two days lying in bed; they ran around on motorbikes, ate from room service … I didn't want to sleep with Paul McCartney, I was too young. But I wanted to be like them.'

The fans' feelings could move quickly from adulation to aggression. 'A Beatle who ventures out unguarded into the streets,' warned *Life* magazine, 'runs the very real peril of being dismembered or crushed to death by his fans.' In a reversal of the usual dynamic, the young women were the sexual predators and the boys from Liverpool the objects of their pursuit. When the Beatles left New York after their second American tour in 1965, a mob of fans cracked the ribs of three policemen, then shattered the airport's plate-glass door and twenty-three of its windows.

In the Beatles movie, *A Hard Day's Night* (1964), the Fab Four cower in cars and scuttle into hotel lobbies, hounded by yelping teenagers. By going wild, the young women have made themselves the story.

☞ *See also:* choreomania, demonomania, laughing mania, trichomania

BIBLIOMANIA

Giacomo 'ran through the store rooms, he ran through the galleries of his library with ecstasy and delight', wrote the fourteen-year-old Gustave Flaubert in his novella *Bibliomanie* (1837). 'Then he stopped, his hair in disorder, his eyes fixed and sparkling. His hands, warm and damp, trembled on touching the wood of his shelves.' Flaubert's book dealer was mad with love for his books. Soon he would give his life for one of them.

The French term *bibliomanie*, derived from the Greek *biblios*, or book, was first recorded in 1734, but the craze reached its zenith at the end of the century, when 'the bibliomania' in Britain became a speculative spending frenzy to rival the Dutch tulipomania of the 1630s. In his poem 'The Bibliomania' (1809) the Manchester physician John Ferrier wondered at his countrymen's obsession with books:

> *What wild desires, what restless torments seize*
> *The hapless man, who feels the book-disease.*

As the private libraries of many French nobles were sold off after the Revolution of 1789, thousands of rare volumes became available to collectors. Meanwhile, a proliferation of new books – reprints, anthologies, compendiums – cast a lustre of rarity on the antique originals. As the literary historian Philip Connell observes: 'The material traces of the literary past now had a price tag, a social cachet and – in a period that saw the introduction of the steam press and stereotype printing – the venerable aura of sacred relics.' The

price of old books, according to one contemporary source, quad-rupled in the first two decades of the nineteenth century.

Those who created private libraries tended to present them-selves as guardians of literary heritage, but in 1801 Isaac D'Israeli likened them to 'gluttons', 'without digestion or taste', who hoarded more than they could consume. Their collections were book prisons, he suggested, in which 'volumes, arrayed in all the pomp of lettering, silk linings, triple gold bands and tinted leather, are locked up in wire-cases, and secured from the vulgar hands of the mere reader, dazzling our eyes like Eastern beauties peering through their jealousies'. These books were not for reading but for viewing, items removed from circulation, locked away like women in a harem. They were put on tantalising display: exuding the scent of flesh, tooled in gold, sensual and desirable but closed and unknowable.

In *Bibliomania, or Book Madness*, the English cleric Thomas Frognall Dibdin reported that aristocrats, antiquarians and entre-preneurs were buying and selling books with abandon: in 1812 the auction of the library of John Ker, 3rd Duke of Roxburghe, became a forty-two-day extravaganza of 'courage, slaughter, dev-astation, and phrensy', at which a 1471 edition of Giovanni Boccaccio's *The Decameron* sold for £2,260 (the equivalent of more than £200,000 today). Dibdin explained that bibliomanes prized 'first editions, true editions, black letter-printed books, large paper copies; uncut books with edges that are not sheared by binder's tools; illustrated copies; unique copies with morocco binding or silk lining; and copies printed on vellum'. They loved the body of a book.

In 1836 Dibdin was shown the collection of 150,000 books left by the renowned bibliomane Richard Heber. 'I looked round me with amazement,' wrote Dibdin. 'I had never seen rooms, cup-boards, passages, and corridors, so choked, so suffocated with books. Treble rows were there, double rows were there. Hundreds of slim quartos – several upon each other – were longitudinally placed over thin and stunted duodecimos, reaching from one extremity of shelf to another. Up to the very ceiling the piles of volumes extended; while the floor was strewn with them, in loose

and numerous heaps.' The dead man's library was a scene of collapse, in which the books stifled and crushed one another, a grave-
yard of learning.

Flaubert created the character of Giacomo the bibliomaniac
book dealer in 1836, after reading an article in a French newspaper
that described the murder trial of the monk-turned-bookseller
Don Vincente. The piece in *La Gazette des Tribunaux* seems
to have been a fabrication, as no other record of this trial has
been found, but according to the article Don Vincente had burned
down a rival collector's house in order to secure a rare book.
His competitor was killed in the fire, and Don Vincente was
charged with murder when the stolen book was found on his
premises. At the trial, his defence lawyer produced a catalogue
that advertised another copy of the rare volume. Don Vincente, he
argued, might have purchased his copy rather than stolen it from
the burning building. But the book dealer gave the game away
when he reacted to his lawyer's revelation by crying out in anguish,
'Alas! Alas! My copy is not unique!' He was convicted and
sentenced to death.

In an age of mass publication, a rare book had become more
alluring than ever. To possess the single copy of a work was
somehow to own it spiritually as well as materially, to take possession of its author's soul. Don Vincente had placed his own life, as
well as that of his rival, second to his longing for such
possession.

Bibliomania has often since led to crime. The Iowan 'Book
Bandit' Stephen Blumberg was charged in 1990 with stealing more
than 23,600 books, worth $5.3 million, from almost 300 universi-
ties and museums across the United States. His spoils included a
Nuremberg Chronicle of 1493, bound in ivory calfskin. According
to a psychiatrist who testified in his defence, Blumberg did not
take the books for financial gain – he had a substantial trust fund.
Rather, he was a compulsive collector whose criminal career
began when he stole stained glass and doorknobs from a Victorian
terrace in his neighbourhood that was slated for demolition.

In 2009 Farhad Hakimzadeh, a multi-millionaire Iranian-born
author and businessman, was found guilty of stealing 150 pages

from works in the Bodleian Library in Oxford and the British Library in London. Hakimzadeh had carefully cut the leaves from the books with a scalpel and taken them home to Knightsbridge to replace damaged pages in his own extensive collection. Most of the volumes that he mutilated were works about European entanglements in the Middle and Far East between the sixteenth and eighteenth centuries; one page that he took was a map by Hans Holbein the Younger, worth £30,000.

The British Library's head of British and Early Printed Collections was 'extremely angry', he told the press: Hakimzadeh was 'somebody extremely rich who has damaged something which belongs to everybody, completely selfishly destroyed something for his own personal benefit which this nation has invested in over generations'. The judge in the case seemed more understanding. 'You have a deep love of books,' he told Hakimzadeh when sentencing him to two years in prison; 'perhaps so deep that it goes to excess.'

☞ *See also: kleptomania, oniomania, syllogomania, tulipomania*

BLOOD-INJECTION-INJURY PHOBIA

Extreme fears of blood, injection and injury (also known as hemophobia, trypanophobia and traumatophobia) are now often considered as one syndrome – blood-injection-injury phobia (BII) – which affects 3 to 4 per cent of the population. The phobic reaction entails dizziness, nausea, a drop in heart rate and blood pressure, and is sometimes accompanied by tunnel vision, tinnitus, sweating and loss of consciousness. The phobia can be so severe that the sufferer refuses blood tests, surgery, vaccinations, and, in extreme cases, all medical treatment.

Individuals with BII phobia usually describe themselves as more disgusted than frightened by blood, injuries or needles, and experiments confirm that disgust, as well as fear, plays a significant part in the condition. When shown a video of surgical procedures, those with a phobia of blood or injury will furrow their eyebrows and raise their upper lips. At the same time, their heart rates rapidly accelerate and then sharply decrease, in a distinctive two-phase pattern that indicates an initial fear-response (an acceleration of blood flow, triggered by the amygdala) followed by disgust (deceleration, triggered by the insula). The speed of the drop in blood pressure causes an overreaction of the vasovagal nerve, leading to faintness and sometimes a loss of consciousness. Very occasionally, the sudden fall in pressure is fatal: in a paper on trypanophobia in 1995, James G. Hamilton cited twenty-three individuals who had died of vasovagal shock after an encounter with a needle. Some speculate that the initial fear-response in blood-injection-injury phobia, indicated by the speeding heart, might in fact be a dread of the impending disgust response, with its unpleasant and even dangerous sensations of nausea, vertigo and faintness.

BII phobia seems to be the most heritable of all the phobias – an estimated 60 per cent of sufferers have a close relative with the condition – though its evolutionary purpose is not obvious. People who freeze, reel or pass out at the sight of blood would not be much use to a group that came under attack: they would be unable to help themselves or their wounded comrades or to inflict injury on the enemy. But a fear of blood and of objects that penetrate the skin may help them to avoid injury in the first place. The phobia may even provide a degree of self-protection in the event of injury, since the drop in blood pressure slightly slows the rate of blood loss. By fainting, BII-phobic individuals might escape the notice of enemies, or at least inhibit their attack reflexes; in effect, they play dead instead of fighting or fleeing.

One hypothesis is that BII phobia evolved as a survival-enhancing trait in some women during the Paleolithic period. Studies of human remains and of DNA lineage indicate that, for several millennia, young men fought one another for females of reproductive age. During these battles, women and children who fainted at the sight of blood may have been more likely to be taken captive than to be killed. If this theory is right, the phobic response would be more advantageous to women of reproductive age than to men, and therefore more prevalent among them. In 2007 Stefan

Bracha and a group of other psychiatrists tested this hypothesis, using an extensive epidemiological survey in Baltimore, and found that, as expected, more than four times as many reproductive-age women as men suffered from BII phobia. In women aged fifty and over, the incidence fell sharply, to a third of the rate of the younger female group. These findings seemed to support the evolutionary explanation.

To avoid fainting, those who suffer from BII phobia can temporarily raise their blood pressure by coughing, swallowing liquid or making themselves angry. In the 1980s the Swedish psychologist Lars-Göran Öst trained a few phobic individuals to increase the blood flow to their brains by tensing the muscles in their arms, torso and legs for ten to fifteen seconds at a time. Öst tested his technique in 1991 by screening a film of thoracic surgery for three BII-phobic groups. One group had been taught his 'applied tension' method, one had received exposure therapy, and a third group had been treated with both. The exposure therapy group experienced twice as many phobic symptoms as the applied tension group, and the group which had undergone both treatments fared best of all.

After watching the video, half of the patients to whom Öst had taught the muscle-tensing technique told him that they had not used it during the film screening. When he asked why, they said that they hadn't needed to. 'If I had the symptoms,' said one, 'I knew I had an effective technique I could use.' Perhaps this confidence itself prevented the vasovagal effect. Having learnt the technique, these individuals may have been so unafraid that they did not experience the initial fear phase of the phobic reaction, and so did not undergo the dramatic, dizzying drop in blood pressure caused by the switch from dread to disgust.

☛ *See also: mysophobia, odontophobia*

BRONTOPHOBIA

In New York in the 1870s George Miller Beard found himself treating several patients who were terrified by the violent thunderstorms in the city. In *A Practical Treatise on Nervous Exhaustion* (1880), he named their condition brontophobia (from the Greek word *bronte*, or thunder) and noted that it was often accompanied by astrophobia (from *astrape*, or lightning). The phobia had a long history – at the rumble of thunder, both Augustus Caesar, the first Roman emperor, and Caligula, the third, would scramble for cover under a bed or in a vault beneath the ground. In Granville Stanley Hall's classic study of 1897, a fear of thunder emerged as one of the most common of all the phobias. 'Perhaps nowhere,' he wrote, 'is the power of noise to control feeling and also to excite imagery so well seen.'

Beard's patients reported feelings of great fear accompanied by headaches, numbness, nausea, vomiting, diarrhoea and, occasionally, convulsions. One woman told him that she was always watching the clouds in summer, dreading the approach of a storm. 'She knows and says that this is absurd and ridiculous,' wrote Beard, 'but she declares she cannot help it.' The woman claimed that she had inherited the phobia from her grandmother and had been told, by her mother, that she showed a terror of thunderstorms even in the cradle. A clergyman brought his wife to Beard, saying that she had been brontophobic for six years. When a storm was coming, he complained, he was 'obliged to close the doors and windows, darken the room, and make things generally inconvenient for himself and his family'.

In 1975, also in New York City, the behavioural therapist Barry Lubetkin treated a forty-five-year-old woman who suffered from brontophobia. She was continually on the look-out for storms, she told him, and when she heard thunder would cower in her basement in terror. The fear had generalised to other sudden loud noises, such as cars backfiring, balloons popping and the roar of low-flying aircraft. She was terrified of New York's summer storms and, having already been treated by two psychotherapists who had failed to cure her phobia, she was thinking of leaving the area. The woman told Lubetkin that she dated her brontophobia to her childhood in wartime Europe, when she had been frightened by the explosions of shells and bombs.

Having taught relaxation techniques to his patient, Lubetkin took her to a local planetarium, where he had arranged for a projectionist to screen a three-minute film of a thunderstorm. The patient relaxed herself before watching the film, then watched it again and again that day, eight times in total. She did the same on seven further visits to the planetarium. She afterwards told Lubetkin that her phobic symptoms had improved. She spent less time worrying about thunder, she said, and during one storm had even felt able to remain on the top floor of a house that she was visiting. Nor was she as disturbed by the sounds of popping or of planes.

In 1978 the psychologists Andrée Liddell and Maureen Lyons analysed the case notes of ten brontophobic and astraphobic women, aged between twenty-three and sixty-six, who had been treated at the Middlesex Hospital in London over the previous fifteen years. The women referred for treatment were constantly anxious about storms: they would obsessively check the sky for dark clouds, tune in to weather reports on the radio, read forecasts in the newspapers and ring the Meteorological Office for up-to-date information. When thunder struck, their hands flew to their ears, they threw themselves under blankets and pillows or dashed to safe corners of their houses. Two chose to lie on the floor at the bottom of the stairs, and two hid in spaces beneath the staircase. They trembled, shook, screamed, cried, went hot and cold.

The researchers noted that in several cases the phobia had been triggered by an adverse life event – a miscarriage, an unhappy second marriage, the death of a parent or a husband – and that three of the patients described being frightened by bombs during the Second World War. One woman said that she developed the phobia on moving to England from Vietnam, where she, too, had been scared by bombing. Yet the researchers reported that most patients could not recall a traumatic incident associated with thunder, and concluded that the phobia was likely to be one of the prepared fears identified by the experimental psychologist Martin

Seligman in 1971. In his influential essay 'Phobias and Preparedness' Seligman argued that evolution had shaped us to learn and retain some associations far more easily than others. He proposed that a fear of thunder, like the fears of heights and darkness, was an adaptive, evolved propensity that had once been useful to the human species and was still latent in many of us.

Yet Seligman believed that to become a phobia even a biologically prepared fear needed to be activated by experience. And though the Middlesex Hospital researchers claimed to have found little evidence of trauma in the cases that they studied, four of the ten patients had mentioned frightening episodes of bombing, one describing herself as 'petrified' by bombs. Most adult Londoners in the 1960s and 1970s would have remembered the Blitz of 1940 and the 'doodlebug' attacks on the city in 1944 and 1945, which between them killed more than 40,000 people. Perhaps the Middlesex researchers considered experiences of bombing too ordinary to be traumatic. But for some of these brontophobic women, as for Lubetkin's European émigré, the boom of thunder might well have recalled moments at which explosions had ripped the air of a city, shaken the walls of homes, shattered windows, torn craters in the streets, and maimed or killed those taken unawares.

 See also: globophobia, phonophobia

CHOREOMANIA

In the midsummer of 1374, an epidemic of manic dancing spread along the river Rhine and out into the surrounding countryside.

'Both men and women,' reported the monk Peter of Herental, 'danced in their homes, in the churches and in the streets, holding each other's hands and leaping in the air.' They danced compulsively, for hours and days, until they fell to the ground with exhaustion. When they stopped, said Peter, 'they felt such pains in their chest, that if their friends did not tie linen clothes tightly around their waists, they cried out like madmen that they were dying'. Some did die. 'Those who were cured said that they seemed to have been dancing in a river of blood, which is why they jumped into the air.' The 'dancing madness', later dubbed choreomania (from the Greek *khoros*, a band of singers or dancers), continued until late October.

Another bout of choreomania broke out on 14 July 1518, when a woman called Frau Troffea began to dance in the streets of Strasbourg. By the end of the week thirty-four people were dancing alongside her, and by the end of the month there were 400. The town tried to control the disorder by providing halls and marketplaces for the dancers, and musicians to accompany them, but these measures seemed only to make it worse. By the time the dancing stopped on 10 August, dozens had collapsed and died with heart attacks and strokes.

These spates of dancing have intrigued historians. In 1832 the German physician Justus Friedrich Hecker described them as a sort of emotional contagion, a 'morbid sympathy', in which people were inspired to dance by the sight of others dancing. He proposed that the original cause was the Black Death, or bubonic plague, which killed half of the people of Europe between 1347 and 1351 and left many survivors mired in despair: a few vented their panic and grief in dance. John Waller, taking up Hecker's interpretation, argues that the dancing epidemics were mass psychogenic illnesses, generated by fear and spread by imitation. The most dramatic outbreaks followed periods of renewed hardship, he observes – the Rhine flooded in 1373 and 1374, submerging streets and homes, while Strasbourg in 1518 had undergone a decade of famine, sickness and savage cold. Kélina Gotman describes the epidemics as symptoms of social upheaval, surges of primitivity and excess. Wild dancers appear, she writes, 'where there is a fault line in civilisation, a rupture and an opening, out of which they seem to spill'.

Some have suggested that the frantic dancing along the Rhine was really an outbreak of delirious convulsions caused by ergot, a psychotropic mould that can form on damp rye – and that the flooding of the fields around the river had poisoned the people's bread. But the sociologist Robert Bartholomew argues that the mania was more likely sparked by pilgrims from Hungary, Poland and Bohemia who danced as a form of worship, and were joined by locals in the towns through which they passed. He cites the French chronicler Jean d'Outremeuse, who wrote on 11 September 1374: 'there came from the north to Liege ... a company of persons who all danced continually. They were linked with clothes, and they jumped and leaped ... They called loudly on St John the Baptist and fiercely clapped their hands.'

Bartholomew points out that in the Middle Ages a dance could be an act of expiation. In the summer of 1188 the royal clerk Gerald de Barri described a ritual at a church in Wales, in which men and women danced at the shrine of St Almedha, then danced 'round the churchyard with song, suddenly falling to the ground as in a trance, then jumping up as in a frenzy'. As they danced, they acted out their misdemeanours, miming the way in which they had unlawfully driven a plough on a feast day, or cobbled a pair of shoes. They were then led back to the altar, where they were 'suddenly awakened, and coming to themselves'. Their dissociated dancing was understood as a spiritual state, through which they touched on their transgressions and sought absolution.

☞ *See also: Beatlemania, demonomania, laughing mania*

CLAUSTROPHOBIA

For 5 to 10 per cent of the world's population, a feeling of panic can be triggered by a small room, a cupboard, a cave, an elevator, a cellar, an aircraft, a tunnel, a mask, an MRI scanner, even a tight-necked shirt. The phobia of confined spaces was identified in the 1870s by the Italian physician Antigono Raggi, who cited the example of a distinguished painter who became so panic-stricken in a narrow gallery showing his work that he rushed for the door and, on finding that he could not open it, leapt from a window and jumped from roof to roof until he reached the ground. Raggi called the disorder 'clithrophobia', from the Greek *kleithron*, a bar that bolts a door, but in 1879 the English-born French doctor Benjamin Ball renamed it 'claustrophobia', from the Latin *claustrum*, or confined space.

One of Ball's claustrophobic patients was a young soldier who when alone in a passage had started to imagine that the walls were getting closer and closer; terrified that he would be trapped, he dashed for the fields outside. Another patient had panicked when climbing the twisting stairs of the Tour Saint-Jacques in Paris. At home, Ball said, both men insisted on keeping the doors to their apartments open so that they could quickly flee if the fear took hold. Claustrophobia, said Ball, was 'apparently different from, but in reality similar to, agoraphobia or the dread of open spaces'. Both were 'closely allied to the causeless depression of melancholy or the furious excitement of mania'. Dr Frederick Alexander, a medical officer in east London in the 1920s, observed that claustrophobia was a 'condition of introspection, i.e. looking inward, contemplating one's own mental processes', as if the feeling of entrapment was a mental state before it became a physical dread.

Because the disorder is so widespread, and acquired at an early age, many psychologists think it a vestige of an evolutionary survival mechanism. In Canada in 1993, Stanley Rachman and Steven Taylor established that the primary component of claustrophobia was a fear of suffocation, closely followed by a fear of restriction. It was more prevalent among those with a heightened response to anxiety, they found, and was often triggered by a frightening experience. In West Germany in 1963, the psychologist Andreas Ploeger decided to follow the fortunes of ten men who had been trapped for fourteen days in a collapsed mine at Lengede; in 1974 he reported that six of the ten had developed a phobia of confined spaces.

At Craiglockhart hospital, near Edinburgh, during the First World War the pioneering psychiatrist William H. R. Rivers took on the case of a young army doctor who suffered from claustrophobia. Before the war, a psychoanalyst had told the young man that his stammer and his terror of confined spaces must be rooted in a repressed memory of a sexual trauma, but the young man had been unable to recall any such incident, and when war broke out he had abandoned his treatment to join the Royal Army Medical Corps.

Rivers learnt that the man's claustrophobia had intensified on the Western Front. 'When he reached the front,' wrote Rivers, 'he had to live and work in dug-outs and was at once troubled by the dread of limited space, and especially by the fear that he might not be able to get out if anything happened. His dread was greatly stimulated on his first day in a dug-out when, on asking the use of a spade and shovel, he was told that they were to be used in case he was buried.' Rather than sleep in the dug-out, he used to pace about all night. Soon he collapsed with exhaustion, was diagnosed with shellshock and sent home.

Rivers offered to analyse the man's terrifying dreams about trench warfare, explaining to him that he thought that Sigmund Freud and his followers were right about the effects of repression but wrong to seek exclusively sexual explanations. He believed that the cause of the young doctor's trouble might lie in other memories. Within days, the man recalled an incident from his childhood in Scotland. He had once, at the age of three or four, visited an old rag-and-bone man to sell him some junk for a halfpenny; as he left the man's apartment had found himself trapped in a dark, narrow passage with a growling brown dog blocking his way. He was too small to reach the door handle to get back into the apartment, he told Rivers, and had felt very scared. He thought the old man's name was 'McCann'.

Rivers checked the facts with the man's parents: an old rag-and-bone man named McCann had lived near the family home, they confirmed, though they hadn't known that their son had ever paid him a visit.

The recovery of this memory seemed to cure the young doctor's claustrophobia. He was so sure that he was better, said Rivers, 'that he wished me to lock him in some subterranean chamber of the hospital, but I need hardly say that I declined to put him to such a heroic test'. Back in London the man found that he was able to sit in the middle of a crowded cinema, an experience that until recently would have filled him with horror, and could travel on the Underground with no discomfort at all. He still suffered from a stammer and from violent nightmares, reported Rivers in 1917, but the lifting of his claustrophobia seemed to prove that this aspect of his anxiety had been rooted in his experience in the rag-and-bone man's corridor.

For Rivers, the case confirmed that repressed memories could cause nervous complaints. In the early days of the war, he observed, doctors had looked for the physical causes of shellshock, 'but as the war has progressed the physical conception has given way before one which regards the shell explosion or other catastrophe of warfare as, in the vast majority of cases, merely the spark which has released long pent up forces of a psychical kind'. Rivers believed that a shock on the battlefield exposed conflicts that were already lodged in a soldier's unconscious mind. Later in 1917 he used these ideas when treating the poet Siegfried Sassoon.

In his poem 'Counter-Attack', published in 1918, Sassoon depicted the choked panic of a soldier on the Western Front:

He crouched and flinched, dizzy with galloping fear,
Sick for escape, – loathing the strangled horror
And butchered, frantic gestures of the dead.

The man is trapped with his dead comrades, caught like them in the stifling clutch of the trench.

☞ *See also: aerophobia, agoraphobia, nyctophobia,*
   siderodromophobia, taphephobia

COULROPHOBIA

The origin of the term coulrophobia, meaning a morbid fear of clowns, is murky. The word is thought to have been invented sometime in the 1990s, perhaps the 1980s. 'Coulro' may be derived from *kōlobathristes*, the Byzantine Greek word for 'stilt-walker', or might be a mangling of the Modern Greek '*klooun*', or clown, which is itself a borrowing from the English. Yet a surprisingly clear sequence of events created the need for the term.

Clowns were much-loved figures in 1960s and 1970s America. The most famous were the children's television star Bozo, with his side-flares of red hair, his round red nose, extravagant painted smile and permanently raised eyebrows, and the similarly red-haired, white-faced Ronald McDonald, mascot for the McDonald's restaurant chain. It was easy to franchise a clown character, as anyone could pull on a wig and apply thick make-up to become Bozo in a local television show or to welcome children to a burger joint as Ronald.

But by the late 1970s the reputation of clowns had been damaged by the conviction of John Wayne Gacy for the murder of thirty-three young men and boys. Gacy, a suburban businessman from Illinois, was found to have been performing at children's parties and local fundraisers as a clown called Pogo. A photograph of Gacy in costume appeared in the press: a plump man in a red-and-white-striped romper suit and ruff, waving to the camera with one gloved hand while holding a bouquet of balloons in the other. A huge red smile was painted across his chalk-white face. 'Nobody ever questions what clowns do,' Gacy was reported to have said after his arrest. 'Hell, clowns can go up to broads on the sidelines and squeeze their tits, and all the women do is giggle. You know, clowns can get away with murder.' Gacy was sentenced to death in 1980. Suddenly a clown's painted white face and rictus grin were sinister, a cartoon mask that could conceal a crazed child abductor, a killer or sexual predator. The goofy smile had become a lascivious leer, a jeer at innocence.

By 1981 there were so many reports of clowns harassing children in Boston, Massachusetts, that the head of the school board issued instructions to all teachers: 'It has been brought to the attention of the police department and the district office that adults dressed as clowns have been bothering children to and from school. Please advise children that they must stay away from strangers, especially ones dressed as clowns.' No sooner was this reported in the press than 'stalker clowns' were sighted nearby in Brookline, then in Providence, Rhode Island, and then in Kansas City, Omaha, Nebraska and Colorado. Fear of clowns had become a mass phobia, especially among children, a kind of collective hysteria.

The figure of the predatory clown gained even more traction in 1986 with the terrifying supernatural jester Pennywise in Stephen King's bestselling novel *It*. Here the clown was a malevolent force who took on the shape of whatever a child most feared. His fixed grin hid a soul full of horrors. When King's novel was adapted as a television miniseries in 1990, the phantom clown sightings multiplied. In 1991 a clown was rumoured to be touring Scotland in an ice-cream van, luring children inside to chop them up. One girl heard that the killer clown was getting rid of the evidence by drizzling his victims' blood onto the ice cream in place of raspberry sauce.

The actor Johnny Depp confessed in 1999 to a longstanding fear of clowns. 'There always seemed to be a darkness lurking just under the surface,' he told the *San Francisco Examiner*, 'a potential for real evil. I guess I am afraid of them because it's impossible – thanks to their painted-on-smiles – to distinguish if they are happy or if they're about to bite your face off.'

When 250 children in a Sheffield hospital were asked for their views on decorating the walls of the ward in 2008, none wanted clown images. 'We found that clowns are universally disliked by children,' said a researcher from Sheffield University. The Association of Hospital Clowns took issue with this blanket con-clusion, and was partly vindicated by an analysis of 124 American hospital trials, published in the *British Medical Journal* in 2020, which found that 'clown doctors' reduced fatigue, pain and distress in children. 'Some may be delighted to see one on the ward,' observed a spokeswoman for the Royal College of Paediatrics and Child Health, but acknowledged that 'others might be alarmed'.

Clowns, jesters and fools have unsettled us for centuries. They are licensed mischief-makers, primed to subvert social norms, and their bright masks and costumes have often been understood as a cover for darkness. Joseph Grimaldi, perhaps the most famous clown ever, was revealed after his death in 1837 to have been a profoundly troubled man. In the memoirs edited by Charles Dickens, Grimaldi's sublime stage antics were set against his private torments: alcoholism, chronic physical pain, grief at the death of his son. Grimaldi's French counterpart, Jean-Gaspard Deburau – the creator of the definitive Pierrot – was so quick to anger that in 1836 he struck and killed a boy who mocked him in a Parisian street.

The French author Edmond de Goncourt observed in 1876 that clowning 'is now rather terrifying and full of anxiety and apprehension': the clowns' violent and despairing gesticulations, he said, were reminiscent 'of the courtyard of a lunatic asylum'. In Ruggero Leoncavallo's opera *Pagliacci* (1892), Canio the clown, in a fit of jealous fury, murders his unfaithful wife.

In the twentieth century the suffering clown mutated into the heartless clown. The most influential of these was Batman's arch enemy the Joker, who appeared in the original edition of the DC comic strip in 1940. Though the Joker was played as a jolly prankster in 1960s television shows, Jack Nicholson made him a nihilistic psychopath in *Batman* (1989), as did Heath Ledger in *The Dark Knight* (2008) and Joaquin Phoenix in *Joker* (2019). The figures who disturb us now seem defined less by their pain than by their incapacity to feel.

☛ *See also: pediophobia*

CYNOPHOBIA

Among people who seek treatment for a specific phobia in the United States, more than a third have a terror of cats (ailurophobia) or of dogs (cynophobia, from the Greek *kyon*, or dog). Since there is more than one dog to every nine people in the world, a phobia of these animals can be a serious obstacle to normal life.

Cynophobia is often diagnosed in children, who are more likely than adults to be chased or bitten by a dog. In 1975, the clinical psychologist Marian L. MacDonald reported on a cynophobic eleven-year-old boy brought by his parents to the University of Illinois counselling centre. The boy was described by his teachers as extremely withdrawn. He would take no part in outdoor sports because he was afraid that he might come across a dog. His mother drove him to and from school in the morning and again in the afternoon, so that he wouldn't bump into any dogs, and his father had given up playing sport because the boy wouldn't accompany him to games. He spent most of his time in his room alone, reading comics and drawing pictures of superheroes.

The boy had become phobic, his parents told MacDonald, after three upsetting encounters with dogs. When he was three, he was startled by a stray dog running through the family's yard. Less than a year later, he and his father were sitting on the back porch when a dog wandered by. The father called it over, patted it, and encouraged his son to touch it too. Unfortunately, as the boy reached out the dog whipped round and nipped his arm. After this, the boy was doubly scared, and his fears started to extend to other creatures (cats, frogs, grasshoppers, bees) and to dog-related sounds, such as barking and the jingle of collar bells.

Another year later, the boy was playing ball in the front yard when a dog burst through an opening in the bushes and knocked him over. He had been terrified of dogs ever since.

The boy's case seemed to illustrate Orval Hobart Mowrer's two-factor model of fear conditioning, formulated in 1947, which proposed that a phobia was created by a combination of classical conditioning and avoidance behaviour. Mowrer explained that a phobic individual first underwent an aversive experience, in which  they came to associate an 'unconditioned stimulus', such as pain, with a 'conditioned stimulus', such as a dog, and then reinforced the association by avoiding the object of fear. The evasive behaviour, though it reduced anxiety in the short term, stopped the individual from gradually uncoupling the object from its scary associations. Mowrer pointed out that the phobia would be even harder to shake if it had started with several experiences that linked the unconditioned and the conditioned stimuli – as in the Illinois boy's three frightening brushes with dogs. Mowrer also described how, in 'second-order conditioning', a phobia could be generalised to other objects, as it had been in this child's case to cats and frogs.

At the counselling centre in Illinois, MacDonald designed a course of desensitisation therapy for the cynophobic boy. She taught him to visualise dog events, starting with mildly alarming scenarios and progressing to intimate contact. 'Alright,' she would say, 'I'd like you to imagine sitting in your back yard, alone, playing with your GI Joe and looking up to see an unfamiliar Collie running down your driveway and past the garage.' In the weeks that followed she taught him relaxation techniques, gave him photographs of dogs to put up in his bedroom, and a tape recording of barking to play on his cassette machine. She asked him to write a happy story about himself and a dog. The two of them discussed the body language of a dog – what it meant for the fur on its neck to bristle, or its tail to wag. She encouraged him to read a dog-training manual and to practise patting and tickling a toy animal. Then she set him real-life tasks: walking to school alone, learning to ride a bike, going to the park to watch a baseball game.

The psychologist gently pointed out to the boy's parents that they might be cueing and reinforcing his phobia, monitoring him too closely and anticipating his anxiety. She suggested that they ignore his hesitations and worries around dogs, praise his positive responses to animals, and generally give him more responsibility and autonomy – 'they were strongly encouraged to allow the child to perform certain basic tasks unassisted', she wrote, 'such as blowing his own nose and opening his bedroom window'. It seemed that the phobia had created a family expectation of the boy's helplessness and need. After a few sessions with the parents, said MacDonald, 'they were more receptive to treating him as if he were competent'.

The intervention was a success. At a follow-up appointment two years later, MacDonald reported, 'the child was regularly playing outdoors both alone and with friends, he was not avoiding confrontation with dogs, and he had not been designated by any teacher as either socially isolated or withdrawn'. The case showed how complex and disabling a single phobia could become, leaking into all aspects of a child's life and into his parents' lives too. Cynophobia had been a vehicle for the family's shared anxieties as much as their cause.

Phobic responses can be conditioned by cultural as well as personal associations. Many Sunni and Shi'a Muslims are taught that dogs are unclean, and are encouraged to undergo a purification ritual after the touch of a dog's mouth or snout. In China, in the 1960s, Mao Zedong banned citizens from keeping the animals as pets on the grounds that dog ownership was bourgeois and decadent: it was not until 2020 that dogs were officially classified by the Chinese ministry of agriculture as 'special companion animals' rather than 'livestock'.

A study by the University of Louisville in 2008 found a higher incidence of cynophobia in African-Americans than in non-Hispanic whites. The researchers suggested that the disparity was caused by Black Americans' history with dogs. In the South in the nineteenth century, some plantation owners instilled a hatred of Black people in their dogs by tying up the animals, instructing slaves to beat them violently, and then setting the dogs on their attackers. These dogs were used to chase down men and women who escaped the plantations, as Solomon Northup described in 1853 in his memoir *Twelve Years a Slave*: 'They were gaining upon me. Every howl was nearer and nearer. Each moment I expected they would spring upon my back – expected to feel their long teeth sinking into my flesh. There were so many of them, I knew they would tear me to pieces, that they would worry me, at once, to death.'

Dogs have continued to be used as weapons of racial violence in the United States. Police set dogs on Black protestors in the civil rights marches of the 1960s, and a study of 2015 found that officers were still twice as likely to unleash 'force by canine' on Black people as on whites.

 See also: doraphobia, hydrophobia, zoophobia

DEMONOMANIA

'For a million years I have been the wife of the Devil,' a French laundress told the psychiatrist Jean-Étienne Esquirol in the early nineteenth century. Ever since one of her children died in her arms, she said, she had been possessed by Satan. The Devil 'lodges with me', she explained, 'and ceases not to say to me, that he is the father of my children. I suffer from uterine pains. My body is a sack, made of the skin of the Devil, and is full of toads, serpents, and other unclean beasts, which spring from devils.' She claimed that the Devil urged her to strike strangers and to strangle her offspring.

Another woman in Esquirol's care said that two demons had taken up residence in her haunches, and would come out of her ears in the form of cats, one yellow and white, and the other black. She put grease in her ears to try to block their passage.

Esquirol interpreted these not as cases of spirit possession but as examples of a psychiatric disorder: demonomania, a word derived from the Ancient Greek *daimōn*. There had been epidemics in the past, he said – in the Netherlands, Belgium and Germany in the fourteenth century, and in Rome in the mid-sixteenth century – but the condition was now rare. Of the many thousand psychiatric patients he had encountered, he wrote in *Mental*

Maladies (1838), fewer than twenty suffered from demonomania. Someone who in the past would have been 'delirious with respect to magic, sorcery and the infernal regions', he said, 'is now delirious, thinking himself threatened, pursued, and ready to be incarcerated by the agents of the police'. The deputies of Hell had been replaced with the deputies of the state.

But Esquirol spoke too soon. Two decades after the publication of his seminal book on mental illness, an epidemic of demonomania broke out in the mountain region of Haute-Savoie, on the borders of France, Switzerland and Italy. Between 1857 and the mid-1860s half of the women in the Alpine town of Morzine, and many of the men and children, reported that they were satanically possessed.

The first victim was Péronne Tavernier, a ten-year-old girl who on leaving church one spring morning in 1857 saw a child being fished out of the river, almost dead. Later that day Péronne fainted and didn't come round for several hours. In the weeks that followed she found herself falling into further fits and trances, and one day while tending goats her friend Marie Plagnat fainted alongside her. Soon afterwards both girls started to hallucinate. When Marie predicted that Péronne's father would sicken and die, he and then his livestock succumbed to mysterious illnesses. Marie's siblings began to behave strangely: her younger sister's eyes swivelled; her older sister complained of demons in her body; her brother was seen scaling a tree with uncanny agility.

Within a few months a hundred townspeople were convulsing, hallucinating, prophesying, frothing at the mouth, speaking in tongues and performing acrobatic feats. In 1858, at their families' request, the town's priest conducted a public exorcism, but chaos broke out in the church: the congregation cursed and convulsed, struck the furniture and screamed abuse. The priest agreed to carry out some private exorcisms – during which spirits apparently spoke through the afflicted, confessing to having sinned when alive – but in 1860 he announced that he did not think that the people of Morzine were possessed, but unwell. At this, several of his parishioners attacked him, and the police had to intervene. The next year the French inspector-general for the insane was sent to restore order, with the help of a troop of soldiers. He dispatched the affected townspeople to hospitals and made sure that they were kept apart from one another.

For a while peace prevailed in Morzine, but by 1864 many of those who had been sent to hospital had returned to the town, and the epidemic flared up again. When a bishop visited in May, he found the cemetery and the floor of the church strewn with dozens of convulsing women. As he approached the altar, several threw themselves at him, blaspheming, tearing their clothes, spitting in his face and trying to bite him.

After this the secular authorities again stepped in. They tried to calm the populace by organising distractions such as concerts and dances; they set up a library, once more sent the afflicted to hospital, and minimised religious activities. These measures were successful. By 1868 only a few women were showing signs of possession, and their neighbours dismissed them as sick, dishonest or imbecilic. 'Perhaps,' writes the sociologist Robert Bartholomew, 'reclassifying them in this way, according to the new way of the scientists rather than the old way of the church and sorcery, was the saving factor. The malady was no longer a collective affliction but had become an individual one.' The events at Morzine embodied the shift from a spiritual to a scientific understanding of the world, and from communal to personal breakdown. Esquirol's definition of demonomania as a mental disorder had been secured.

Catherine-Laurence Maire, the French historian who first detailed the episode at Morzine, suggests that demonomania took hold of this town because it had been suddenly exposed to modern, secular society. For centuries its people had been cut off from other communities, hemmed in by mountains, adhering to ancient beliefs in magic and the Devil as well as the tenets of the Roman Catholic Church. They knew little of the world beyond the mountains – only 10 per cent of the town's 2,000 citizens could read. But by the 1850s, transport and communications had started to open up the region, and more than half of the Morzine men were travelling to Geneva and Lausanne for work, returning only at Christmas. For the most part, their wives, mothers and daughters were left to care for the livestock and the land.

It was at this moment of social and demographic upheaval that the women of Morzine succumbed to demonomania. They deployed 'the most extreme possibilities of language and gesture', argues the American author Allen S. Weiss, 'to express the pains and desires inherent in a culture on the way to its final dissolution'. The demonomaniac fits at Morzine were the dying spasms of the medieval world.

☞ *See also: Beatlemania, choreomania, kayak phobia, laughing mania*

DERMATILLOMANIA

The word *dermatillomanie* was first used by the French dermatologist Louis-Anne-Jean Brocq in 1889 to describe the behaviour of an adolescent girl who compulsively picked her acne. *Derma* means skin in Ancient Greek, and *tillo* is to pull out or pluck. The condition is also known as excoriation or skin-picking disorder. 'The habit is not controllable,' wrote George Miller MacKee in 1920, 'and the person finds it difficult, if not impossible, to avoid picking at little islands of epithelial débris, follicular plugs, comedones, stubby hairs, acne lesions, milia, crusts etc.'

Dermatillomania was recognised as a psychiatric problem in the American Psychiatric Association's *Diagnostic and Statistical Manual 5* of 2013, and – like trichotillomania, or hair-plucking, and onychotillomania, or nail-pulling – is classified variously as an obsessive-compulsive, impulse-control or body-focused repetitive disorder.

Most dermatillomanes use their fingernails as tools, though teeth, tweezers, pins and knives are sometimes deployed. It is a relatively common condition, affecting about 3 per cent of the population, but only 20 per cent of sufferers seek treatment. The behaviour often begins in the teenage years, and the goal is usually to smooth the skin, whether by scratching, digging, squeezing or rubbing. Dermatillomanes worry at spots, papules, scabs, scars and insect bites. Many focus on the face, though others pick at any place that they can reach – the butterfly-shaped zone between the shoulder blades is sometimes the only zone that remains untouched.

Dermatillomania can stem from a skin condition such as psoriasis or scabies, or from an illness that causes strange sensations on the flesh, such as diabetes or liver disease, but it is usually psychological in origin and can be treated with drugs or cognitive behavioural therapy. Occasionally it is dangerous. A study from 1999 described a woman who so compulsively picked her neck that she exposed the carotid artery, and another who picked her hands so severely that the doctors considered amputation.

Skin-picking, especially when focused and deliberate, can be a self-punishing behaviour. But it can also be a pleasurable, automatic, absent-minded activity. The dermatillomane's fingers work on the flesh as if scratching an itch, tweaking and pinching, inflaming and soothing, creating a self-contained cycle in which the body enters an intimate conversation with itself, fidgety and fuzzy, and the conscious mind and the wider world recede.

'Well, doctor,' a female patient told the American dermatologist Michael Brodin, 'you know I'm a picker. My mother was a picker, I'm a picker, and my daughter's a picker.' She announced it, Brodin told the *Journal of the American Academy of Dermatology* in 2010, 'in the same tone of voice and with the same demeanor and conviction as if she had just told me they were all Republicans, and proud of it.'

☞ *See also: acarophobia, haphemania, onychotillomania, trichotillomania*

DIPSOMANIA

The term dipsomania (from *dipsa*, which means thirst in Greek), coined in 1819 by the German physician Christoph Wilhelm Hufeland, was used in the nineteenth century to refer both to a morbid craving for alcohol and the crazed state that alcohol could induce.

Of all the Victorian words for excessive drinking (among them inebriety, intemperance, habitual drunkenness, sottishness, crapulence), dipsomania was the term favoured by British doctors. It gave a scientific gloss to the behaviour, casting it as a sickness rather than a moral failing. Once the term alcoholism entered medical discourse, in 1882, dipsomania came, more specifically, to mean an intermittent, episodic form of drunkenness. The dipsomane was a binge drinker, who had periods of abstinence between bouts of boozing. In 1892 the English alienist Daniel Hack Tuke characterised the mania as 'an irresistible obsession and impulse to drink, coming on in attacks, during which the patients are in a condition of impotence of will and manifest great anguish'.

At the turn of the twentieth century, the psychiatrist Pierre Janet described a well-born, well-educated woman of thirty who, since the age of nineteen, had experienced periodic cravings for whisky. Hers, said Janet, was 'the classic form of dipsomania'. She would start by taking just a sip of whisky, aware of how dangerous the liquor was to her, but before she knew it would have taken a gulp, and then another, and from there would continue, said Janet, 'ashamed and unhappy, to drink in secret more and more'. She would consume half a bottle a day, falling into stupors from which she came round with a feeling of profound despair: 'She speaks of killing herself, and only consoles herself with difficulty, by making the most solemn promises.'

After a prolonged binge, the woman would drink just water for a few weeks or months, she told Janet, but then her mood would shift, at first gradually and then in a rush, until 'a veil of sadness spread over everything, a discouragement, a disgust for all action, a profound ennui'. Once she was in this state, she said, 'I am weary of everything. Nothing is worth the trouble of an effort. I can no longer even get angry, for nothing is worth getting angry about, and I am astonished when I see people who have the courage to get angry.' She felt neither happy nor unhappy, she said; she desired nothing. 'You cannot imagine this feeling of a shadow which, little by little, invades the whole of life, like an eclipse of the sun.'

Janet's patient would feel so bleak, so empty of love even for her husband and children ('What a horror it is to lose all feelings of affection!'), that she couldn't see why not to kill herself. She turned to whisky. 'After I have taken a drink of it everything changes colour and becomes interesting again,' she said. 'I no longer feel stupid; I can see, read, speak, and act. It makes life worth living; it gives a fictitious value to everything.' She knew that the uplift of alcohol was false, and she knew that its after-effects were terrible, but it was sometimes the only thing that she was capable of wanting.

☛ *See also: kleptomania, lypemania, nymphomania, pyromania*

DORAPHOBIA

In 1897 the American psychologist Granville Stanley Hall documented 111 cases of 'fur-aversion', a condition that he dubbed doraphobia – from the Greek *dora*, meaning the hide or skin of an animal. Most of his doraphobic subjects hated the feel of fur, whether soft as mink, bristly as a terrier's coat, or coarse and greasy as a rat pelt. A fourteen-year-old girl had a particular horror of fur that was parted or blown to reveal the flesh beneath.

In a famous experiment in the United States in 1919, the behavioural psychologists John Broadus Watson and Rosalie Rayner tried to establish that a phobia could be induced. The pair were inspired by the work of the Russian physiologist Eugene Pavlov, who had discovered in the 1890s that animals could be conditioned to respond physically to specific stimuli – dogs, for instance, would salivate at the clicking of a metronome that they had been taught to associate with the arrival of food.

Watson and Rayner hoped to make a baby fear white rats. The experimental subject was 'Albert B', the 'stolid and unemotional' child of a wet nurse in the Johns Hopkins University Hospital in Baltimore, Maryland. When Albert was nine months old, Watson and Rayner arranged for him to be brought to their laboratory for tests. In the first session, they presented him with a white rat, then with a rabbit, a dog, a monkey, masks and cotton wool. He showed no fear of any of these. He did, however, react violently to the sound of a hammer striking a steel bar just behind his head. The baby not only started and froze at the noise but burst into tears.

At his next session, two months later, the researchers tried to teach Albert to associate the loud noise with the white rat. Each time he stretched out his arm and touched the rat, they struck the steel bar with the hammer. A week later the rat was presented to Albert again. This time he was hesitant. Though he tentatively reached towards the creature with his left forefinger, he stopped short of touching it. At intervals throughout the day, the psychologists showed the rat to the boy and at the same time whacked the steel bar. By the end of the session Albert was reacting with terror to the sight of the rat alone.

'The instant the rat was shown to him, the baby began to cry,' noted Watson and Rayner. 'Almost instantly he turned sharply to the left, fell over on left side, raised himself on all fours and began to crawl away so rapidly that he was caught with difficulty before reaching the edge of the table.' The experiment had been successful. 'This was as convincing a case of a completely conditioned fear response,' they wrote, 'as could have been theoretically pictured.'

A week later, Albert reacted with fear to a rabbit, a dog and a sealskin coat. It seemed that his terror of the rat had spread by association to other furry things. The experiments ended soon afterwards, because the baby's mother left her job at the hospital.

Fears were not innate but learnt, Watson maintained, and the same applied to most human traits. 'Give me a dozen healthy infants, well-formed, and my own specified world to bring them up in,' he proclaimed in 1930, 'and I'll guarantee to take any one at random and train him to become any type of specialist I might select – doctor, lawyer, artist, merchant, chief and, yes, even beggar-man and thief, regardless of his talents, penchants, tendencies, abilities, vocations, and race of his ancestors.' The behaviourist theory that Watson developed was an alternative both to eugenics, which emphasised the role of heredity in human psychology, and to Freudianism, which emphasised the role of repressed sexual desire. Watson joked that if Albert B were to undergo psychoanalysis in later life, his therapists, puzzling over his fear of sealskin coats, might 'tease from him the recital of a dream which upon their analysis will show that Albert at three years of age attempted to play with the pubic hair of the mother and was scolded violently for it'.

Watson and Rayner claimed that their interventions with Albert B would do the boy little harm: the shocks to which they had exposed him, they argued, were similar to those that any infant might encounter. But they said that, given the chance, they would have tried to remove Albert's fears. To recondition his responses, they had planned to feed him sweets when he was shown the rat, they said, or to stimulate his erogenous zones: 'We should try first the lips, then the nipples and as a final resort the sex organs.' The baby Albert may have got off lightly: the scientists had succeeded in terrifying him, but they had at least not had the opportunity to sexually abuse him.

In 2014 Albert B was plausibly identified as Albert Barger, the illegitimate son of a young woman who had worked at Johns Hopkins. His niece told journalists that Albert had died in 2007, having known nothing of the experiments performed upon him as a baby. He seemed to have had a happy life, she said, but he did not like animals. When he called round to see her, she recalled, she used to lock away her dogs for the duration of his visit.

☛ *See also: ailurophobia, cynophobia, musophobia, phonophobia, pteronophobia, zoophobia*

DROMOMANIA

The compulsion to wander was given the name dromomania – from the Greek *dromos*, or running – by the French physician Emmanuel Régis in 1894. Also known as pathological tourism, wanderlust and vagabondage, the mania seems to have proliferated in France in the last decades of the nineteenth century. It sometimes manifested in unconscious states such as ambulatory amnesia and dissociative fugue, and sometimes – in its most benign form – in the behaviour of the *flâneur*, a man who cruised the streets, a wanderer-about-town.

For most of the eighteenth and nineteenth centuries, extended walking was seen as an accomplishment – in Britain in 1809, the 'celebrated pedestrian' Captain Robert Barclay won £1,000 for walking 1,000 miles in 1,000 consecutive hours – and many artists and philosophers exulted in wandering. 'Walking has something about it which animates and enlivens my ideas,' said Jean-Jacques Rousseau in *Confessions* (1789): 'I can hardly think while I am still; my body must be in motion to move my mind.' Friedrich Nietzsche walked eight hours a day while writing *The Wanderer and His Shadow* (1880). 'Sit as little as possible,' he advised his readers; 'do not believe any idea that was not born in the open air and of free movement – in which the muscles do not also revel. All prejudices emanate from the bowels.' But these authors made the choice to walk, as a means of communing with nature and themselves. By the 1890s there seemed to be an epidemic of people who could not stop walking.

Jean-Albert Dadas, a gas fitter from Bordeaux, was the first famous dromomane. As Ian Hacking recounts in *Mad Travellers* (1998), Dadas sustained a head injury after falling out of a tree in 1868, when he was eight, and experienced his first wandering episode four years later when he disappeared from the gas factory to which he was apprenticed. He was discovered in a nearby town working as an assistant to a travelling umbrella salesman, seemingly unaware of how he had got there. Throughout his life, he claimed, he would lapse into fugue states, and come round, bewildered, to find himself in far-flung locations – on a bench in Paris, scrubbing pots in Algeria, in a field in Provence. In 1881 he absconded from the French army in Mons, and walked to Berlin and then to Moscow, where he was arrested and deported to Constantinople. Once he had been returned to Bordeaux in 1886, he was treated by the young neuropsychiatrist Philippe Tissié, whose account of Dadas's adventures popularised the mania. Many cases were identified over the next two decades, some of them by military doctors seeking to save deserters from the death penalty.

In 1906 the psychiatrist Pierre Janet described a fifty-one-year-old male dromomane, 'H', whose compulsive walks included a 140-mile hike from Paris to Lille. Before he embarked on one of his epic treks, H explained: 'I feel a hidden sorrow, a deadly tediousness, an unknown dread ... everything oppresses me, everything makes me uneasy, everything seems flat, the whole world seems not worth anything and I in it, of less account. Then I feel the need of moving, of rousing myself.' To try to prevent himself from setting out on a walk, H would lock his house from the inside and throw the key out of the window. But eventually the yearning overpowered him. 'I break open the door and run out without knowing it,' he said. 'I know only that when I come to myself I am already on the road.'

Janet encountered a young woman who suffered from a similar restlessness, and would repeatedly break out of the asylums in which she was confined. 'She must have exercise,' he wrote, 'and it is absolutely necessary for her to walk every day, without exception, forty or fifty kilometres on a public highway.' She could not relax until she had counted off forty-six of the highway's kilometre posts. 'Sometimes she has a carriage accompanying her,' wrote Janet, 'but she never enters it; she runs beside it while the horse is trotting.' This 'mania for walking', said Janet, 'seems very strange; it is, however, more common than is supposed. There are in Paris unfortunate persons who have a cement track built in their yards on which they walk during the hours when they cannot cover kilometres on the highway.'

The urge to walk was interpreted by some as a resurgence of ancient impulses, a throwback to man's nomadic, pre-agrarian past. Female wanderers were especially disturbing, as they seemed to disown their domestic vocation. 'I could not help it,' says the narrator of Charlotte Brontë's *Jane Eyre* (1847): 'the restlessness was in my nature; it agitated me to pain sometimes.'

Perhaps only a society that idealised domestic and family life would classify the urge to wander as a sickness. During the First

World War, when women were called to work in factories and men to fight for their countries, the diagnosis of dromomania fell away. We now admire walking again – in 2020, during the Covid-19 crisis, the ninety-nine-year-old Captain Tom Moore raised more than £30 million for the British National Health Service by walking a hundred times around his garden before his hundredth birthday, and was knighted for his achievement.

☞ *See also: monomania*

EGOMANIA

The English critic William Sidney Walker first used the word egomania, to mean 'obsessive self-centredness', in a letter of 1825: in Latin and Ancient Greek, *ego* means 'I'. The term entered common usage in Britain in 1895, with the publication of Max Nordau's *Degeneration*. Nordau condemned the avant-garde artists and writers of his generation as egomaniacs, men who were fixated on themselves to the point of delusion. The egomaniac, said Nordau, did not believe that he was better than everyone else. Rather, he 'does not see the world at all. Other people simply do not exist for him … he is alone in the world; more than that, he alone is the world'.

☞ *See also: graphomania, megalomania*

EMETOPHOBIA

Emetophobia is an intense and persistent fear of vomiting (*emeo* means 'vomiting' in Greek). Those who suffer from this phobia dread the loss of control that vomiting entails, and the disgust that it arouses in themselves and others. They avoid all kinds of situations that might expose them to vomit: being around small children or people who are drunk or unwell, going to parties or hospitals, being pregnant, visiting foreign countries, drinking alcohol or taking drugs, boarding boats, planes, trains or rollercoasters.

The condition, also known as Specific Phobia of Vomiting, or SPOV, is much more common in women than in men – the ratio is almost five to one – and often goes undiagnosed because it forms part of an eating disorder, an obsessive-compulsive disorder or a general health anxiety. Emetophobes can feel sick with worry about vomiting. They are desperate not to spew, fearing that if they do so they will humiliate themselves, disgust themselves, reveal their disgustingness. A violent attack of vomiting can feel like being turned inside out, emptied and exposed.

In 2018 a synthesis of the scanty research on the disorder found that 80 per cent of emetophobes reported intrusive images of vomiting, including 31 per cent who had flashbacks to early experiences of throwing up. When asked which features of vomiting they dreaded, four-fifths cited gagging, more than half said that they feared contamination and illness, a third feared a heart attack, a panic attack, suffocation or shame, more than two-thirds feared the sight, sound and smell of vomit, and a twentieth feared the taste.

Emetophobes tend to be more sensitive to disgust than other people. This makes them hypervigilant to gastrointestinal changes, and perhaps prone to misinterpret internal sensations as signs of danger. Many feel nauseous almost every day. They avoid eating out (especially at buffets and salad bars) and are wary of certain foods (such as shellfish, eggs, foreign dishes). To guard against vomiting, they may check sell-by dates repeatedly, wash food several times and follow strict diets.

A survey in Britain in 2013 asked people with this phobia for specific memories of vomiting. Several recalled the negative reactions of others, whether anger, mockery or disgust: 'My dad got mad and was shouting'; 'My sister and some kid laughed at me'; 'Reaction from relative – horror.' Some had been very scared: 'I collapsed afterwards'; 'I felt I nearly died.' Others associated vomiting with another distressing event: 'I was upset having learnt my teenage brother had cancer'; 'My grandmother took me to my father's business and there was a smashed window as it had been unsuccessfully petrol-bombed the night before.' Most also had memories of seeing other people throw up – 87 per cent of emetophobes could recall seeing another person vomit, compared to 23 per cent of a control group. But it was unclear whether these memories were a cause or consequence of the phobia.

Emetophobia is difficult to treat. Gradual exposure to feared images and situations can be effective, but a survey of 2001 found that only 6 per cent of emetophobes were willing to engage in such a process. In 2012 Ad de Jongh of the University of Amsterdam reported on an emetophobic woman – Debbie – whom he had treated with four sessions of EMDR (Eye Movement Desensitisation and Reprocessing) therapy, a technique used since 1987 for post-traumatic stress disorder. In this intervention, the patient is encouraged to summon a distressing memory while concentrating on an external bilateral sound or sight, such as the back-and-forth movements of the therapist's fingers. The idea is that by focusing on a distracting stimulus, the patients tax their cognitive capacity and so reduce the vividness and emotional force of the disturbing memories that they retrieve. When the memories are reconsolidated, they will be less powerful; they may even have been modified.

Debbie was a Dutch office worker, aged forty-six, who had suffered from emetophobia for as long as she could remember. She was so afraid of vomiting that she avoided hospitals, television dramas, travel and much else. 'Her world had shrunk considerably,' wrote de Jongh.

When de Jongh talked to Debbie about her early memories of vomit, she recalled that a child in her kindergarten class had once thrown up over a table. He asked her to think about this while undertaking an EMDR exercise. Debbie put on a pair of headphones and concentrated on the clicks that switched from one earpiece to the other as she described the horrible mess on the table of her kindergarten classroom. 'An intense flow of thoughts immediately started in Debbie's mind,' wrote de Jongh. 'She suddenly burst into tears when she realised how much fun she had actually missed because as a child she had been so fearful.'

During the next sequence of clicks, Debbie said that the memory of the vomit-splurged table was altering, 'changing from very small and detailed into something much broader'. After another series of clicks, she seemed calmer, and said: 'The picture that I always had of it in my mind's eye seems to be simply disappearing.' She recalled other aspects of the classroom, as if she were zooming out from the scene of her distress: a set of jars that she had liked filling with glue; the teacher's sweet smile. And then she had a new memory, of her little brother throwing up in the kitchen while she was babysitting him one night. Her father had come home and cleaned up but then left again. Debbie felt deserted: 'No one even saw my fear,' she said. 'Not heard, not seen. I am not there.'

Over the next three sessions Debbie recalled other upsetting encounters with vomit. Each memory seemed to be made less potent by the EMDR techniques. In the final session Debbie told de Jongh that her phobia was subsiding: she had found herself able to tolerate the sound of her husband retching, and she was soon planning to take a coach trip, a prospect which until recently would have filled her with dread. She was also sticking up for herself at work, she said. Addressing her fearful memories seemed to have boosted her confidence. The treatment came to an end.

Three years later, de Jongh sent Debbie an email to ask how she was doing. 'I'm still not entirely happy when I see someone vomit,' she wrote back, 'but the violent panic reaction doesn't happen.' She told him that she had changed jobs, and now worked for an undertaker. She was frequently required to clean a dead body. 'It's not always fresh,' she said, 'and it often happens that some comes out through the mouth.' She couldn't quite bring herself to use the word 'vomit', but she was evidently able to deal with whatever leaked from the corpse's lips. 'I am really amazed at myself for doing this!' she said, understandably impressed by how far she had come.

☛ *See also: aerophobia, agoraphobia, mysophobia, osmophobia, pnigophobia, tokophobia*

ENTOMOPHOBIA

Salvador Dalí suffered from such severe entomophobia – a term derived from the Greek *entoma*, or insects – that he claimed to find some insects more terrifying than death. 'If I were on the edge of a precipice,' he said in 1942, 'and a large grasshopper sprang upon me and fastened itself to my face, I should prefer to fling myself over the edge rather than endure this frightful "thing".' The film star Scarlett Johansson told a journalist in 2008 that she had had a terror of cockroaches ever since waking up as a child to find one crawling across her face. Dalí, too, traced his horror to his childhood. When he was a boy, he recalled, a female cousin once crushed a large grasshopper under the collar of his shirt: 'though it was eviscerated and abundantly sticky with a loathsome fluid, it still stirred, half destroyed, between my shirt-collar and my flesh, and its jagged legs clutched my neck'.

The English physician Millais Culpin believed that an aversion to insects was a conditioned fear, instilled by a disturbing experience. In *The Lancet* in 1922, he described his work with a veteran, a recipient of the Distinguished Conduct Medal, who during the First World War had developed a phobia of flies and bees. When the former soldier visited his consulting room, said Culpin: 'I purposely closed the window and imprisoned a stray bee. As the insect drummed on the pane the patient, who had once possessed sufficient courage to win the DCM, cowered in his chair and sweated with terror; his condition was so pitiable that I at once opened the window, and regained his confidence only by assuring him, with truth, that I had not realised what a serious thing his fear was.' Culpin attributed the man's terror of the bee to his repressed memory of the buzz of German planes over the trenches of the Western Front.

Entomophobia can also be understood in evolutionary terms: maggots are associated with putrefaction; cockroaches and ticks carry disease; slugs and worms resemble slimy waste such as mucus and faeces. We flinch from these creatures to guard against infected, toxic or rotten matter. As we recoil from them, we usually curl our upper lips, narrow our brows, wrinkle our noses and push out our tongues – this is a classic disgust response, a function of the 'behavioural immune system' that helps to stop pathogens from entering our bodies. For those of us especially prone to disgust, even insects not obviously associated with threats to health, such as beetles and crickets, may stir anxieties about infestation.

The Hungarian philosopher Aurel Kolnai proposed that entomophobia was rooted partly in existential dread. Swarms of insects, he wrote in *On Disgust* (1929), exude a 'restless, nervous, squirming, twitching vitality', a 'senseless, formless surging', an 'interminable directionless sprouting and breeding'. We are disgusted by insects' mindless fecundity, said Kolnai: they seem 'pregnant with death', pulsing with regeneration and decay. We fear that they will not only invade our bodies but breach our symbolic boundaries with the natural world, reminding us of our own grossness and finitude. Similarly, the environmental scholars Mick Smith and Joyce Davidson argued in 2006 that we might feel threatened by insects 'not because they pose a physical danger (evolutionary naturalism), nor because they are associated with the polluting effects of human bodily waste (psychoanalytic naturalism), but because they are indicative of nature itself transgressing the very basis of the symbolic order on which modern society and self-identity are founded'.

Smith and Davidson suggest that a society's choices of phobic objects reveal its collective needs and nightmares. Perhaps, they say, we are phobic about creatures that threaten our assumption that we can control and commodify nature: 'these phobias might indeed crystallise something seriously wrong with modernity's cultural logic, with its relations to a nature that it believes it has suppressed and surpassed but which threatens to return in myriad uncontrollable ways'. In this analysis, entomophobia is an expression of our unease about how we have treated the natural world.

Several commentators have suggested that we are secretly attracted to creatures that repel us. Kolnai said that our aversion to a disgusting object lies in 'the shadow of a desire for union with the object'. Culpin observed that 'fear and desire, phobia and obsession, are to one another as the obverse and reverse of a coin'. The entomologist Jeffrey A. Lockwood notes that the physiological effects of horror – heavy breathing, a racing pulse – can be similar to those of sexual arousal, and that some people find it thrilling to use ants or spiders in erotic foreplay.

William Ian Miller, in *The Anatomy of Disgust* (1997), says that disgust is a clue to our 'unconscious desires, barely admitted fascinations, or furtive curiosities'. Disgust, he points out, is intimately connected to the senses: 'It is about what it feels like to touch, see, taste, smell, even on occasion hear, certain things.' It is provoked by the rustle and hiss of a cockroach, the squelch of a slug, the feathery tickle of ant legs or the powdery brush of a moth's wing.

In 2002 the United States Justice Department authorised the CIA to use insects in the interrogation of Abu Zubaydah, an entomophobic Saudi-born Palestinian captive who was refusing to answer questions about his associations with Al-Qaeda. At secret locations in Thailand, Poland and Lithuania, the CIA subjected Zubaydah to 'enhanced interrogation techniques' including waterboarding, sleep deprivation, beatings, loud noise, extreme temperatures and proximity to insects. They slipped a caterpillar into his narrow, coffin-like 'confinement box', and then a swarm of cockroaches, hoping that the creatures' presence would make him so desperate that he would give up his secrets. There is conflicting testimony about whether these methods were successful, and in 2005 the CIA destroyed the relevant videotapes. Though Zubaydah was not officially charged with any crime, he was transferred in 2006 to Guantanamo Bay, where he was still being held sixteen years later.

☛ *See also: acarophobia, arachnophobia, trypophobia, zoophobia*

ERGOPHOBIA

Ergophobia, or the fear of work (*ergon* in Greek), was identified as a condition by William Dunnett Spanton, a Staffordshire surgeon, in the *British Medical Journal* in 1905. Spanton blamed the rapid spread of the disease on the Workmen's Compensation Act of 1897, which required employers to pay wages to staff who took time off after being injured at work. An ergophobe, Spanton wrote, was a fellow who liked nothing better than smoking cigarettes, watching football matches and staying out late; he would spend weeks off work with a minor injury such as a crushed finger. The press understood what Spanton was getting at: ergophobia, said the *Baltimore Sun*, was a 'new name for laziness'. Or, as *The Bystander* of London put it, in a poem published that June:

> You feel a bit tired in the morning,
> You've a disinclination to rise,
> And the knock on your door is a bit of a bore,
> For you really can't open your eyes ...
>
> You feel that you're fitted for nothing
> But to lie on the flat of your back;
> If your symptoms are these, then you've got a disease,
> You're an Ergophobiac.

☛ *See also: giftomania, siderodromophobia*

EROTOMANIA

Erotomania (from the Greek *eros*, or passionate love) was originally a term for the deranging desperation of unrequited love; in the eighteenth century it came to mean an excess of sexual desire; and now it describes the delusion that one is secretly adored by another person, a condition also known as de Clérambault's Syndrome. In 1921 the French psychiatrist Gatian de Clérambault outlined the case of Léa-Anna B, a fifty-three-year-old Parisian milliner who was convinced that George V was in love with her. On her many trips to London, she would stand for hours outside the gates of Buckingham Palace, waiting for the king to send her coded messages with twitches of the royal curtains.

As de Clérambault explained, the heady early days of an erotomaniac fixation often give way to periods of frustration and resentment. The three stages of the syndrome, he said, are hope, vexation and grudge. The condition is assumed to be more common in women, but in men it is more likely to end in violence, either against the imagined lover or against someone who seems to be obstructing the love affair. As a result, male erotomanes are more likely to come to the attention of psychiatrists and the police, and their stories to be recorded.

In 1838, Jean-Étienne Esquirol described a male patient who suffered from this 'disease of the imagination', a small, thirty-six-year-old black-haired clerk from southern France, who on a visit to Paris had conceived a great passion for an actress. He waited outside her house in all weathers, hung about at the stage door, followed her on foot when she took a carriage ride, and once climbed onto the roof of a hansom cab in the hope of catching a glimpse of her through a window. The actress's husband and her friends did their best to discourage him – they 'revile this wretched man', wrote Esquirol, 'repulse, abuse and maltreat him'. But the clerk persisted, convinced that the actress was being prevented from expressing her true feelings for him. 'Whenever the object of his passion appears upon the stage,' said Esquirol, 'he attends the theatre, places himself on the fourth tier of seats opposite the stage, and when this actress appears, waves a white handkerchief to attract her attention.' And she looked back at him, the clerk claimed, with flushed cheeks and shining eyes.

After a violent altercation with the actress's husband, the clerk was sent to a mental hospital, where Esquirol interviewed him. Finding that the man was perfectly rational on most subjects, Esquirol tried to reason with him about the actress. 'How could you believe that she loves you?' he asked. 'You have nothing engaging, particularly to an actress. Your person is not handsome, and you possess neither rank nor fortune.'

'All that is true,' replied the clerk, 'but love does not reason, and I have seen too much to doubt that I am loved.'

In London in the 1850s a claim of female erotomania was invoked in the new English divorce court. A prosperous engineer called Henry Robinson filed for a dissolution of his marriage to his wife Isabella in the summer of 1858, submitting her diaries as proof of her adultery with a prominent physician, Dr Edward Lane. Mrs Robinson's lawyers replied that their client was suffering from erotomania: her diary entries were fantasies, they said, based on the delusion that Dr Lane was in love with her. Isabella Robinson succeeded in defeating her husband's suit, but her private correspondence suggests that she had done so only to save the young doctor's reputation. She had pretended to be suffering from erotomania in order to spare her lover.

In some instances of erotomania, the fixations multiply. In 2020 a team of Portuguese psychiatrists outlined the case of Mr X, an unemployed fifty-one-year-old who lived with his widowed mother in a small village in southern Portugal. Mr X became convinced that Mrs A, a married woman who frequented his local coffee house, had fallen in love with him: she sent him signals, he said, and looked at him longingly. He started to follow her around, eventually making such a nuisance of himself that she physically assaulted him. At this, he became convinced that the coffee-shop owner, Mrs B, was also in love with him, and, out of jealousy, had maligned him to Mrs A. He was angry with Mrs A for believing the gossip about him and for not being brave enough to leave her marriage.

Soon afterwards, when his mother fell ill and was moved to a care home, Mr X developed a belief that Mrs C, another coffee-shop regular, had fallen for him. She turned him down when he invited her on a date but he reasoned that, because she was married, she was ashamed of admitting her feelings for him. He began to stalk Mrs C, and at one point accused her of using witchcraft to stop him from sleeping and to shrink his genitals. At knifepoint, he demanded that she undo the spell that she had cast. Mrs C reported the incident, and Mr X was admitted to a psychiatric unit, where he was prescribed anti-psychotic drugs. His persecutory delusions abated, but he remained convinced that all three women were in love with him, and declared himself still devoted to Mrs A.

Erotomanes live in a world of their own devising. In Ian McEwan's novel *Enduring Love* (1997), the erotomaniac anti-hero is convinced that another man is secretly in love with him. Wherever he looks, he sees hidden messages of desire. 'His was a world determined from the inside,' writes McEwan, 'driven by private necessity ... He illuminated the world with his feelings, and the world confirmed him at every turn his feelings took.'

☛ *See also: egomania, megalomania, monomania, nymphomania*

ERYTHROPHOBIA

The word erythrophobia was coined in the late nineteenth century to describe a morbid intolerance for things that are red (*erythros* means 'red' in Greek). Physicians had noticed an aversion to the colour in patients whose cataracts had been surgically removed. But by the early twentieth century the word had been adopted to describe a pathological fear of blushing, a dread of going red.

Erythrophobia is a self-fulfilling syndrome, which brings about the physiological change that the sufferer fears. The feeling that one is about to blush summons a blush; as the skin grows hot, the embarrassment intensifies and the heat seems to deepen and spread. The condition can be severely debilitating. In 1846 the German physician Johann Ludwig Casper described a young patient who had started to blush at the age of thirteen and by the time he turned twenty-one was so tormented by the fear of blushing that he avoided even his best friend. That year he took his own life.

People blush when they believe that they are the centre of attention, whether as objects of admiration, ridicule or censure. If others point out that they are blushing, they feel their skin burn all the more furiously. The reddening extends across the area in which the veins are close to the surface of the skin – the cheeks and forehead, the ears, neck and upper chest. The phenomenon is more visible and therefore more likely to become a phobia among fair-skinned people.

Blushing is 'the most peculiar and most human of all expressions,' wrote Charles Darwin in 1872; it is induced by 'shyness, shame and modesty, the essential element in all being self-attention ... It is not the simple act of reflecting on our own appearance, but the thinking of what others think of us which excites a blush.' In fiction, a flush of the skin can reveal a character's hidden feelings. The literary essayist Mark Axelrod counted sixty-six blushes in *Anna Karenina*, Leo Tolstoy's novel of 1878. Anna blushes repeatedly upon hearing the name of her beloved Vronsky. When she and her friend Kitty converse they take turns blushing, as if letting off flares of submission, embarrassment, modesty, pleasure. The rich landowner Konstantin Levin blushes when complimented on his fancy new suit, 'not as grown-ups blush who hardly notice it themselves, but as boys blush who are aware that their shyness is ridiculous and who therefore feel ashamed of it and blush still more, almost to tears'. He blushes at his blushing.

'The fear of blushing,' said the psychiatrist Pierre Janet in 1921, 'like the fear of exhibiting deformity or a ridiculous aspect of oneself, are varieties of pathological timidity, of the fear to be obliged to show oneself, to speak to others, to expose oneself to social judgments.' Yet we sometimes blush when we are alone, and sometimes when a private preoccupation is raised in conversation, such as the name of a person to whom we are secretly attracted. The blush here, too, may indicate a fear of exposure; or, as Freudian theorists propose, a desire for such exposure. 'By blushing,' wrote the Austrian-American psychoanalyst Edmund Bergler in 1944, 'the erythrophobe makes himself really conspicuous.' The wish to be noticed is so strongly repressed, Bergler suggested, that it emerges in the unconscious exhibitionism of the blush.

Biologists have puzzled over the evolutionary purpose of blushing. Some speculate that, as an involuntary response that cannot be faked, it serves a social purpose: by showing that a person is capable of shame and wishes for the group's approval, the blush works to prevent deception and build trust. Granville Stanley Hall argued in 1914 that all blushing sprang from fear. 'Its most generic cause,' he said, 'seems to be a sudden change, real or fancied, in the way in which others regard us. A too frank compliment, a sense that we have betrayed something we want to conceal and that our give-away would cause censure or criticism.' Women blush far more than men, he observed, and a 'blush storm' could be set off by male attention. 'To be stared at by men has for ages been for women the prelude to assault,' he added. 'Even the blush at compliment may have been because once the sense of being admired was associated with greater danger.'

Many erythrophobes suffer from social phobia. Either they blush because they are pathologically shy, or they fear social interaction because they blush. The Chilean psychiatrist Enrique Jadresic was sure that his blushing had a physiological cause: a chronic blusher has an overactive sympathetic nervous system, Jadresic said, which causes the face and chest quickly to light up. As a university professor, he was mortified by his tendency to redden whenever he unexpectedly met a colleague or student. 'There you go up the cherry tree again, doctor,' teased a woman in his department.

Jadresic became exhausted by the need always to be guarding against situations in which he might blush. Having tried several cures, including psychotherapy and medication, he decided to undergo a procedure to cut off the nerve that causes blushing and sweating, which runs from the navel to the neck and can be accessed through the armpit. Many who submit to this operation are afterwards afflicted by pain in the chest and upper back and by compensatory sweating in other parts of the body. Even though Jadresic suffered some of these side-effects himself, he was delighted to be no longer besieged by blushes.

But an experiment reported in the *Journal of Abnormal Psychology* in 2001 suggested that people who feared blushing might not blush more than others at all. The researchers recruited fifteen socially phobic people who were anxious about blushing, fifteen socially phobic people who were not, and fourteen people without social phobia. Among the erythrophobic subjects was a lawyer who had quit her job because she blushed so much in the courtroom. The researchers asked each participant to watch an embarrassing video (of him or herself singing a nursery rhyme), to hold a five-minute conversation with a stranger and to deliver a short talk. During these tasks an infra-red probe would measure the intensity of their blushing and an electrocardiogram would record their heart rates.

To the researchers' surprise, the erythrophobes did not blush more intensely than either the other socially phobic people or the non-phobic control group. During the conversation task, for instance, the non-phobic participants blushed just as much as the others, but did not report it: they did not notice that their skin had reddened. The erythrophobic group, however, did have higher heart rates than the others during each task. The researchers wondered if a socially phobic person who detected a rise in his or her own heart rate might become instantly and vividly aware of other bodily processes, especially those – like blushing or sweating – that they thought could be perceived by other people. They were so worried about their anxiety being seen that they experienced a fast-beating heart as a fast-heating skin.

☛ *See also: agoraphobia, gelotophobia, glossophobia, public urination phobia, social phobia*

F

FYKIAPHOBIA

In 1970, the American psychiatrist Charles A. Sarnoff reported on a two-year-old girl called Jan whom he had treated for a phobia of seaweed, an aversion sometimes referred to as fykiaphobia, from the Greek *phykos*.

Shortly before developing the phobia, Jan had shown distress about being separated from her mother: she would wake crying in the night, and she panicked when left with a babysitter. One afternoon, while the family was staying at her grandmother's seaside home, Jan became upset about the 'green stuff' on the beach, and asked her father to carry her.

At the water's edge the next day, she again took fright at a piece of algae and turned to her mother. 'What's that?' she asked, pointing to its slippery, entangling tendrils. 'Just seaweed,' said her mother, holding out a piece, 'like spinach, like lettuce, like grass.'

The girl quailed in horror and begged to be carried away from the beach. Later in the day she played for a while in a paddling pool in her grandmother's garden, but when she saw some grass in the water, she screamed for help.

That evening, while her parents were out at dinner, Jan woke several times, crying hysterically and kicking her legs. When her grandmother tried to soothe her, Jan said that she was trying to get her feet out of the water, away from the green stuff.

Jan's parents took her to see Sarnoff the next day. She sobbed and trembled as she spoke to him. 'I'm afraid of seaweed,' she said.

'What are you afraid it will do?' he asked. 'Are you afraid it will hurt you?'

'No.' she replied. 'I'm afraid it will hurt Mommy.'

It occurred to Sarnoff that though seaweed could not really attack Jan's mother, Jan herself might fantasise about doing so. He asked Jan if she were the seaweed.

'Yes,' said Jan.

'Are you ever angry at Mommy?'

'Yes. When she goes away.'

Sarnoff assured the child that this was normal, and that her mother would not be angry if she were to tell her how she felt. He encouraged the mother to talk to Jan about her worries. Soon afterwards, Jan's parents told him that the girl was no longer scared of seaweed.

Phobias are very common in childhood, and usually fleeting. Jan's terror of seaweed would probably not have lasted anyway. But Sarnoff used the girl's two-day-old fykiaphobia to work out what was bothering her, and also to reflect on the role of symbols and phobias in child development. Sarnoff felt that Jan's hostility towards her mother had been projected onto the seaweed. The phobia did not necessarily indicate that her anxiety had intensified, he said. Rather, it showed that she had reached a developmental stage in which she was able to express her distress symbolically. She had learnt to displace her anger onto an external object instead of experiencing it physically. This capacity was an intrinsic part of human development, observed Sarnoff: 'Symbols are the basis of culture and civilisation as well as neurotic symptoms.'

Sarnoff noted that the Swiss psychologist Jean Piaget dated a child's capacity for symbolic play from about fifteen months: it was then that an infant might use an object to represent something or someone else – for instance by punishing a doll for being naughty. Between the ages of two and four, Piaget had found, the child developed a capacity for secondary symbolisation, in which threatening thoughts and feelings were unconsciously displaced onto external objects, and the link to the original source of anxiety was repressed. This repression was fairly shallow in a child, which was why Jan had so easily been able to recognise and accept Sarnoff's interpretation of her phobia. Teasing out the source of an adult phobia was far harder.

In 1972 Sarnoff's fellow analyst Otto Renik took issue with his reading of Jan's fykiaphobia. It was Jan who fled the seaweed, Renik pointed out, as if it posed a danger to herself rather than to her mother. She had not just identified with the seaweed, endowing it with her anger, but separated herself from it, in order to feel free of the bad feeling. This showed how a phobic object held two contrary impulses: identification and rejection, a statement and a denial, an embodiment of forbidden feelings and a fear of being punished for them. But Renik praised Sarnoff for keeping things simple: sometimes, an inexact or incomplete interpretation was extremely effective at solving a patient's problem.

☞ *See also: pediophobia, thalassophobia*

GELOTOPHOBIA

Gelotophobia – the fear of being laughed at, from the Greek *gelōs*, or laughter – is a paranoid, touchy form of social phobia. It was first identified as a clinical condition in 1995 by Michael Titze, a German psychotherapist who noticed that some of his patients were tormented by the feeling that they were being mocked. These patients would mistake a cheery grin for a contemptuous sneer, affectionate teasing for aggressive ridicule. When they heard laughter, their facial muscles congealed, said Titze, producing the 'petrified countenance of a sphinx'. Some so braced themselves for mockery that they acquired a stiff, jerky gait, and moved like wooden puppets. Titze described their syndrome as 'Pinocchio complex'. People with gelotophobia often reported having been bullied, Titze found, but it was not clear whether the bullying caused gelotophobia, or whether gelotophobic types interpreted teasing as bullying.

A woman in Titze's care traced her gelotophobia to her school-days. Her mother, a refugee from Eastern Europe, liked to cook with garlic, and the girl found herself being mocked at school because of the smell that emanated from her. A classmate dubbed her 'Miss Garlike', and other children joined in the jeering. 'As soon as they caught sight of me they started grinning in a filthy way,' said Titze's patient. 'Frequently they cried things like, "Ugh!"' Her schoolmates ostentatiously avoided her, not only in the schoolyard but in the street. 'Some covered their face with their cap or their schoolbag,' she said. 'Everyone facing me with a smiling face caused me to panic.' She described how her body responded. 'I grew more and more stiff out of shame.'

Since then, researchers have studied the prevalence of geloto-phobia as a personality trait as well as a pathological condition. Willibald Ruch of the University of Zürich has argued that the highest incidence of gelotophobia is found in 'hierarchically organised societies where the main means of social control is shame'. In one survey, 80 per cent of Thai participants said that they became suspicious if other people laughed in their presence, but fewer than 10 per cent of Finns. Another study found that Chinese students were significantly more afraid of being laughed at than their Indian counterparts. At the International Symposium on Humour and Laughter, held in Barcelona in 2009, Ruch claimed that gelotophobia was most common in British people. 'Within Europe, Britain is on the top,' said the Swiss psychologist. 'Absolutely on the top.'

☞ *See also: erythrophobia, glossophobia, public urination phobia, social phobia*

GERASCOPHOBIA

Gerascophobia – from the Greek word *gerasko*, 'to grow old' – sometimes describes a horror of old age and sometimes a horror of growing up. In 2014 three psychologists in Mexico reported on a fourteen-year-old boy whom they had treated for this condition. As he turned twelve, the boy had become alarmed by how his body was changing. In response, he began to eat less, to stoop to disguise his height, and to speak in a high-pitched whisper. He searched the internet for details of operations that might reverse the effects of puberty.

The boy's parents took him to a clinic in Monterrey, northern Mexico, where he was interviewed by psychologists. He agreed with them that his fear of growing older was excessive, but said that the burdens of adulthood seemed terrible to him: he could not face the idea of finding a partner, looking after a home, holding down a job. Growing up, he said, would only bring him closer to illness and death. He told the psychologists that he admired all things American and longed to look like a Hollywood film star.

The psychologists noticed that the boy's mother tended to infantilise him (singing him lullabies, combing his hair) and his father to treat him harshly (in an attempt to correct his stoop, he used to strap him into a posture belt and squeeze his spine hard with both hands). They recommended that the boy take anti-depressant medication and have two or three psychotherapy sessions each week; and that his parents attend a three-month course of family therapy.

Over the next year, the psychologists talked to the boy about his aversion to growing up. They learnt that he had been treated for separation anxiety when he was five, and had been bullied at school when he was eleven. Most significantly, they discovered that at the age of six he had been sexually abused on several occasions by a sixteen-year-old neighbour. They suggested to him that his experience of abuse had instilled in him a terror of sexual maturity. As the psychologists helped the boy to find causes for his feelings, he started to adopt a more upright posture, to speak and eat normally, and to be less worried about becoming a man.

A child's fear of ageing is portrayed in J. M. Barrie's stage play *Peter Pan, or The Boy Who Wouldn't Grow Up* (1904), in which Peter urges Wendy to follow him to Neverland. 'Come with me,' he coaxes, 'where you'll never, never have to worry about grown-up things again.' And an adult's fear of old age is depicted in Oscar Wilde's novel *The Picture of Dorian Gray* (1891), in which a young man envies the undying freshness of his oil portrait. 'I shall grow old, and horrible, and dreadful,' laments Dorian. 'But this picture will remain always young. It will never be older than this particular day of June ... If it were only the other way! If it were I who was to be always young, and the picture that was to grow old! For that – for that – I would give everything!' Dorian's fear of ageing is not only a fear of physical decay, but a dread of moral responsibility. For a while, he succeeds in swapping his fate with that of the portrait. Though he devotes himself to debauchery and crime, his skin stays taut, his lips soft and his eyes bright. The face in the oil painting, meanwhile, sags, withers and sneers.

☞ *See also: trichomania*

GIFTOMANIA

In London in January 1897, Elise Brown, a dressmaker, sued the Reverend Frederick Hetling for the return of £1 which she had placed on the collection plate at Christ Church in Albany Street, near Regent's Park. She had not intended to donate so much, she told Bloomsbury County Court, and could only suppose that she had been suffering from a temporary bout of insanity. She pointed out that a rich American tourist had recently claimed in another London court that her shoplifting was a symptom of kleptomania.

'My malady is just the reverse,' said Elise Brown. 'Mine is giftomania.'

'What was that?' asked the judge sharply.

'Giftomania,' repeated Miss Brown.

'Oh, nonsense,' said Judge Bacon, dismissing her case.

☞ *See also: kleptomania*

GLOBOPHOBIA

Globophobia (from the Latin *globus*, or sphere) is an aversion to balloons, usually rooted in a fear of the pop made by a balloon when it bursts. The sound 'reminds me of gunfire', said Oprah Winfrey in 2013, 'and perhaps somewhere in my life or in a past childhood I must've had something to do with gunfire, because it just really freaks me out being around balloons'. The South Korean film star So Ji-sub confessed to a television presenter in 2017 that being anywhere near a balloon made him feel that his 'insides were going to burst', as if his body was itself a sac of air, preserved by pressure, poised to explode.

☛ *See also: brontophobia, phonophobia*

GLOSSOPHOBIA

For many of us, public speaking is a terror – known as glosso-phobia, from the Greek *glossa*, or tongue – that manifests in symptoms such as sharpened hearing, an increased heart rate, raised blood pressure, sweating, rapid breathing, stiffening of the neck and back, shaking, a dry mouth, flushed skin and dilated pupils. The blood seems to pump hard and then drain away. 'I turn pale at the outset of a speech,' wrote the Roman orator Marcus Tullius Cicero, 'and quake in every limb and in all my soul.'

Public speaking is a very widespread fear, a phobia often cited as more common than the dread of spiders or snakes. A survey of 1973 found that more people named public speaking as a fear than they did death. 'This means to the average person,' observed Jerry Seinfeld, 'if you have to be at a funeral, you'd rather be in the casket than doing the eulogy.'

The condition can afflict even seasoned performers. In *The New Yorker*, John Lahr described the 'unmooring terror' of stage fright, 'a traumatic, insidious attack on the performer's instru-ment: the body'. He cited actors who had been suddenly overcome by fear, among them Ian Holm, who in 1976 abandoned the stage for fifteen years after being paralysed by fright during a preview of *The Iceman Cometh* at the Aldwych theatre in London. 'The experience,' said Lahr, 'with the metabolic changes it sets off – sweating, confusion, the loss of language – is a simulacrum of dying.'

Glossophobia can be treated with hypnosis, cognitive behavioural techniques, or practical advice (for instance: speak slowly, breathe deeply, take pauses, focus on one face in the audience). In 2003 the social psychologists Kenneth Savitsky and Thomas Gilovich devised an experimental treatment at Cornell University in New York. First, they ran trials to verify the 'illusion of transparency', our tendency to overestimate the extent to which others can perceive our internal states. They then asked a cohort of Cornell students to deliver three-minute speeches on race relations at the university, and split them into three groups. The control group was given no guidance about performing the speeches, while the second group was reassured that it was normal to be anxious, and that they might even be nervous about looking nervous. The third group was given the same message and then also told: 'I think it might help you to know that research has found that audiences can't pick up on your anxiety as well as you might expect.' They explained that most people had an 'illusion of transparency', a belief that their strong emotions would 'leak out' and be seen by others. In reality, said Savitsky and Gilovich, this was very rarely the case. 'If you become nervous,' they told the students, 'you'll probably be the only one to know.'

Once all the participants had delivered their speeches to a video camera, they were invited to rate the confidence and effectiveness of their own performances. Members of the group that had been informed about the 'illusion of transparency' gave themselves the highest scores. A further set of students recruited to watch the videos also rated this group's speeches the most highly.

'Knowing about the illusion of transparency,' concluded the researchers, 'allows speakers to be better speakers. Our results thus lend credence to the notion that "the truth can set you free": knowing the truth about the illusion of transparency set participants free from the cycle of anxiety that can plague those who engage in public speaking.'

Most of us are better than we think at concealing our anxiety. And once we realise that others can't detect our fear, we are less afraid.

☞ *See also: erythrophobia, gelotophobia, social phobia, telephonophobia*

GRAPHOMANIA

As a literary term, graphomania (from the Ancient Greek *graphein*, 'to write') has been used to denigrate prolific authors. The Hungarian critic Max Nordau dismissed Oscar Wilde as a graphomane. 'He has an insatiable desire to write though he has nothing to write about except his own mental and moral ailments,' complained Nordau in *Degeneration* (1895). He accused Wilde of writing for writing's sake, indulging in 'idiotic punning' in which words bred words. It was the culmination of a century that had been flooded with words, as the literary scholar Lennard J. Davis observes: 'Dickens, Balzac, Trollope, Zola, Goncourt, and many less well-known writers have an output, an opus, that is staggering and awe-inspiring. These writers wrote not only novels but journalism, criticism, and letters – they were in effect writing all the time. They had become obsessives in the cause of letters.'

As a clinical condition, compulsive writing is usually referred to as hypergraphia, a term coined in 1974 by the American neurologists Stephen Waxman and Norman Geschwind. They observed that some patients with temporal lobe epilepsy compulsively kept diaries, composed poetry, made lists, copied out aphorisms and song lyrics. The neurologists speculated that epileptic fits had realigned the activity in these patients' brains. In 2013 *New Scientist* reported on a seventy-six-year-old woman with epilepsy, a patient at University College Hospital, London, who when given drugs to stop her seizures had started to turn out poetry. She produced more than ten verses a day, having shown no interest in literature before, and reacted with anger if anyone interrupted her. A typical poem ended:

> To *tidy out cupboards, throw rubbish from sight*
> *(Even the poems you write up at night)*
> *Is morally wrong.*
> *So I'm keeping this one.*

The doctors guessed that the woman's temporal lobe seizures had reorganised the linguistic and emotional-reward mechanisms in her brain, forming a new circuit in which the composition of poetry was peculiarly gratifying.

Automatic writing can be eerie. Psychics and mediums enter trances in which they seem compulsively to scrawl messages from the dead. In Stanley Kubrick's film *The Shining* (1980), Jack Torrance sits typing in his room in a deserted hotel, apparently writing a novel but in fact – as his wife discovers, to her horror – repeatedly clattering out the phrase: 'All work and no play makes Jack a dull boy.' He is mindless as a machine, the torrent of words a cover for emptiness.

 See also: arithmomania, onomatomania

H

HAPHEMANIA

An overpowering desire to touch things – known as haphemania, from the Greek *haphe*, or touch – is common in obsessive-compulsive disorders. Often, a haphemane adheres to a ritual: tapping a doorframe, lifting and replacing an object, patting a person on the top of the head, rapping an item a set number of times or tracing a pattern upon it. The act of touching is usually designed to avert harm and, like a machine or like a spell, it works its magic by repetition. Sometimes the need to touch is so recurrent that callouses form on the tips of the haphemane's fingers and thumbs.

☞ See also: arithmomania, dermatillomania, haphephobia, mysophobia

HAPHEPHOBIA

The term *haphéphobie* was coined in France in 1892 by two physicians – Drs Maurice Lannois and Edmond Weill – who had a patient who could not bear to be touched.

'Jean B', fifty-eight, worked in a laundry in Lyon by the river Saône. He was taken to hospital after he collapsed at work and temporarily lost the power of speech, but the doctors soon noticed another peculiarity: Jean pulled away violently if anyone tried to touch him. For as long as he could remember, he told them, he had reacted with terror to the idea of contact with another person. A hand reaching towards him was frightening, a finger near the face even more so, and if someone came up from behind, the shock would run right through his body: he would almost explode with fright, and spring away.

At work one day, Jean had been carrying a bundle of laundry across a bridge from the quay to the wash house when someone approached him from behind. He dropped the laundry into the river in fright. Jean's friends and family all knew about his phobia. An acquaintance had once teased him by suddenly touching him from behind, at which Jean instantly jumped from a window into the street, a floor below.

In the hospital ward, Jean would look furtively to his left and right, turn round to check behind him, and he sometimes stood against the wall behind his bed so that he could not be taken by surprise. There seemed no physical cause for the phobia – he had no skin conditions or sensitivities; he was not even ticklish – but he was constantly suspicious, watchful, uneasy and, if touched, consumed by anguish.

The doctors tentatively attributed Jean's disorder to 'hereditary degeneration', noting that his father (who had killed himself aged fifty-six) had shared the terror of being touched, as had a nephew who had died of absinthe poisoning on his return from Africa a few years earlier. Yet many members of Jean's family seemed perfectly well. Jean himself could find no reason for his phobia. 'I'm scared,' he said. 'That's all.'

☛ *See also: claustrophobia, haphemania, mysophobia, social phobia*

HIPPOPHOBIA

In 1909 Sigmund Freud published an influential analysis of a five-year-old Viennese boy, 'Little Hans', who in 1908 had developed a severe fear of horses (or hippophobia: *hippo* being Greek for 'horse'). Horses were common on the streets of Vienna, and Hans was so scared of them that he often refused to leave the house. 'The fear of horses was two-fold,' wrote Freud: 'a fear that a horse might fall down and a fear that the horse might bite him.'

Hans's father, a friend and admirer of Freud, said that the phobia had taken hold when the child saw a heavy carthorse fall over in the street and thrash its legs in panic. Freud believed that the sight of the fallen horse, vulnerable and violent, had fixed a pre-existing psychosexual fantasy in the boy's mind. Hans had already shown curiosity about the animals' 'widdlers' ('*Wiwimacher*'), and recently had been told off by his mother for masturbating. He had also remarked on the small 'widdler' of his baby sister.

For the next four months Hans's father conducted a psycho-analysis of his son, under Freud's supervision. He would take notes on what Hans said and did, then discuss the case with Freud before talking to the boy about his wishes and behaviours. Freud believed that the case confirmed his theories of spontaneous infantile sexuality and the Oedipal complex. He speculated that Hans, like other boys of his age, secretly wanted to replace his father as his mother's lover, and that he feared both the harm that this might inflict on his father (making the horse fall down) and the revenge that his father might take (the horse's bite, representing castration).

Freud met Hans only twice. On the second of these occasions, the child said that he was now less frightened by horses but still feared the black things around their eyes and mouths: the blinkers and bridle. Freud asked whether these trappings reminded him of his father's spectacles and dark moustache.

Freud was convinced that Little Hans, in order to deal with his ambivalent feelings towards his father, had displaced his fear and aggression onto horses. The phobia was a compromise, which at once repressed and expressed his feelings. By avoiding the animals in the street, he could disown his own bad thoughts towards his papa.

The analysis ended soon afterwards. It seemed that Little Hans had overcome his phobia. His father thought that it might have been sublimated into his growing interest in music. In May 1908 Freud paid a visit to the family's apartment in Vienna with a belated birthday gift for the child: a rocking horse.

The publication of the Little Hans case the next year was highly controversial, being the first account of the psychoanalysis of a child. It was also the clearest elucidation yet of Freud's theory of Oedipal conflict, and a prototype for the analysis of phobias. Freud described phobias – or 'anxiety-hysterias' – as 'par excellence, the neuroses of childhood'. Most such neuroses were discarded as a child grew up, he said, but the traces often remained. 'It may be that Hans now enjoys an advantage over other children,' wrote Freud, 'in that he no longer carries within him that seed in the shape of repressed complexes.'

In about 1920 Herbert Graf, the seventeen-year-old son of the Austrian musicologist Max Graf, read Freud's case study of Little Hans and recognised himself. He went to his father, who had recently divorced. 'What *is* this?' he asked. 'It obviously concerns *me*?!' His father acknowledged that he was Little Hans: 'Yes, this is so.'

In 1922 Herbert Graf turned up at Freud's studio. 'He looked at me, of course,' said Graf, 'not recognising me. And I said: I am the Little Hans. And it was very touching. He came to me and embraced me, and said, sit down! And then we had a long discussion in which he asked me what I am doing, what I am planning to do, and so forth, at the end of which he said that he felt that the treatment must have done some good because I spoke or acted – at least in his presence – quite normally.'

Freud wrote a postscript to his study. 'Little Hans' was now a 'strapping youth', he reported, who suffered from no obvious troubles or inhibitions. He had coped well with the divorce and remarriages of his parents and remained on good terms with both. The analysis had not damaged him as critics had predicted.

In his early twenties, Herbert Graf became a celebrated opera director in Salzburg and Zürich, and he went on to direct the Metropolitan Opera in New York. In an interview with *Opera News* in 1972, a year before his death, he revealed his identity as Little Hans. He alluded to himself as an 'invisible man', a figure behind the scenes both of opera productions and of the evolution of psychoanalysis. It has since emerged that he had endured tragedies in his adult life. His younger sister killed herself, as did his first wife.

It has also emerged, in interviews with Herbert Graf and his parents made available by the Freud archive only in 2000, that Freud suppressed many facts in his study. He did not mention, for instance, that he had treated the boy's mother, Olga Hönig, in the 1890s, that he encouraged Max Graf to marry her, and that he knew in 1908 that the marriage was extremely unhappy. Freud was eager to use the Little Hans case to substantiate his theories about childhood sexuality. He may not have wanted to muddy the waters by describing the emotional disorder of this particular family – nor his involvement with it. In 1953 Olga Graf remarked that Freud 'wreaked havoc on us'.

Several commentators have questioned Freud's conclusions about Little Hans. Some suggested that both Freud and Max Graf had put ideas in the boy's head, eliciting the elements that supported Freud's new theories. Freud himself acknowledged that: 'Hans had to be told many things which he could not say himself' and 'had to be presented with thoughts which he had so far shown no signs of possessing.' In the 1950s the British psychoanalyst John Bowlby argued that the boy was suffering from separation anxiety: he found evidence in the case study of Hans's insecure attachment to his mother and his fear that she would leave him. The French critic Julia Kristeva, too, thought that Freud underplayed the importance of Hans's mother: she argued in 1982 that the horse symbolised the boy's fear of his mother's body as well as his anxieties about his father. 'The phobia of horses,' she wrote, 'becomes a hieroglyph that condenses all fears.'

With the Little Hans case, Freud had placed phobia at the heart of psychoanalytic theory. To him, Herbert Graf's fixation was a demonstration of how we all unconsciously disown and displace our feelings, transforming our desires into symbols and, sometimes, our fears into art.

☛ *See also: musophobia, zoophobia*

HIPPOPOTOMONSTROSESQUIPEDALIOPHOBIA

Hippopotomonstrosesquipedaliophobia is a partly nonsensical word that was invented, probably in the 1970s, to describe a fear of long words. 'Sesquipedaliophobia' alone would do the job – 'sesquipedalian' has been used since at least the eighteenth century to mean 'many-syllabled' – but the term has been extended to include 'hippopoto' (a slapdash abbreviation of 'hippopotamus') and 'monstro' (from *monstrum*, or monster in Latin). The word enlists a large and slightly comical creature to make itself large and silly. It mimics the phobic object it describes – a long, abstruse word – and it makes fun of phobia coinages, which use Greek and Latinate prefixes to give off an air of antiquity and scientific authority.

Hippopotomonstrosesquipediophobia seems first to have been recorded in a footnote to Dennis Coon and John O. Mitterer's

Introduction to Psychology (1980) and may have been designed to be one letter longer than 'supercalifragilisticexpialidocious', a famously long and fanciful word popularised in 1964 by the movie *Mary Poppins*.

☞ *See also: aibohphobia, onomatomania*

HOMICIDAL MONOMANIA

A homicidal monomaniac, according to Jean-Étienne Esquirol's definition of 1810, is an otherwise sane person who is seized by an irresistible impulse to kill. Esquirol's formulation expanded the possibilities of the insanity defence: seemingly rational killers could now contend that they had fallen prey to a murderous compulsion, a specific and often momentary madness, and should therefore be sentenced as lunatics rather than criminals. When a person is in the grip of homicidal monomania, wrote the American psychiatrist Isaac Ray in 1838, 'the reflective powers are paralyzed, and his movements are solely the result of a blind, automatic impulse with which the reason has as little to do, as with the movements of a newborn infant'. An individual with this affliction, added Ray, should not be punished for killing someone.

In a landmark case in the British courts, the Scottish wood-turner Daniel M'Naghten was acquitted of murder in 1843 on the grounds that he had been suffering from 'homicidal monomania' when he shot the civil servant Edward Drummond, apparently having mistaken him for the prime minister, Robert Peel. Instead of being hanged, M'Naghten was admitted to the Bethlem asylum for criminal lunatics. The diagnosis saved his life, but it also masked his political anger: rather than being remembered as a violent protester against aristocratic Tory rule, M'Naghten went down in history as a madman.

A homicidal monomaniac, said Esquirol, often appeared to return to sanity once the murder was done. 'The act accomplished,' he wrote, 'it seems that the attack is over; and some homicidal monomaniacs, seem to be relieved of a state of agitation and anguish, which was exceedingly painful to them. They are composed, and free from regret, remorse or fear. They contemplate their victim with indifference; and some even experience and manifest a kind of satisfaction.' The act of killing seemed to expunge the madness.

Michel Foucault pointed out in 1978 that Esquirol's concept of homicidal monomania 'transformed a criminal into a madman whose only illness was to commit crimes'. Nineteenth-century psychiatry had 'invented an entirely fictitious entity', he argued, 'a crime which is insanity, a crime which is nothing but insanity, an insanity which is nothing but crime'.

Though the diagnosis had fallen out of favour in psychiatric circles by the 1860s, it continued to be invoked in the courts. Between 1857 and 1913 a defence of homicidal monomania was advanced in forty-three murder trials at the Old Bailey in London. In the trial of Robert Coombes, a thirteen-year-old who stabbed his mother to death in the east of the city in 1895, the prosecution ridiculed the defence's claim that the boy suffered from homicidal monomania: the child had bought and hidden a knife with which to kill his mother, the crown's lawyers reminded the jury. But the jurors chose to accept the diagnosis – and found Coombes guilty but insane.

Coombes was sent to the Broadmoor asylum for criminal lunatics, where he was held alongside others who had been spared the death penalty by merciful juries. Most of the inhabitants of the women's wing (and several of those in the men's quarters) had been diagnosed with homicidal monomania after killing their own children, apparently in fits of panic or despair. Robert Coombes was discharged from the asylum in 1912, aged thirty. Three years later he was awarded the Military Medal for his calm courage as a stretcher-bearer at Gallipoli; and, twenty years later, as a farmer in the Australian countryside, he rescued an eleven-year-old boy from a violent parent on a neighbouring property. His compulsion to kill, if it had ever existed, did not return.

☞ *See also: kleptomania, monomania, pyromania*

HOMOPHOBIA

In 1965 the psychotherapist George Weinberg coined the term homophobia, to mean an aversion to homosexuality, after hearing a stranger insulting a lesbian friend. Though the word literally means a phobia of sameness (*homos* in Greek), Weinberg chose it for effect rather than accuracy – it was pithier than previous attempts to name anti-gay sentiment, such as 'homoerotophobia'. Two other friends of his used the word in an article in *Screw* magazine in 1969: 'What a pitiful state of affairs has been brought about by *homophobia*!' wrote Jack Nichols and Lige Clarke, explaining the condition as 'an intense and neurotic fear of being thought attracted to one's own sex'.

Weinberg, who was himself heterosexual, elaborated on his word's meaning in *Society and the Healthy Homosexual* (1972): the term homophobia ascribed anti-gay feeling to fear, suggesting that a prejudice against homosexuality was a disguised anxiety, an unnatural fixation. 'Discriminatory practices against homosexuals,' he wrote, 'have deep psychological motives.' Homosexuality was then still categorised as a psychiatric disorder, and Weinberg hoped to turn the tables, pathologising the enemies of homosexuality instead of homosexuals themselves. His coinage seemed to work. In 1973 the American Psychiatric Association decided unanimously that homosexuality should no longer be classified as a mental illness. 'Although homophobia was not itself then listed as a clinical disorder,' observes the cultural historian Daniel Wickberg, 'it basically came to supplant homosexuality as the sickness in need of cure.'

Some psychologists argued that the word 'homophobia' was misleading, since anti-gay feelings often seemed rooted more in hate and anger than in fear, but Weinberg pointed out that these emotions were entwined: the dread of homosexuality 'led to great brutality, as fear always does'. As early as 1914 the Hungarian psychoanalyst Sándor Ferenczi had argued that an aversion to homosexuals was a defence reaction, a symptom of repressed desire for one's own sex. A few studies seem to have supported this proposition. In 1996, for instance, an experiment at the

University of Georgia with sixty-four avowedly heterosexual men showed that those who were most hostile to gay men were also the most aroused by homoerotic imagery.

Some LGBT activists have taken issue with the term homophobia on the grounds that it turns an ideological problem into a disturbance of personal psychology. It absolves individuals of responsibility, by describing their prejudice not as a choice but as a psychiatric condition beyond their control. 'While it may be convenient to label one's political enemies mentally ill,' said the radical lesbian feminist Celia Kitzinger in the 1980s, 'to do so removes the argument from the political arena.'

In 2012 the Associated Press banned its reporters from using the term homophobia, along with other politically strategic 'phobia' constructions (such as fatphobia, which dates from the 1980s, and transphobia, from the 1990s). The term homophobia was 'off the mark', said a spokesperson for the news agency. 'It's ascribing a mental disability to someone and suggests a knowledge that we don't have.' But Weinberg stood by his coinage. 'The word homophobia,' he wrote in the *Huffington Post* that year, 'was exactly the concept that gay men and lesbians needed to achieve liberation.'

☞ *See also: xenophobia*

HYDROPHOBIA

The Greek compound 'hydrophobia' – from *hydro*, or water – was formed in the fourteenth century as an alternative to the Old English word *wæterfyrhtness*, to describe a rabies victim's terror of water. Hydrophobia was a physical condition, caused by the bite or scratch of a rabid animal, in which drinking, and even the idea of drinking, could cause agonising spasms in the larynx. Once this symptom had emerged – often alongside other signs of neurological damage such as agitation, hallucination, paralysis, hypersalivation – rabies was almost always fatal. Hydrophobia, as rabies became known, was widespread in Europe and America until Louis Pasteur developed a vaccine in 1885.

In a well-known case of 1819, the Duke of Richmond, Governor-General of British North America, fell ill at a camp near the Ottawa River. On the first day of his illness he was unable to swallow fluids, writes Don James McLaughlin in 'Infectious Affect'; on the second he was so alarmed by water that he could not bathe; and on the third he leapt out of a canoe that was carrying him to Montreal to see a doctor, and tore into the forest to escape the river. When his men caught up with him, they took him to a farmhouse to recuperate, but he was horrified by the sound of running water nearby. They moved him to a bed of straw in a barn behind the house, where he died.

Perhaps the duke had been bitten by a rabid fox while out hunting, his companions speculated, or by his beloved dog, Blucher, who was known to share his bed. It was clear to them that the duke had fallen victim to hydrophobia.

The most unsettling aspect of the duke's illness was not his physical condition, but the way that his fear of drinking became a fear of all water: the aversion spread into his imagination, transforming into a sickness of the psyche. McLaughlin notes that the same pattern was observed in a ten-year-old English girl, Hannah Springthorpe, who was bitten by a dog in Leicester in 1793. Hannah hallucinated that dogs and cats were attacking her, snapped her jaws as if she were becoming a dog herself, shouted in horror at the sound of water. 'The nurse happening to pour some mint tea incautiously,' noted the physician who was attending her, and Hannah 'cried out that it hurt her much, and begged her immediately to desist.'

The idea of hydrophobia was itself disturbing. As a disease caught from an animal, it was a signal, even before the publication in 1859 of Darwin's *On the Origin of Species*, of the kinship between humans and beasts. 'It threw into question the fantasy of human difference,' writes McLaughlin, 'and the hermetic integrity of the species.'

Hydrophobia was characterised by chronic dread and foreboding. Anyone bitten by a dog or other animal fearfully awaited the onset of hallucination and water-fear, since the incubation period was thought to last for weeks, months or years. This lag made hydrophobia a paranoia as well as a disease, a fear of incipient madness. Some people developed the symptoms even when they had no recollection of being bitten. In these cases, McLaughlin observes, 'spontaneous hydrophobia' was diagnosed, a purely psychological sickness contracted by reading or thinking about the disease. The illness named 'fear of water' had come also to mean 'fear of fear of water', fusing the sensations of aversion and dread, imaginative and bodily apprehensions. In 1874 this paranoid condition acquired its own name: lyssophobia, from the Greek *lyssa*, or rabies.

Pasteur's vaccine marked the start of a new age of microbiology in which rabies became rare. But hydrophobia had established itself as a template for phobias, not least in the way that it unsteadied the boundary between the emotional and the physiological. Many of the phobias identified in the eighteenth and nineteenth centuries partook of both realms: they had bodily symptoms such as shaking, trembling, sweating, reeling, shivering, flushing, but were also defined by ineffable feelings of horror and dread. Sometimes they seemed to be mentally transmitted, sometimes inherited, sometimes inflicted. Usually it was unclear whether they were rooted in experience, or in human prehistory, or had been generated spontaneously by the body.

In his novel *Ulysses* (1922), James Joyce depicts hydrophobia as both a mental torment and a physical substance, at once gross and invisible. Garryowen the dog is 'Growling and grousing and his eye all bloodshot from the drouth is in it and the hydrophobia dropping out of his jaws.' The animal's saliva is thick with sickness.

☞ *See also: aquaphobia, cynophobia, mysophobia, thalassophobia*

HYPNOPHOBIA

Hypnophobia – from the Greek *hypnos*, sleep – is a morbid fear of sleep, usually associated with a terror of dreams or nightmares. The condition was identified in a medical dictionary in 1855, and vividly dramatised in Wes Craven's *A Nightmare on Elm Street* in 1984. In this film, a group of teenagers are visited in their sleep by a disfigured and insane child murderer who has the power to kill them as they dream. 'Whatever you do,' ran the tagline, 'don't fall asleep.'

An editorial in *Sleep Medicine Reviews* in 2021 observed that trauma victims can develop hypnophobia because they dread the dreams that will come if they sleep; other hynophobes try to stay awake because they experience the nightly slide into oblivion as a terrifying loss of self; and yet others fight against sleep because they have survived a nocturnal heart attack or stroke, and fear that the next time they fall asleep they will not wake at all.

☞ *See also: nyctophobia, sedatephobia*

HYPOPHOBIA

The psychiatrists Isaac Marks and Randolph Nesse used the term hypophobia in 1994 to describe an abnormal and dangerous lack of fear (*hypo* means 'under' or 'below' in Greek). They pointed out that anxiety is a useful trait, which protects us from external threats: to be immune to fear is to be vulnerable. Many people are diagnosed with anxious complaints, but there may be lots of dangerously fearless individuals who, by definition, do not seek help. 'People with too little anxiety do not come to psychiatrists complaining of deficient fear,' Marks and Nesse observe, 'so their disorders, the "hypophobias", still await formal description.'

Granville Stanley Hall, in his essay of 1897, argued that fear was the most important emotion in our evolution as a species: our capacity for 'anticipatory pain' has enabled us to predict and therefore avoid danger. Marks and Nesse remind us that creatures on isolated islands can become so hypophobic that they lose their ability to flee, fight or hide. When humans arrive, bringing other predators, the tame indigenous species fail to protect themselves. 'The point is captured,' say Marks and Nesse, 'in the phrase "Dead as a Dodo".'

☞ *See also: pantophobia*

KAYAK PHOBIA

When posted to the West Greenland coast in 1902, the Danish medical officer Alfred Bertelsen learnt that a number of Inuit men had abandoned the kayaks in which they traditionally hunted seals, having become paralysed with fear while out at sea. In some coastal districts, he found, more than one in ten of the adult males had 'kayak phobia'. This was a serious problem in a Danish colony that, since the decline of the whaling industry in the late eighteenth century, had become dependent on seal hunting.

Inuit hunters and fishermen faced many dangers – icebergs, storms, attacks from wounded animals – but the kayak panic usually struck while the sea was smooth as a mirror. The kayaker would become convinced that his craft was narrowing, or looming above him; he might feel the boat growing heavier and the paddle lighter. Sometimes he found it difficult to judge distance, grew confused and dizzy and convinced that his kayak was filling with icy water. Often, said Bertelsen, phobic kayakers felt that 'something from the ocean would come and harm them, something that no one dared or could look at'. A few became so disturbed that they abandoned their communities or took their own lives.

A thirty-seven-year-old sealer told Bertelsen that one July day in the 1890s he was out fishing for cod in his kayak at noon. It was hot and the sky was clear, the sun shining in his eyes. He had already caught several fish when he felt a tug on his line. As he pulled it in, he was unnerved to see that a sea slug had bitten at the lure. He let go of the line and began to tremble and sweat; his head hurt, spots danced before his eyes, the bow of the kayak seemed to stretch away and tilt. He was seized by the conviction that something was coming for him from behind, but he felt unable to move. Eventually he managed to rouse himself and paddle towards the land. He told Bertelsen that he no longer went to sea.

Kayak phobia among the Greenlandic Inuit had been observed by Danish doctors since the middle of the nineteenth century. At first, physicians attributed the phenomenon to intoxication by tobacco or coffee – in effect, they blamed it on the stimulants that Denmark had introduced to the colony – but in 1892 the psychiatrist Knut Pontoppidan suggested that it was a form of agoraphobia. Bertelsen, too, classified it as a phobia, and in 1940 introduced a racial element to his analysis. Kayak angst, he said, seemed 'to point to a certain primitiveness in the Eskimo brain' – among Aryans, he added, only women and children were as susceptible to pathological fear.

The Danish authorities were becoming less worried about kayak phobia in any case, as fishing was replacing seal hunting in Greenland and fishing boats were taking over from kayaks. But a few scholars have returned to the subject. In the 1960s the American psychiatrist Zachary Gussow speculated that kayak phobia stemmed from sensory deprivation, a loss of orientation provoked by the still, featureless landscape of the North Atlantic. In 1996 Klaus Georg Hansen, a Danish ethnographer, pointed out that the Inuit had their own explanation for the phenomenon. According to Greenlandic folklore, the phobia was caused by a *tupilak*, a monster sent to kill a hunter by a jealous rival. Sometimes the monster took the form of a seal, which when harpooned would drag the hunter overboard, and sometimes it was an invisible malevolent force that induced a trance. If a kayaker survived an encounter with a *tupilak*, he could arrange a seance at which an *angakok*, or shaman, would try to destroy the creature. But if the attacks continued, the kayaker might give up hunting. Whereas Western doctors interpreted kayak phobia as an individual pathology, wrote Hansen, the Greenlanders thought that it emanated from social tensions. For them, the trouble expressed by a phobia was not personal but communal.

☞ *See also: agoraphobia, demonomania, laughing mania, thalassophobia*

KLAZOMANIA

The word klazomania – from the Greek *klazo*, 'to scream' – was coined by the Hungarian psychiatrist L. Benedek in 1925 to describe a compulsion to shout. Benedek had a patient who would succumb to paroxysms of very loud and apparently uncontrollable hollering: single vowels, syllables, animal noises. In 1927 two of Benedek's colleagues reported on further cases, noting how angry the patients seemed during a fit (extremely restless, their faces flushed) and how apologetic afterwards. They seemed to have remained conscious throughout their surges of yelling.

Similar characteristics were observed in 1996 by the British psychiatrist G. D. L. Bates when he treated a sixty-three-year-old man who was prone to shouting attacks. For the previous two years, the patient reported, he had experienced these outbursts once or twice a month. Bates observed the fits for himself. The patient would become agitated, shout at the top of his voice, issue cries of distress such as 'aargh!' and 'help!' When the shouting ended he would jolt forwards, as if surprised. Father Jack, the elderly Irish priest in the 1990s British sitcom *Father Ted*, has similar shouting jags, though his favoured ejaculations are 'Feck!', 'Arse!', 'Drink!' and 'Girls!'

Though it resembles Tourette syndrome, klazomania is not thought to be an inherited or genetic condition but a symptom of injury to the brain. Bates speculated that his patient's ailment was caused by excessive alcohol consumption and believed that the syndrome could also be caused by carbon monoxide poisoning. The klazomanes described by Benedek and his colleagues in the 1920s were survivors of encephalitis lethargica, the mysterious 'sleeping sickness' that killed half a million people between 1915 and 1927 and left many more with Parkinsonism and other neurological conditions.

☞ *See also: graphomania, onomatomania*

KLEPTOMANIA

The Swiss physician André Matthey first identified the compulsion to steal as *klopémanie* in 1816 – 'a unique madness characterised by the tendency to steal without motive and without necessity' – and in 1830 the word entered the English language as kleptomania (*klepto* is 'to steal' in Greek). One kleptomaniac inmate at a British asylum was allowed to indulge his madness, reported the *Journal of Psychological Medicine* in 1852. He hid the items that he stole from the institution in his clothing: forks, spoons, nightcaps, handkerchiefs, rags, tobacco pipes, bits of cheese. Before his sprees, the doctors noted, 'he appeared a thin and lathy figure; but presently his clothes would begin to expand around him, and he would increase in size until it became necessary to unpick the lining of his coat, waistcoat, breeches, and relieve him of his imaginary booty'.

Kleptomania soon became associated with affluent women rather than pauper lunatics. *The Lancet* pointed out in 1861 that the syndrome was invoked in the courts almost exclusively on behalf of the more prosperous classes: 'where so-called respectable persons commit theft without sufficiently obvious motive for the act, they have their crime extenuated on the plea of kleptomania'. By definition, kleptomania required that the thief had no need for the objects that he or she had taken.

In a notorious case in 1896, Ella Castle, the thirty-seven-year-old wife of a San Francisco tea merchant, was charged with stealing fur from six London stores. She was staying with her son and husband at the Hotel Cecil in the Strand, the biggest and most sumptuous hotel in Europe. When the police raided the Castles' room, they found purloined sable and chinchilla skins, ermine ties and boas, gold watches, lorgnettes, hand mirrors, clocks, fans and tortoiseshell combs, some of them with price tags attached. A few silver-plated toast racks, embossed with the Hotel Cecil insignia, were also discovered in their trunks.

Both Mr and Mrs Castle were arrested – it seemed impossible that Walter Castle was unaware of the thefts, since many of the items had been stolen in his presence and stowed among his belongings – but the charges against him were dropped when several medical men testified that Ella Castle was suffering from kleptomania. The case was a sensation, reported avidly on both sides of the Atlantic. Even Arthur Conan Doyle weighed in. 'If there is any doubt of moral responsibility,' he wrote to *The Times*, 'the benefit of the doubt should certainly be given to one whose *sex* and *position* … give her a double claim to our consideration. It is to the consulting room and not to the cell that she should be sent.'

The magistrates sentenced Mrs Castle to three months in prison, but the Home Secretary directed that she quietly be released after only a week. She and her family sailed for America, where she submitted to two operations to fix her 'ovarian insanity'. By tracing kleptomania to the female reproductive system, argued the feminist scholar Elaine S. Abelson in 1989, doctors conflated women's sexuality with sickness and strangeness. 'Even as it became a socially and medically credible diagnosis,' observes Abelson, 'kleptomania reinscribed beliefs about female weakness.' As more shoplifters pleaded temporary insanity, the kleptomaniac woman became a music-hall staple, 'a stock character, a popular joke'.

With the rise of department stores in the late nineteenth century, impulsive theft became easier than ever. In these emporiums of plenty, well-heeled women could circulate freely on their own, handling – and sometimes pocketing – the dazzling treats arrayed before them. 'The temptation was acute,' Émile Zola noted in *The*

Ladies' Paradise in 1883; 'it gave rise to an insane wave of desire which unhinged every woman'. Zola depicts the Parisian department store as an erotic wonderland, a gorgeous fusion of fabric, flesh and cash. In one scene in his novel, salesgirls search the comtesse de Boves for stolen goods, 'even taking off her dress to inspect her bosom and hips. Apart from the Alençon flounces, twelve metres at a thousand francs a metre, which were hidden in the depths of a sleeve, they found a handkerchief, a fan and a scarf hidden squashed and warm in her bosom, making a total of about fourteen thousand francs' worth of lace. Ravaged by a furious, irresistible urge, Madame de Boves had been stealing like this for a year.'

In the aftermath of the Castle case, Clara Bewick Colby suggested in *The Woman's Signal* that some compulsive shoplifters were granted too little financial independence by their husbands. The items that qualified as kleptomaniac spoils were typically luxuries and fripperies and unnecessary gewgaws – just the objects that a woman, however affluent, might feel ashamed to want, or expenses that she might feel unable to justify. The solution, said Colby, was to grant wives more autonomy: the married woman 'must have freedom to control what is justly her own'. She might otherwise end up like Madame G, one of the women interviewed by Paul Dubuisson in *Les Voleuses de Grands Magasins* (1902), whose first theft marked the beginning of a new existence. She was transformed, writes Dubuisson. Her household and her husband were no longer her priorities. Instead, she had just one overriding thought: to return to the department store to shoplift. Kleptomania had become a form of rebellion against the home.

Sigmund Freud's followers firmly linked kleptomania to female sexuality. In 1924 Wilhelm Stekel argued that the condition always had sexual roots: the kleptomane wants 'to do something forbidden', he wrote, 'to secretly take hold of something'. Or as Fritz Wittels put it in 1942: 'to steal is actually the sex life of Kleptomaniacs'.

From the start, psychologists noticed that kleptomanes found release in shoplifting. In 1840 the French alienist Charles Chrétien Henri Marc observed that the act could bring exhilaration and the relief of anxiety. In 2000 the American Psychiatric Association's *Diagnostic and Statistical Manual 4* described the kleptomane's 'rising subjective sense of tension before the theft' and the 'pleasure, gratification or relief when committing the theft'. Kleptomania is now often considered an impulse-control disorder, and is treated with drugs that dull the thrill of theft or reduce the anxiety that is otherwise alleviated by stealing. Some kleptomanes try to cure their compulsion with aversion therapy – for instance, they are taught to hold their breath to the point of pain when they imagine an act of theft, or to associate shoplifting with images of arrest and imprisonment. In cognitive behavioural treatments, they learn to interrupt shoplifting patterns and to banish recurring thoughts such as: 'They deserve it', or 'I want to see if I can get away with it', or 'My family deserves better things.'

In Hermann Hesse's short story 'Kinderseele' (1919), quoted by Stekel, an eleven-year-old boy is seized by a kleptomaniac desire. The child walks home from school one day in a state of unease, as if guilty of something. 'A feeling of dread came over the boy. It began with a sense of tightness in the breast reaching up to his throat and there culminated in a feeling of suffocation and of nausea.' Filled with foreboding, he enters the hall of his home: 'the Devil is loose today', he thinks, 'something is going to happen'. He finds himself walking into his father's study. 'Inwardly I wished father might stir in the next room and come in to break the terrible spell that drew me on.' But no one comes, and the boy begins to open his father's drawers, one by one. 'The feeling of being a criminal knotted my stomach and made my finger tips grow cold. I had no idea, as yet, what I was about to do.' In one drawer, he finds a garland of white candied figs, and – as if to break the tension – he pulls a few figs off their string, pushes them into a pocket, slams the drawer and flees the room in fright and shame.

☛ *See also: giftomania, monomania, oniomania, syllogomania*

KOUMPOUNOPHOBIA

Steve Jobs, the co-founder of Apple, was reputed to wear turtleneck jumpers because he suffered from koumpounophobia, or a fear of buttons (*koumpouno* is Modern Greek for 'button'). According to the design engineer Abraham Faraq, Jobs's phobia extended to the buttons on machines. In the 1990s, said Faraq, Jobs walked past a prototype computer mouse on which the buttons had yet to be installed. 'That's genius,' he remarked. 'We don't want to have any buttons.' On hearing this, the engineers scrambled to design a button-free version. Similarly, the touchscreen on the iPhone was sometimes said to be inspired by Jobs's dislike of push-button keypads.

Koumpounophobes hate the idea that they might touch a button. Lisa Cross, a microbiologist from Devon, told the *Guardian* that she had been averse to buttons since she was a child. She was especially repelled by slippy plastic buttons and by buttons that had come loose. 'A toggle on a duffel coat is fine,' she said; 'the metal ones on jeans are fine, but anything else on a shirt or similar is awful. Worse than that would be one on the floor, not attached to the garment – even worse if it has a bit of cotton in it.'

A few koumpounophobes can identify the circumstances that triggered their phobia. One woman had been repeatedly warned off buttons by her mother, a dressmaker, who was afraid that the child might put one in her mouth and choke on it. A button-phobic man remembered that as a boy he had once stared at the buttons on his dentist's shirt while being subjected to painful dental work – perhaps buttons came to remind him of teeth, hanging from the gum on stringy threads or clacking against a dentist's metal dish. Buttons are to clothes as teeth are to bodies: bits that can come loose, fall off. And perhaps a dangling or detached button implies not just loss but exposure, an inadvertent opening.

A nine-year-old Hispanic-American boy in Miami dated his phobia to the moment that he accidentally tipped a giant bowl of buttons over himself in a kindergarten art class. After this, he began to hate wearing a buttoned shirt to school and to fear any object that a button touched. The buttons were a reminder of a terrible scattering, a loss of control, and they were also agents of constraint: to be fastened into his school shirt was to be consigned again to the classroom, the scene of his horror. The sense that buttons are toxic or contaminating is common among koumpounophobes. 'For me, touching a button would be like touching a cockroach,' Gillian Linkins, a twenty-two-year-old from Hampshire, told the London *Metro* in 2008. 'It feels dirty, nasty and wrong.'

Psychologists have started to explore the link between button phobia and disgust. In 2020 researchers at Stanford University studied a twenty-nine-year-old Asian-American woman who was averse to buttons, especially those that she saw dangling from a piece of clothing or astray on the floor. She reported feelings of disgust as well as fear in such scenarios, and showed an 'elevated early attention' response to buttons, a heightened awareness typically triggered only by 'biologically relevant' objects such as cockroaches or blood. The Stanford team wondered whether koumpounophobia was a form of trypophobia, a disgust-related aversion to clusters of holes, but they found that their subject was more disturbed by 'canonical' four-hole plastic buttons than by buttons with twenty closely packed punctures. The phobia was about the button as a whole, not its perforations.

'This is the first demonstration,' write the study's authors, 'that the same properties of biologically prepared phobias can be present in phobia for a nonthreatening, noncontamination risk, nonbiologically prepared object.' The koumpounophobe recoils from buttons as if they are a disease.

☞ *See also: bambakomallophobia, pnigophobia, odontophobia, trypophobia*

L

LAUGHING MANIA

Several epidemics of wild, prolonged laughter were reported among African schoolchildren in the 1960s. According to Robert Bartholomew and Bob Rickard's *Mass Hysteria in Schools* (2013), the first known outbreak took place in January 1962 at a Christian missionary college in Tanganyika, as Tanzania was then known. Three girls at a boarding school in Kashasha, on Lake Victoria, started to laugh uncontrollably, then to weep, then to laugh again. The fits seemed infectious – several of the girls' classmates joined in, more of them each day. Some of the children grew restless and violent, running around the grounds, saying that something was chasing them. Others claimed to feel things moving in their heads.

The *endwara ya Kucheka*, or laughing trouble, became so severe that in March the school was closed and the girls sent back to their villages to recuperate. They seemed to get better but when the school reopened in May the fits of cackling and sobbing started up again. Over the next eighteen months more than a thousand children in the region succumbed to manic laughter, often accompanied by crying and running. A team of investigators tested for food poisoning and viral disease but found evidence of neither. The girls' parents believed that the spirits of dead ancestors might be working through them.

The crazed laughter recurred in 1966, when two schools on Lake Victoria had to be closed. 'It spreads like wildfire among schoolchildren, particularly girls,' a health ministry official told *The New York Times*. 'One girl starts to laugh her head off and all the others follow. Nobody can control them and the only answer is to separate them for a couple of weeks.' Over the next decade further cases were reported in schools and colleges in Uganda, Zambia and northern Botswana.

Psychogenic surges of this kind have taken place among school-children, especially adolescent girls, since at least the nineteenth century, and seem to spread by a process of unconscious imita-tion. Dozens of girls trembled and vibrated at schools in Basel, Switzerland, in 1893 and 1904, and in Meissen, Germany, in 1905 and 1906. At a secondary school in Blackburn, Lancashire, in 1965, eighty-five girls were taken to hospital with a mysterious illness characterised by fainting and spasms, and in 2001 about a hundred students at a camp in Thailand developed breathing dif-ficulties after seeming to see ghosts. In 2011 it was reported that a group of teenage schoolgirls in Le Roy, New York, began to writhe and twitch, and in 2014 a group in El Carmen, Colombia, con-vulsed and fainted.

These group manias, writes the neurologist Suzanne O'Sullivan, show us that sickness has social as well as biological and psycho-logical components. 'Sometimes,' she notes, 'doctors are so busy looking inside people's heads that they forget the social factors creating illness. Or, more likely even, they are afraid to look too closely at their patients' social worlds for fear that they will be accused of blaming the person, their family or their community for the illness.' O'Sullivan points out that adolescent school-children are especially vulnerable to 'social contagion', and that media attention often acts as a further agent of infection, spread-ing and prolonging an epidemic. Having travelled round the world to study outbreaks of mass mania, she wonders whether 'eradicat-ing these disorders was, in fact, the wrong thing to hope for. For many of the people I met, psychosomatic illness served a vital purpose ... Sometimes, embodying and enacting conflict is either more manageable or more practical than articulating it.' She urges us to attend to the stories that these involuntary actions tell.

G. J. Ebrahim, a Tanzanian paediatrician, suggested that the laughing sickness in central and eastern Africa of the 1960s played out anxieties about social change. At home, the children were immersed in a traditional, conservative tribal ethos, while in the missionary schools they were exposed to ideas that challenged the beliefs of their parents and grandparents. At the same time, gov-ernment officials were forcing many families to move off their tiny farmsteads and into planned villages in urban areas. They were being driven away from their ancestral lands, away from the graves of their forebears and the protection of the spirits. Caught up in these upheavals, and caught also in the physiological and emotional upheavals of adolescence, the children ran, they cried, and they laughed.

☞ *See also: Beatlemania, choreomania, demonomania, kayak phobia*

LYPEMANIA

A lypemane, wrote Jean-Étienne Esquirol in 1838, was a victim of pathological mournfulness, an overwhelming sadness akin to the state of mind that Benjamin Rush called 'tristimania'. Though Esquirol's term didn't catch on, his analysis of the condition laid the groundwork for the modern understanding of clinical depression. Among his case studies was a 'Mademoiselle W', who in 1804, at the age of about sixteen, fell into a profound melancholy upon the death of her childhood playmate, the duc d'Enghien. Napoleon Bonaparte had ordered the assassination of the duke because he suspected him of plotting to overthrow the government. When Mademoiselle W heard of the killing, her abundant hair turned grey and her big blue eyes glazed over. She stopped speaking and was sent from her home in the Château de Chantilly to the Salpêtrière asylum in Paris, where she would sit on the bolster of her bed, her long, thin legs drawn up against her belly, her elbows on her knees and her chin resting on her right hand as she gazed out of the window, murmuring to herself.

Esquirol named lypemania after Lype, who in Greek mythology was the personification of grief. Her mother was Eris, the goddess of strife, and her sisters were Akhos and Ania, spirits of anguish and sorrow.

☞ *See also: dipsomania, monomania, monophobia*

MEGALOMANIA

The term megalomania – from the Greek *mega*, large – is often used to mean a lust for power or a desire for absolute control, but it was coined in France in 1866, as *mégalomanie*, to describe insane delusions of grandeur. Delusions are common in psychosis. They are experienced by half of those suffering from schizophrenia and two-thirds of those with bipolar disorder, often as part of a manic state of hyperactivity, euphoria, rapid speech, racing thoughts and sudden switches of mood.

On a family skiing holiday to Innsbruck, Austria, in 2018 the British author Horatio Clare became convinced that he was an MI6 agent who had been enlisted in an international espionage plot to save the world, part of his mission being to marry the Australian pop star Kylie Minogue. 'Madness of this kind is like a sunrise of the self,' writes Clare in *Heavy Light* (2020), 'a flood of light banishing the shadows of the relative, of perspective … I feel myself infused with this light, which feels like knowledge and power and significance; a light which seems tangible and almost visible to others, judging by the way they look at me … It is exhilarating and it is exhausting.'

In the nineteenth century, people with this form of mania imagined themselves to be figures such as Napoleon, Joan of Arc or Jesus Christ. In 2005 a British megalomane told researchers that he was a cousin of the then prime minister, Tony Blair, and another reported: 'I am God; I created the universe and I am a son of Prince Philip. I am also a famous DJ. I have Superman-type powers.' A third claimed scientific genius: 'I was spitting on a light bulb,' he said in 2009, 'thinking if I watched the saliva burn, the different colours and shapes, I could find the cure to cancer.' Very rarely, megalomania issues in violence. The millionaire philanthropist John du Pont, a wrestling enthusiast who killed his friend Dave Schultz in Philadelphia in 1996, believed himself variously to be the Dalai Lama, a CIA operative, and the last Russian tsar.

☛ *See also: egomania, erotomania, mythomania, plutomania*

MICROMANIA

By 1899 'micromania' (from the Greek *mikros*, or small) was being used to mean a deranged belittling of oneself, or pathological self-deprecation. But it was originally defined in 1879 as a condition in which people thought themselves, or some part of themselves, to have shrunk. The French president Paul Deschanel refused to be seen out of doors in 1920, having convinced himself that his head had shrivelled to the size of an orange.

In Lewis Carroll's novel *Alice's Adventures in Wonderland* (1865), Alice seems to shrink when she drinks from a bottle marked 'Drink me'. 'I must be shutting up like a telescope,' she thinks, and soon finds herself standing just 10 inches high. She grows enormous when she nibbles on a cake labelled 'Eat me', but abruptly contracts again when she takes a bite of a mushroom offered to her by the Blue Caterpillar: 'Her chin suddenly dropped to her feet.'

In 1952 the American neurologist Caro Lippman wondered whether Lewis Carroll's migraines might have inspired his depiction of the shrinking (and expanding) Alice. Lippman had observed migraine-induced hallucinations in several of his patients. One woman said that before or during a severe headache she became convinced that she was only a foot tall, a belief that she could correct only by staring at herself in a mirror.

☛ *See also: megalomania*

MONOMANIA

Edgar Allan Poe was the first to use the term monomania in fiction: the narrator of his short story 'Berenice' (1835) has such a monomania for his fiancée's teeth that he digs them out of her mouth as he buries her live body. His mania, he says, gripped him with a savage fury: 'I struggled in vain against its strange and irresistible influence. In the multiplied objects of the external world I had no thoughts but for the teeth. For these I longed with a frenzied desire.'

The psychiatrist Jean-Étienne Esquirol invented the word *monomanie* in about 1810 to describe individuals possessed by a single delusional compulsion (in Latin, *monos* means one, single or only). They were otherwise rational beings, said Esquirol, whose partial and elusive insanity might be visible only to the expert eye. In the law courts, a diagnosis of monomania became a strategy for defending all sorts of criminals. A sketch by Honoré Daumier in the magazine *Le Charivari* in 1846 shows a prisoner slumped against the wall of his cell, his lawyer standing beside him. 'What really bothers me,' says the despondent cook, 'is that I've been accused of 12 robberies.' 'Twelve of them,' muses the lawyer. 'So much the better. I will plead monomania...'

By the middle of the century Esquirol's term was being derided in the press as an excuse for arson, murder, theft, adultery and drunkenness. Nonetheless, the idea had taken hold in the popular imagination and was invoked often in novels, as Lindsey Stewart shows in her study of the idea. In Emily Brontë's *Wuthering Heights* (1847), Heathcliff is accused of a monomaniac love for Cathy. In Herman Melville's *Moby-Dick* (1851), Captain Ahab has a monomaniac desire to avenge himself on a whale. In Anthony Trollope's *He Knew He Was Right* (1869), Trevelyan develops a monomaniac jealousy of his wife's friendship with another man.

To suspect oneself of monomania became a horrible form of self-doubt. In *Lady Audley's Secret* (1862), Mary Elizabeth Braddon depicts a man fixated on proving that his uncle's young wife has committed murder. 'Was it a monition or a monomania?'

he asks himself. 'What if I am wrong after all? What if this chain of evidence which I have constructed link by link is constructed out of my own folly? ... Oh, my God, if it should be in myself all this time that the misery lies.' Braddon's portrayal drew on the experiences of the real-life detective Jack Whicher, a Scotland Yard officer who tried to solve the murder of a three-year-old boy at Road Hill House in Wiltshire in 1860. Whicher's obsession with the case brought on a breakdown, and he retired early from the police force in 1864 with 'congestion of the brain'.

Monomania has become a discredited concept, partly because of the difficulty of distinguishing normal from pathological obsession; and partly because mental illnesses rarely manifest as single symptoms. But a few specific monomanias are still diagnosed, among them kleptomania and pyromania, which are usually classified as obsessive-compulsive or impulse-control disorders.

Perhaps the notion of monomania was so seductive because it gave a modern, medical twist to the classic literary idea that a person could be undone by a tragic flaw. Stewart credits Esquirol's word with popularising psychology itself. 'Once the exclusive domain of the priest or doctor,' writes Stewart, 'the health of the psyche became a talking point for all and, on the back of a proliferating print culture, the diagnosis of monomania at its apogee enabled a new generation of armchair clinicians.' With the idea of monomania, Esquirol had opened up the possibility that rational people were streaked with madness. His term could be used to describe consuming love, corrosive envy, unconscious compulsion, pathological brooding – the many insanities of the sane.

☛ *See also: bibliomania, demonomania, dermatillomania, dipsomania, erotomania, homicidal monomania, kleptomania, lypemania, nymphomania, oniomania, pyromania, trichomania, trichotillomania*

MONOPHOBIA

Monophobia, or the fear of being alone, was identified as a specific phobia in 1880 by George Miller Beard. In 1897 Granville Stanley Hall diagnosed the condition in a woman who loathed being at home by herself. Everything felt gloomy and awful, she reported, the silence of her farmhouse broken only by the loud ticking of a clock. 'It felt as if everybody was dead,' she said. 'I would sing and do the most unusual things, watch the clock, the approach of night, dread every preposterous accident, seek companionship with the animals in the barn, and even with the flowers in the garden.'

☞ *See also: lypemania, nyctophobia, sedatephobia*

MUSOPHOBIA

A horror of rats and mice, named musophobia after the Greek *mus* for 'mouse', may stem from our innate wariness of creatures that contaminate food and carry disease. It is often sparked by an early shock – the sight of a small, furry body racing across the ground – and reinforced by cultural attitudes. In the medieval legend of the Pied Piper of Hamelin, rats are agents of death. When mice appear in cartoons, people jump and scream. Sigmund Freud, in a famous case of 1909, analysed a young lawyer who had developed the phobia after hearing of a 'horrible Chinese torture' in which a rat was strapped to a man's buttocks and left to gnaw its way through his anus.

George Orwell was terrorised by rats while fighting in the Spanish Civil War. In a barn in which he slept in 1937, he wrote in *Homage to Catalonia* (1938), 'the filthy brutes came swarming out of the ground on every side'. One day he was so startled to see a rat beside him in a trench that he pulled out his revolver and shot the creature. Upon hearing the loud bang in the ditch, both the Republican and the Nationalist soldiers thought that the other side had launched an attack, and immediately retaliated. The ensuing skirmish destroyed his militia's cookhouse and two buses used for ferrying troops to the front.

A variation on the Chinese rat torture appears in *Nineteen Eighty-Four*, Orwell's novel of 1949. The story's hero Winston Smith refuses to betray his girlfriend, Julia, even when he is beaten and electrocuted, but his gaolers know how to break him. 'Have you ever seen a rat leap through the air?' asks his tormentor in Room 101, brandishing a cage that holds two of the creatures. 'They will leap onto your face and bore straight into it. Sometimes they attack the eyes first. Sometimes they burrow through the cheeks and devour the tongue.' When Winston smells the 'foul, musty odour of the brutes' and feels the wire of the cage glance against his cheek, he at last surrenders his beloved. 'Do it to Julia!' he cries out in horror. 'Do it to Julia! Not me! Julia! I don't care what you do to her. Tear her face off, strip her to the bones. Not me! Julia! Not me!'

☛ *See also: doraphobia, zoophobia*

MYSOPHOBIA

'Under the name of Mysophobia,' wrote the American neurologist William Alexander Hammond in 1879, 'I propose to describe a form of mental derangement ... characterised by a morbid, overpowering fear of defilement or contamination.' Hammond created his term from the Greek *musos*, or uncleanliness. Over the previous decade, he said, he had treated ten patients with the syndrome.

'MG', an affluent widow of thirty, consulted Hammond in 1877. Six months earlier, she said, she had read a newspaper article about a man who contracted smallpox by handling contaminated bank notes. 'The circumstance made a deep impression on my mind,' she explained, 'and as I had only a few moments before counted quite a number of notes, the idea struck me that perhaps they had been handled by some person with a contagious disease of some kind or other.' She had washed her hands after touching the notes, but she now washed them again and went to bed feeling uneasy. In the morning she cleaned her hands meticulously. Realising that the bank notes were in the same drawer of her dressing table as her linen underclothing, she sent the linen to the laundry, and dressed herself in garments from another drawer. She put on a pair of gloves, placed the bank notes in an envelope and asked a servant to thoroughly wash the dressing-table drawer with soap and water.

It then struck her that she had touched many other things since touching the notes, and any one of them might now infect her. 'I was still in danger.' She removed her dress, which she had been wearing the previous day, and put on a new one. 'From that,' she said, 'I went on from one thing to another. There was no end to the series. I washed everything I was in the habit of touching, and then washed my hands. Even the water was a medium for pollution. For no matter how thoroughly I wiped my hands after washing in it, a portion still remained, and had to be washed off, and then again the hands washed.'

MG gave up reading, for fear that she might be poisoned by the pages of a book or newspaper, and would shake hands only when wearing gloves – 'and lately, even gloves do not seem to afford me entire protection', she told Hammond. 'I know they are porous.' Hammond noticed that she kept a close watch on her hands as they spoke, rubbing them against each other to get rid of contaminating particles. After he took her pulse, she pulled a handkerchief from her pocket, moistened it with a drop of cologne, and wiped the spot that his finger had touched. She put the handkerchief back in a different pocket, reserved for soiled items. MG said that there was no particular disease that she feared. It was just 'an overpowering feeling that I shall be defiled in some mysterious way, that presses on me'.

Another of Hammond's patients – 'Miss F', a slender young woman of eighteen – became mysophobic in 1877 after a severe infestation of head lice. 'Little by little,' he wrote, 'the idea became rooted that she could not escape sources of contamination, that other persons might defile her in some way or other, and that the various articles about her might also possess a like power.' By the time she consulted Hammond, in 1879, the phobia had come to dominate her existence – 'her whole life is one continued round of trouble, anxiety and fear', said Hammond. 'She is suspicious of every person and every thing.' In the street she would gather up her skirts so that they wouldn't brush against anyone. She spent hours examining and cleaning her combs and brushes, washed her hands more than 200 times a day, and in the evenings undressed without touching her clothes – after a servant had undone the fastenings, she let the garments fall to the floor, from where they were taken to be laundered. In the laundry, she knew, her clothes would encounter the clothes of others. 'She sees no practicable way of escape from this circumstance,' wrote Hammond, which 'makes her very unhappy.'

Like MG, Miss F could not quite name what she feared: 'She imagined it to be something that was capable of doing her bodily injury in some subtle manner, by being absorbed into her system through her hands or other parts.'

The fear of dirt was not new. In the 1830s Esquirol had treated 'Mademoiselle F', a tall, auburn-haired, blue-eyed woman of thirty-four who avoided touching anything with her hands or her clothing, constantly rubbed and washed her fingers, shook out books and needlework to dislodge any dirt, and had a waiting-woman spoon food into her mouth. Like the ladies who consulted Hammond, she was perfectly aware that her behaviour was irrational. 'My disquietude is absurd and ridiculous,' she said, 'but I cannot prevent it.'

But when scientists discovered that disease could be spread by invisible microbes, in the second half of the nineteenth century, the fear of contamination became much more common, and it was then that Hammond identified it as a distinct mental disorder. The world seemed suddenly rife with hidden agents of infection, notes Don James McLaughlin, and the fear of these agents seemed to spread just like the microbes themselves. The names for the condition multiplied, too – the fear became known not only as mysophobia but also as germophobia, germaphobia, verminophobia, bacteriophobia, bacillophobia.

All kinds of distress could be communicated through the fear of dirt. In 1880 Dr Ira Russell treated a forty-seven-year-old bachelor, a graduate of Harvard Medical School, who had been seized by the 'filth dread' after his brother died suddenly in his arms. Russell's patient avoided touching doorknobs, chairs and other furniture, and his night-time cleaning rituals took several hours. In the 1890s, Freud treated a woman who constantly washed her hands and touched door handles only with an elbow. 'It was the case of Lady Macbeth,' he wrote. 'The washing was symbolic, designed to replace by physical purity the moral purity which she regretted having lost. She tormented herself with remorse for conjugal infidelity, the memory of which she had resolved to banish from her mind.'

Freud explained why it was so difficult to wean people off these ritualistic behaviours: 'If we try to hinder them in the performance of their compulsive acts, or their washing or their ceremonials, or if they dare to give up one of their compulsions, they are seized with terrible fear that again exacts obedience to the compulsion. We understand that the compulsive act had veiled fear and had been performed only to avoid it.' Such compulsions, Freud argued, were symptoms of magical thinking. Mysophobes feared that their feelings and wishes were seeping out, and external influences leaking in. The washing rituals were designed to prevent this contamination, the breaching of the porous boundaries of the self.

Hammond treated his mysophobic patients with bromides, a type of sedative, while Freud tried to cure them by exploring their unconscious fantasies. In the late twentieth century psychologists experimented with behavioural therapies. In 1975 the British psychiatrist Isaac Marks was consulted by a woman who was washing her hands at least fifty times a day and using seven giant packs of soap flakes each week. She threw away 'contaminated' clothing, which she could barely afford to replace, and moved house five times in three years to escape 'infected' environments. She associated many places with dirtiness, wrote Marks, chief among them the English town of Basingstoke: 'the mere mention of the word Basingstoke evoked washing rituals'. In the course of her treatment, Marks accompanied her to the dreaded town, an outing that 'resulted in total contamination, severe depression, and a threat to discharge herself'. However, said Marks, the depression lifted after twenty-four hours and the woman persevered with her treatment, eventually finding herself able to dispense with her cleaning rituals altogether.

At a north London psychiatric hospital in the middle of 2019, the artist Cassandre Greenberg embarked on a course of exposure therapy to treat her phobias of contamination and vomiting and her mania for cleanliness. But in February 2020 her treatment was abruptly halted. The Covid-19 virus and been detected in Britain and hospitals had been told to offer only emergency treatment. At the same time, the government began instructing people to take up the compulsive behaviours that Greenberg had been trying to let go.

'Hand-washing suddenly became an act of saving the nation,' wrote Greenberg in the magazine *White Review*. 'As people stormed supermarket aisles for antibacterial soap, the very thing that made me "sick" had become the picture of health.' She watched people strive to acquire 'behaviours and patterns of feeling that I have long held as personal indicators of a disease of my mind, my own ritualistic mitigations against exaggerated expectations of danger. The previously "pathological" has been recast as the sensible and responsible.' All of a sudden, the public were being encouraged to adopt attitudes that would only recently have marked them out as phobic about germs, and as manic about cleanliness.

We might expect the incidence of mysophobia to rise when a dangerous virus spreads swiftly across the world, and studies have confirmed that many obsessive-compulsive behaviours were exacerbated by the Covid-19 pandemic. But in the *Journal of Obsessive-Compulsive and Related Disorders* in 2020, Frederick Aardema observed that what a compulsive handwasher really fears is not physical illness but psychic violation: germs are emblems of desecration; obsessive washing rituals 'are carried out to safeguard and protect against dangers to the self, as opposed to the physical body'. One person with OCD told Aardema that instead of feeling more frightened of infection during the spread of Covid-19, she felt relieved to find others adopting her behaviours. 'She no longer had to feel embarrassed using protective gloves,' he wrote, 'or refusing to shake hands.'

In the early stages of the Covid-19 pandemic, we redefined – at speed – what was rational. 'I have seen people's fears externalised in the space around me,' wrote Greenberg, 'in a way that collapses any conceptions I previously had of mental "health" or illness.' It was an accelerated instance of how a historical event could transform perceptions as well as behaviours. The display of fear itself became normalised: to be afraid was to be logical, conscientious, informed. To be compulsive, now, was a way of caring for oneself and others.

☛ *See also: ablutophobia, arithmomania, dermatillomania, emetophobia, haphephobia, trypophobia*

MYTHOMANIA

In a paper of 1905, the French psychiatrist Ernest Dupré described the pathological tendency to exaggerate or lie as mythomania, from the Greek *muthos*, or myth. True mythomania, he said, is apparently purposeless. Mythomanes either believe their own lies or know them to be lies but cannot stop telling them. Usually, they move fluidly between fantasy and reality, shuttling, as a child might, between conscious lies and daydreams. The condition is also known as pseudologia fantastica (a term coined by Anton Delbrück in 1891), or as pathological lying. Documented cases include a maidservant who wandered across Austria and Switzerland in the late nineteenth century, claiming sometimes to be an impoverished medical student, sometimes a Romanian princess; and a Frenchman whose reckless inventions culminated in 1993 in the murder of his wife, his children and his parents.

'The pathological liar,' observed the Polish psychoanalyst Helene Deutsch in 1922, 'relates a piece of daydreaming or fantasy as if it were a real experience.' One of her patients, she said, claimed to have had a masochistic teenage affair with an older boy and she produced a diary that described their erotic encounters. Deutsch knew that her patient's story was invented, but sought to understand why she persisted with it. Eventually it emerged that her older brother had sexually assaulted her when she was about three years old. The repressed event, which might have emerged in a somatic symptom, had instead found expression in a fictional story. In Britain in the 1930s, the Hungarian ghost-hunter Nandor Fodor came to believe that some women who professed supernatural powers – such as Alma Fielding, a London housewife who seemed to be generating poltergeist phenomena – were compulsively spinning tales to convey secret truths about their lives.

'There is a pretty widespread view,' wrote Deutsch, 'that fantasy liars tell their stories in order to arouse the admiration, envy, etc., of their listeners.' But she had found, she said, that a mythomane 'merely follows an inner urge to communicate without really caring about the reaction'. A profitable response was just a welcome side-effect. 'In this,' Deutsch wrote, 'the fantasy liar resembles the true creative writer, who produces without regard to the reception of his work, and not the inferior artist who adapts his work to public taste.' Mythomanes, like novelists, follow an impulse to escape – or discover – themselves in made-up stories.

In 2015 the French psychoanalyst Michèle Bertrand encountered a patient called Alex, a tall young man with a hunched posture, who announced himself with the words: 'Madame, I am a liar!' Ever since his schooldays, he told her, he had disguised his dyslexia, pretending to be highly literate when in fact he could barely read or write. He would leave jobs and romantic relationships as soon as he felt in danger of being discovered. Alex was tormented by anxiety and guilt, but he kept fabricating stories. 'The mythomaniac,' wrote Bertrand, 'is one who has not been able to build up a consistent image of himself. He doesn't know who he is ... He does not invent stories to hide what he is, but ... to acquire a content, a density of being, a consistency. What makes his situation inextricable is that without this pretension to be what he chose to be, he is nothing in his own eyes.'

In *The Examined Life* (2013), the psychoanalyst Stephen Grosz describes a television producer, 'Philip', who was referred to him for pathological lying. One of Philip's first lies – at the age of eleven or twelve – had been to tell his headmaster that he had been recruited by MI5 to train as an agent. More recently, Philip had falsely told his wife that he had lung cancer; he had pretended to his daughter that he could speak French; and to his father-in-law that he had once been selected as a reserve for the British men's archery team. Soon enough he was lying to Grosz about why he hadn't paid his bill. Grosz was baffled by his patient's blatant, pointless and often ridiculous inventions, until Philip recounted a childhood memory. From the age of about three, he said, he often woke to find that he had wet himself in the night. When he dressed in the morning, he would push his damp pyjamas under the bedclothes, and in the evening he would return to find them, clean and folded, beneath his pillow: his mother had quietly removed and washed them in the course of the day. She never mentioned his problem, nor reprimanded him, nor told his father about it. This silent ritual continued until Philip was eleven, when his mother died.

Though Philip afterwards outgrew his bed-wetting, Grosz guessed that pathological lying had taken its place. 'He told lies that would make a mess,' writes Grosz, 'and then hoped that his listener would say nothing, becoming, like his mother, a partner in a secret world.' His lying was not intended to deceive, but to create a bond of complicity. It was 'his way of keeping the close-ness he had known, his way of holding onto his mother'.

Occasionally, the diagnosis of mythomania can itself be used to deny reality. In the first monograph on pathological lying, pub-lished in 1915, the child psychologists William and Mary Tenney Healy described some of the compulsive liars they had treated in Chicago. One, they said, was 'Bessie M', aged nine, who told a woman who was looking after her that she had been sexually assaulted by several men, including her father and brother. Her guardian, 'Mrs S', informed the police, who charged Bessie's father and brother with incest. When Bessie gave her testimony in court, she provided detailed and horrifying descriptions of the assaults, but the judge thought that her stories 'savoured of untruth' and found that her brother's 'demeanour', in particular, was 'quite out of keeping with the grave accusations against him'.

The Healys, as experts in juvenile delinquency, assessed Bessie for the court. They learnt that her family had moved to Chicago from Ireland when she was five, her mother and several siblings having died in 'the old country'. The girl had boarded in many households in the four years since, and for six months had shared a bed with her father and brother. Bessie claimed that she had been involved in sexual activity with different men in almost all of the places in which she lodged. The psychologists were astonished by the extent of her sexual knowledge, but they noted that Mrs S, her current guardian, had fostered a 'love of the dramatic' in the girl by taking her to theatres and picture shows and by encouraging her to read aloud. A physician who examined Bessie found that her hymen was unbroken, and the Healys decided that she must be lying about the most serious assaults upon her. They reported their findings to the court.

Mrs S and other women attending the hearing were outraged when the judge dismissed the case against Bessie's father and brother. 'The girl's first story,' observed the Healys, 'was so well told that many had been irrevocably convinced of the utter guilt of the father.'

The Healys had enlisted the concept of pathological lying to explain why Bessie should tell a lie from which she had so little to gain. But it has since been established that the condition of the hymen does not indicate whether a woman or girl has been assaulted. A survey of child rape cases in 2010 found that only 2 per cent of victims had sustained 'visible lesions'. 'An examination of the hymen,' according to a paper by several international experts on sexual violence in 2019, 'is not an accurate or reliable test of a previous history of sexual activity, including sexual assault.' Bessie's story may have been so persuasive to Mrs S and the other women who knew her not because she was a mythomane but because she was telling the truth.

☞ *See also: erotomania, megalomania, plutomania*

NOMOPHOBIA

The term nomophobia – a jokey contraction of 'no-mobile-phone-phobia' – was coined in a Post Office survey of British mobile phone owners in 2008. The study, carried out when such devices had been on the market for twenty-five years, found that almost 53 per cent of participants felt anxious when their phone was mislaid, or had poor network coverage, or was short of battery or credit. A further 9 per cent were anxious when their phone was switched off. The levels of anxiety were comparable to those triggered by wedding-day nerves or trips to the dentist, the survey reported.

Mobile- or cell-phone dependence has continued to rise all over the world. A study of 2012 described phones as 'possibly the biggest non-drug addiction of the twenty-first century'. When used to lift low moods, they seem to activate the same neurobiological reward and reinforcement pathways as gambling and alcohol. Spending too much time on a smartphone can increase anxiety and depression, cause wrist and neck pain, impair sleep, concentration and educational performance. A series of national surveys between 2014 and 2018 found that excessive phone use was especially prevalent among teenagers: it was estimated at 10 per cent in Britain, 17 per cent in Taiwan and Switzerland, 31 per cent in Korea and India. Nomophobes were often stricken by the 'Fear of Missing Out' (FoMO) and the closely related 'Fear of Being Offline' (FoBO).

In 2014 the Italian psychiatrists Nicola Luigi Bragazzi and Giovanni Del Puente listed the signs of overdependence on a telephone. Nomophobes tended to carry a charger at all times, they said, and to avoid places, such as theatres and planes, in which use of a phone was banned. They repeatedly checked their phones, always left them switched on, and kept them close at night. Many preferred communicating by phone to speaking in person. Some heard phantom ring tones and felt phantom vibrations. Some incurred debts by spending too much money on data or on phones themselves. The capacities of smartphones are developing so swiftly that these criteria change but, generally speaking, said Bragazzi and Del Puente, nomophobia is the pathological fear of being technologically disconnected.

Bragazzi and Del Puente pointed out that a phone can carry different emotional meanings – it may be used as a protective shell or shield, as an imagined friend, or as a way of avoiding social interaction (they described this as part of the 'new technologies paradox', whereby electronic devices simultaneously connect and isolate us). The anthropologist Amber Case argued in 2007 that phones allow us to occupy a 'betwixt and between' social space, in which we are able to control and mediate our public selves. By composing a text message or staging a photo, we manage what we show and say; even a phone call withholds non-verbal cues such as posture or facial expressions. A nomophobe may feel comfortable only in this liminal world, and horribly exposed by live contact with other people.

Many of us feel incomplete when separated from our phones. In an experiment at a university in the American Midwest in 2014, forty iPhone users were asked to work for five minutes on a word-search puzzle, and to ignore their phones while doing so. Some of the group were physically separated from their phones, having placed them in a nearby cubicle, while others had the phones on their desks as they undertook the task. Each student worked on the puzzle in isolation. After three minutes, a researcher rang the student's phone, using the number provided on the registration form. All the participants ignored the ringing phones, as they had been instructed, but the blood pressure and heart rate of the students separated from their devices rose significantly more than those of the students with the phones on their desks. The group separated from their phones also showed a greater decrease in cognitive capacity while the device was ringing – they managed to find fewer words in the puzzle – and they reported higher rates of anxiety and discomfort. The researchers hypothesised that all of the students had imaginatively incorporated their iPhones, unconsciously perceiving them as extensions of their own bodies, and those who could not reach the devices had felt disturbingly, distractingly separated from a part of themselves.

But our dependence on phones is becoming so great that it is hard to gauge where it shades into unnatural obsession at all. In the years since the term nomophobia was coined, we have learnt to use phones to shop, to gamble, to arrange dates with strangers, to navigate from one place to another, to consult doctors, to gain entry to clubs, theatres, planes, trains, to watch films, sports events and television shows, to translate languages, to follow the news and to post our own news, to keep track of our health and levels of activity, to read books, to control other devices, to prove our identity, to monitor our homes and friends and families from afar, to do our jobs. The fear of being separated from our mobile devices has come to seem less pathological, and more a very reasonable concern.

☞ *See also: monophobia, social phobia, syllogomania, telephonophobia*

NYCTOPHOBIA

Nyctophobia, from the Greek *nyx* (night), is a disabling fear of the dark. Freud described it as the first fear that we experience, along with the fear of solitude. Once, he said, he heard a child who was afraid of the dark call into an adjoining room: 'Auntie, talk to me, I am afraid.' 'But what good will that do you?' asked the woman. 'You cannot see me!' The child answered: 'If someone speaks, it is brighter.' The child's fear of the dark was a terror of being alone, Freud surmised: 'The yearning felt in darkness is converted into the fear of darkness.'

We are not born scared of the dark – after all, at the moment of birth we have spent several months bobbing about in the womb with our eyes shut – but most of us become scared by the time we are four. In a study of Dutch primary school pupils in 2001, 73 per cent reported night-time fears, including 85 per cent of seven- to nine-year-olds. The primary school parents dramatically under-estimated the extent of their children's fear – when interviewed, only 34 per cent thought that they were frightened at night.

A fear of the dark is often expressed indirectly: a child may just seem slow to go to bed, or reluctant to be left at bedtime; the only sign of their anxiety may be that they talk about burglars, ghosts or monsters, that they cry in the night, or slip quietly under someone else's duvet. Among adults, too, the phobia may be more widespread than we think, being sometimes interpreted as insomnia or general anxiety. In a survey of British adults in 2012, 40 per cent of respondents said that they were afraid to walk around the house in the dark, and 10 per cent said that they wouldn't get out of bed at night even to use the bathroom. Queen Elizabeth I was so afraid of the dark that she had a lady-in-waiting share the royal bed every night.

To fear the dark is innate and sensible. Because our night vision is poor, we are more vulnerable to attack in the dark, less competent, less fast. If we wake in the night, our eyes struggle to adjust to the lack of light and we see shadowy figures take shape, as if the darkness is materialising. 'Children strain the eyes to see in twilight, and even inky blackness,' wrote Granville Stanley Hall in 1897, 'till perhaps darkness is reified as if it could be felt or cut.' We may fear that the 'big dark' outside will swallow us like a monster, he wrote, while the 'little dark' indoors is 'close and smothery'. The psychoanalyst George Devereux argued in 1949 that the loss of vision at night deprives the ego of its most important ally, physical reality. 'The fear of darkness,' he wrote, 'is, to some extent, a symptomatic expression of the ego's fear of being overwhelmed by instinctual forces.' When we are robbed of sight, the vacancy may be filled by irrational fears and desires.

Benjamin Rush had a simple remedy for nyctophobia. 'The fear which is excited by darkness may easily be overcome,' he wrote in 1786, 'by a proper mode of education in early life. It consists in compelling children to go to bed without a candle, or without permitting company with them until they fall asleep.' Nowadays, psychologists are more likely to recommend that we comfort frightened children by reading them stories in which the characters overcome their fear of the dark, or by introducing them to games that help to reduce the anxiety (shadow-animals on the walls, blindfolded treasure hunts). Children can be taught to soothe themselves by imagining that their heroes are guiding them through their bedtime rituals: 'Inspector Gadget thanks you for helping him in his mission and gives you a medal. Then he takes you back inside, removes your special undercover uniform and puts you to bed. You fall asleep...'

David A. Kipper, an Israeli psychologist, reported in 1980 on two nyctophobic patients whom he had treated with desensitisation therapy. One was a man of twenty-one who suffered from horrifying nightmares, having undergone a traumatic experience while serving with the Israeli army. The other was a thirteen-year-old girl who had been nyctophobic for five years but whose only frightening memory was of hearing the next-door apartment being burgled when she was twelve. Neither patient would stay in a dark room or leave the house after sunset. The man slept only in the daylight hours, while the girl insisted on light and company at night.

Kipper took the former soldier to a dark street, encouraged him to relax, walked alongside him and then moved ten yards away before letting him join him. He walked a little further away before inviting the man to follow. Once the patient got used to Kipper being several hundred yards away, the psychologist put himself out of sight, hiding at a prearranged spot until the man came to find him. The process was repeated over several weeks until the former soldier was able to walk alone in the dark. Kipper found that the same routine cured the thirteen-year-old girl of her fear, though she needed an extra treatment to feel safe in her bedroom: she was allowed at first to keep the door to her room ajar, to let in light, and asked to close it a little more each night.

Darkness has long been a cover for illicit activities – criminality, sedition, sexual transgression – and a metaphor for ignorance and sin. In *Rethinking Darkness* (2020), Tim Edensor describes how the scientists and philosophers of the Enlightenment spoke of banishing the darkness of unreason, while colonists and missionaries strove to civilise the 'Dark Continent' of Africa. In Christian writings, light is a symbol of salvation. 'You were once darkness,' Saint Paul tells the Ephesians, 'but now you are light in the Lord. Walk as children of the light.' The behavioural psychologist John B. Watson said that he was instilled with a fear of the night by his childhood nurse, who warned him that the Devil was lurking in the dark, waiting to snatch him off to Hell.

Edensor suggests that it may be time to rehabilitate darkness. In a world bright with electricity, the night can be a haven. Shadowy caves and dim rooms offer privacy, intimacy, an escape from surveillance. In his essay on fear, Granville Stanley Hall hailed the creative power of the dark: 'We know not what the imagination would be but for darkness, its great school,' he wrote, 'or if the eye, like the ear, could not close; or if eye pictures, like noises, had no night.' In the dark, observes the nature writer John Tallmadge, we not only imagine but feel, hear, taste and smell more intensely; the body 'relaxes, opens, breathes, extends its attention outward into the world the way a plant feels its way into the soil with roots or into the air with leaves'. We should cherish the gloom.

☛ *See also: hypnophobia, monophobia, thalassophobia, xylophobia*

NYMPHOMANIA

The word nymphomania, meaning an insatiable sexual appetite in women, is usually traced to the Greek word *nymphē*, meaning a young woman or bride. The concept was adopted in Britain and America in about 1775, after the translation into English of Jean Baptiste Louis de Thesacq de Bienville's *Nymphomanie*. In previous centuries, writes the historian Carol Groneman, women were often assumed to be as lustful as men, and their fertility was thought to depend in part on their sexual pleasure. But in an increasingly industrial society, women became defined by their roles as wives and mothers, and encouraged to adopt the self-denying, morally pure womanhood of evangelical Christianity. Any sign of sexual intent in a woman could be classified as excessive: not only her wish to masturbate or to have sex outside marriage, but also her wish to have more (or more satisfying) sex with her husband.

In 1856 'Mrs B', the twenty-four-year-old wife of a Boston wine merchant, told Dr Horatio Storer that she kept having erotic dreams about men of her acquaintance. In the seven years that she had been married, she said, she and her much older husband had engaged in sex every night, but lately there had been difficulties: 'he found obstruction to intercourse on her part', wrote the doctor, 'though she thinks it rather an increasing failure by him in erection'. Dr Storer diagnosed nymphomania and recommended that Mrs B abstain from sex for a while, avoid brandy and all other stimulants, refrain from writing (she was working on a novel), and swab her vagina with a borax solution. Unless she reined in her fantasies, he warned, she might end up in a lunatic asylum.

Physicians agreed that nymphomania was an organic disease, though they were not sure whether it emanated from the genitals or the brain. Perhaps the two were linked, they speculated: an irritation in a woman's reproductive organs could travel along the spinal column to madden the brain, and vice versa. When confronted with sexually restless women, doctors usually prescribed sedatives, cold baths or bloodletting (by the application of leeches to the perineum, for instance). Later in the century, a few undertook surgical operations such as oophorectomies (removal of the ovaries) or excisions of the clitoris or labia.

Some doctors were cautious about these interventions, notes the historian Sarah W. Rodriguez. In Brooklyn in 1896 Dr John Polak examined Lizzie B, a pale and emaciated twenty-nine-year-old who had been brought to his consulting room by her father. Mr B said that Lizzie had been morose and withdrawn for a decade, and would sit masturbating at home for hours on end, both alone and in front of others. He asked the doctor to remove Lizzie's clitoris – he was prepared to take full responsibility for the consequences, he said – and Polak reluctantly agreed. Three months later, Polak was relieved to report in *Medical News* that

Lizzie 'has shown no desire to return to her former habits; she seems happier, and her mental condition clearer'. The doctor did not specify the source of this information. Perhaps it was again Mr B, whose claims over his daughter's body seemed absolute.

In the 1920s and 1930s nymphomania was treated as a purely psychological disorder, an excessive hunger for sex that indicated a damaged psyche. After the Second World War many questioned whether there was such a condition at all. In *Sexual Behaviour in the Human Female* (1953), Alfred Kinsey argued that it was normal for women to masturbate and to fantasise about sex. A decade later, Albert Ellis and Edward Sagarin observed: 'What is often termed nymphomania is usually promiscuity, relatively well controlled, probably highly selective, and of a nature that would be considered relatively normal if found in almost any male in our society.' The licensing of the contraceptive pill in 1960 made it less risky for women to have sex outside marriage, and in the 1970s 'happy nymphos' appeared in women's magazines such as *Cosmopolitan* and in pornographic films such as *Deep Throat*.

Nymphomania was coming to seem a dubious concept, designed to make female desire look deranged or ridiculous. 'All too often,' observed the American sex therapist Dr Ruth Westheimer in the 1970s, 'a man calls a woman that because she likes a lot more sex than he does.'

As medical terms, nymphomania and its rarely diagnosed male equivalent, satyriasis, have been replaced by 'sex addiction', 'sexual compulsive disorder' and 'hypersexuality'. There is still difficulty about how to quantify excessive erotic appetite. One measure is whether people experience their behaviour as damaging, to themselves or others. In a study of 940 men and women in New Zealand in 2005, all of them thirty-two years old, 13 per cent of men and 7 per cent of women reported that they had engaged in 'out-of-control' sexual activities in the past year, though only 3.9 per cent of the men and 1.7 per cent of the women in the sample believed that these behaviours had interfered with their lives.

An Italian study in the *Journal of Affective Disorders* in 2021 found a statistically significant link between traumatic experience and hypersexuality. The authors argued that compulsive sexual

behaviour was a dysfunctional strategy for dealing with psychological suffering, mediated by depression and guilt, and they confirmed that the condition was much more common among men
than women. The clinical psychologist Richard B. Gartner
describes how this mechanism could work in a man who had been
sexually abused as a child. 'He may feel ambivalent about sexual
pleasure, since a certain amount of physical pleasure may have
accompanied the traumatic abuse ... Hungry for interpersonal
contact but phobic about it, believing that sexual closeness is his
chief opportunity to feel loved but experiencing love as abuse, a
sexually abused man who allows himself to be sexual at all often
solves his dilemma by engaging in frequent, indiscriminate, and
dissociated sexual encounters.' The description might even apply
to Lizzie B's glazed, repetitive sexual encounters with herself in
Brooklyn in the 1890s, compulsions that her father decided to
eliminate through surgery.

☛ See also: *erotomania, monomania*

ODONTOPHOBIA

About 15 per cent of us are averse to dental treatment, and 5 per
cent avoid visits to the dentist altogether. This can result in severe
damage to the teeth and gums, and sometimes to general health.
In 1897 Granville Stanley Hall named the fear odontophobia,
from the Greek word *odous*, or tooth.

Most odontophobes recall painful or frightening incidents in
the dentist's chair. Their experiences may have left them terrified
by the jab of a needle or the whirr of a drill. They may fear gagging
or choking or fainting, or just the helpless sensation of opening

their mouth wide to let a stranger dig about inside. During a dental examination, we cannot speak or even swallow easily. Our lips and tongues are stilled. The dentist works in there, out of sight, grinding and scraping and chipping with sharp and noisy tools.

In their analysis of the evolutionary origins of anxiety, Isaac Marks and Randolph Nesse explain how a terror of the dentist taps into an ancient, self-preserving impulse. Just as we can quickly become phobic about new diseases because we are hardwired to avoid infection, we can quickly learn to dread the dentist because we are primed to avoid injury. 'Head and heart unite more easily when new threats relate to earlier ones,' say Marks and Nesse. 'When they do, then fears of those threats may develop easily, but often in unmodulated fashion.'

To alleviate an odontophobe's anxiety, dentists may explain and demonstrate what they are going to do (the 'tell-show-do' approach), what the patients might feel ('sensation information') and how they can halt the procedure (with an agreed stop signal). To deal with conditioned fears of needles or drills, a dentist may recommend a course of exposure therapy, suggest that patients learn relaxation or distraction techniques, or even reduce their anxiety with benzodiazepine or nitrous oxide (the first person to use the gas to treat a patient was an American dentist, Horace Wells, in 1844). But if an individual has avoided the dentist for years, the work required may be so extensive that it will worsen the phobia. In this case, the odontophobe may choose to be knocked out with intravenous sedation or general anaesthesia while the dentist carries out the intricate procedures in the mouth.

☛ *See also: blood-injection-injury phobia, pnigophobia*

ONIOMANIA

The French psychiatrist Valentin Magnan coined the term oniomania – from the Greek *oninēmi*, 'for sale' – in 1892, and the German psychiatrist Emil Kraepelin included it in his influential psychiatric textbook of 1909. The 'buying mania', as Kraepelin described it, has since been dubbed compulsive shopping, spendaholism, shopaholism and compulsive buying disorder. The first epidemiological studies, in the US in the 1990s, found that between 2 and 8 per cent of the population were compulsive shoppers, most of them young women with relatively low incomes. Online shopping has made impulsive purchases all the easier.

Abraham Lincoln's wife Mary was a compulsive shopper. During Lincoln's presidency, from 1861 to 1865, she spent so much on redecorating the private and public rooms of the White House that Congress had to pass two bills to cover the expense. While civil war was raging between the northern and southern states of North America, Mary Todd Lincoln was running up huge debts with her favourite jeweller, Galt & Brothers, for gold bracelets, diamond rings, gem-encrusted brooches, fans and teaspoons. Some historians have speculated that the First Lady's oniomania was part of a psychiatric condition – she suffered from headaches, mood swings and outbursts of temper that may have been symptoms of bipolar disorder. Her compulsion may also have issued from grief. Mary Lincoln outlived three of her four sons, and was unable to function for several months in 1862 after the death of the twelve-year-old Willie.

Shopping can dispel feelings of emptiness and depression. 'When I shop,' explains Becky Bloomwood in the movie *Confessions of a Shopaholic* (2009), 'the world gets better, *is* better. Then it's not any more. And I have to do it again.' At the moment of transaction, a shopper both expresses and gratifies a yearning. The vulnerable and the victorious versions of herself fleetingly co-exist – the wanting and the having, the hunger and the satisfaction. Owning a thing is not the point: buying it is. The British psychoanalyst Darian Leader described a patient who spent thousands of pounds on clothes that she did not even take out of their bags and boxes. They were 'costumes for people I could be', she told him, 'a wardrobe of unactivated props'. By staying in their wrappings, the clothes retained their potency; they were still charged with the fantasy and promise of that instant of purchase.

☛ *See also: giftomania, kleptomania, monomania, syllogomania*

ONOMATOMANIA

Onomatomania is an obsession with a particular word. The French psychiatrists Jean-Martin Charcot and Valentin Magnan, who created the term in 1885 from the Greek *onomato* (word), outlined the three forms that the disorder could take: an agonised search for a specific, forgotten word; a compulsion to repeat a word, like an incantation; and a terror of hearing or uttering a word that is felt to be dangerous. In *Imperative Ideas* (1894), Daniel Hack Tuke described a young Englishwoman – 'Miss B' – who was so averse to a man of her acquaintance that she hated any word containing the syllable that was his name. Even after his death, she would wash her hands and arms if she heard such a term. An onomatomane ascribes magic force to certain words. Tuke – perhaps to preserve the anonymity of his patient, perhaps to honour her taboo – did not disclose the monosyllable by which Miss B was haunted.

☛ *See also: aibohphobia, arithmomania, hippopotomonstrosesquipediophobia, monomania*

ONYCHOTILLOMANIA

The destructive picking, pulling or filing of the fingernails or toenails was given the name onychotillomania, from the Greek *onyx* (nail) and *tillo* (to pull), by the Polish dermatologist Jan Alkiewicz in 1934. Though nail-biting and pulling are common habits, severe nail-picking is fairly rare. A survey carried out in Warsaw in 2013 identified only three cases among 339 medical students, a prevalence of less than 1 per cent. Like hair-pluckers and skin-pickers, onychotillomanes pull at the body's surfaces, probing the boundaries between the intrinsic and the extra, unpicking the flesh from its outgrowths.

'T', a married thirty-seven-year-old engineer with two children, was treated for onychotillomania at the University of Wisconsin-Milwaukee in 2014. He had been picking his nails since he was ten, he told the psychologists, a habit he shared with his mother and sister. He picked both his toe- and fingernails, keeping his thumbnails relatively long in order to use them to dig into the other digits. He would stroke the thumbs over the fingertips to find 'chinks in the armour': nicks, tags or tears that could be used to winkle out bits of nail.

When prevented from picking his nails, T felt tense, and the picking brought him relief. He claimed to pick his nails for eight or ten hours every day, and to play with, nibble and eat the pieces that he pulled free. In company, he would try to hide his actions by putting his hands behind his back or under the table. His nails were badly damaged: the nail beds on the middle fingers were 75 per cent exposed, and two toenails were missing altogether.

T was distressed by his condition: ashamed of his deformed nails, angry with himself for being unable to control the behaviour and frustrated at the way that the habit interfered with his life. He was too embarrassed to take his children swimming because of his stunted toenails, and tried to avoid handing things to colleagues at work for fear that they would be shocked by his mutilated fingers.

In the Milwaukee psychology department, T underwent an eight-month course of habit-reversal and other behavioural therapies. Having devised a series of interventions with the psychologists, he learnt to 'ruin the picking tools' by keeping his thumbnails short and smooth; to wear gloves when driving; to squeeze stress balls at work; to tape up 'target' nails when watching television; and to nibble on celery and beef jerky in lieu of chunks and slivers of nail. By the end of the treatment, reported the psychologists, the feeling was returning to T's traumatised nail beds, his nails were slightly longer, and he was able to take his children swimming at the local pool.

☛ *See also: dermatillomania, trichotillomania*

OPHIDIOPHOBIA

Snakes have always inspired awe and terror. They appear as gods and monsters in the myths of ancient Greece and Rome, of India, China, Mexico and Egypt. In the Bible, the serpent in the Garden of Eden brings knowledge, shame and ruin to mankind. Nowadays, about half of us are made anxious by snakes and about 6 per cent suffer from an excessive fear of them. In 1914 Granville Stanley Hall described this condition – the most common specific phobia in the world – as ophidiophobia, from the Greek *ophis*, or serpent. Ophidiophobes dread the snake's slither and hiss, its flickering tongue, its scaly limbless length and its unblinking stare. They hate the speed at which it slips across the ground, and whips round.

Since 600 of the 3,500 known species of snake are venomous, and even now 100,000 people die of their bites each year, it seems logical that we fear them. Charles Darwin believed that the response was instinctive and outside conscious control, a theory he tested on a visit to London Zoo. 'I put my face close to the thick glass-plate in front of a puff-adder in the Zoological Gardens,' he reported in 1872, 'with the firm determination of not starting back if the snake struck at me; but, as soon as the blow was struck, my resolution went for nothing, and I jumped a yard or two backwards with astonishing rapidity. My will and reason were powerless against the imagination of a danger which had never been experienced.'

Darwin tried putting a stuffed snake in the primate house at the zoo to see if the chimpanzees would rear back in terror as he had done. 'The excitement thus caused was one of the most curious spectacles which I ever beheld,' he wrote. The monkeys 'dashed about their cages, and uttered sharp signal cries of danger'. Afterwards he presented them with a mouse, a turtle and a dead fish, but they barely responded to these. He speculated that humans and chimps had evolved an inbuilt classification system that prompted a fearful response to certain creatures. This would explain why primates from areas where there were no poisonous snakes – lemurs in Madagascar, for example – showed no fear of them.

In experiments at the Wisconsin Primate Research Center in the 1980s and 1990s, the psychologist Susan Mineka found that young monkeys raised in a laboratory showed no horror of snakes but quickly learnt the fear when shown a film of other monkeys reacting to snakes with fright. When the film was spliced to show monkeys apparently being alarmed by flowers or rabbits, the lab monkeys were much slower to adopt these anxieties: they seemed to have at least a predisposition to learn and retain snake-fear. Further experiments showed that they were also able to spot snakes in grass much more quickly than they could pick out frogs, flowers or caterpillars.

In a laboratory in Sweden in the 1990s, Arne Öhman showed photographs of snakes to a group of human subjects, flashing them up for just 30 milliseconds and then immediately replacing them with other pictures to stop the pre-frontal cortex, which usually mediates visual stimuli, from processing the snake images. Despite this 'masking', those with ophidiophobia responded physically to the snake pictures – with sweating palms, for instance – confirming that the fear was relatively independent of conscious cognition. Öhman attributed the response to a self-contained survival circuit in the amygdala, a part of the brain that pre-dates the evolution of the pre-frontal cortex. In a joint paper of 2003, he and Mineka demonstrated that humans and monkeys were primed rapidly to detect and respond to certain threats.

In *The Fruit, the Tree and the Serpent* (2011), the animal behaviourist and anthropologist Lynne Isbell argues that the threat posed by snakes shaped the evolution of the human brain. When venomous serpents emerged in Asia and Africa, she says, they became the chief predators of our ancestors, who were small, nocturnal, mole-like creatures, guided chiefly by smell. Those that survived the advent of the snakes were those that developed better sight, a capacity to function by day, and an integration of their visual and fear systems. Their brains evolved much more cortex than the brains of other creatures, with enhanced powers to identify and decode visual and social cues. They became able not only to spot a snake but to alert others to danger, learning to communicate by pointing, the key precursor to language.

Isbell's theory of language evolution is contentious but, if she is right, the advent of snakes encouraged the changes to the cortex that enabled us to use words, to imagine and to reflect. This part of our brain, says the philosopher Stephen T. Asma, allows us to 'take our memories, ideas, goals, and emotions offline, so to speak, and entertain them in a parallel universe of mental space. The frightening monsters of the savanna can be decoupled from realtime and represented on cave walls and in stories, and we can embellish them without constraint.' It may be thanks to the snake that our species' cognitive and imaginative world has expanded. We now not only have specific, automatic behavioural reactions to danger, but we can also analyse, elaborate, invent and amplify our anxieties. We have fantasies as well as memories, ideas as well as perceptions. We have phobias.

☛ *See also: arachnophobia, zoophobia*

ORNITHOPHOBIA

In 2012 the One Direction singer Niall Horan confessed to a terror of pigeons. 'One once flew in through my bathroom window,' he told an interviewer, 'and went for me while I was having a wee. That was enough. I think pigeons target me.' On the band's tour of America that year, security guards swept the outdoor venues for birds. 'Niall's really scared of pigeons,' confirmed his bandmate Harry Styles. 'We have to protect him.'

Dell Catherall, a Canadian poet, attributed her fear of birds to two childhood incidents. In the first, she was attacked by a green budgerigar while she was being fitted for a ballet tutu. In the second, she accidentally hooked a seagull with her rod while out fishing with her father on Howe Sound, a fjord near Vancouver.

The bird screamed, flailed, thrashed its wings against the dinghy's stern as the girl's father tried to prise the hook from its leg. Meanwhile a horde of angry gulls started to dive at the boat, pecking and clawing at the man's face and neck. The girl picked up an oar and struck out wildly at them. By the time the injured gull was freed, and the girl had been gathered into her father's bleeding arms, her aversion to birds was complete.

Ornithophobia – from the Greek *ornis*, or bird – is commonly treated with exposure therapy. A three-day course in England in 2015 encouraged participants first to put out seed for birds in a park, then to handle tame doves at an aviary, then to catch and weigh turkeys on a farm, and finally to allow birds of prey – such as falcons, hawks, owls or vultures – to hop onto their hands.

The phobia was dramatised in Alfred Hitchcock's film *The Birds* (1963), based on a short story that Daphne du Maurier wrote after seeing a flock of seagulls dive-bombing a farmer in Cornwall. In the movie version, ravens, gulls and crows attack the people of Bodega Bay in California. The film's characters suspect one another of being somehow implicated in the birds' malevolence. 'Why are they doing this?' a local woman demands of the recently arrived Melanie Daniels, played by Tippi Hedren. 'They said when you got here, the whole thing started. Who are you? What are you? Where did you come from? I think you're the cause of all this. I think you're evil. Evil!' In this film the Freudian mechanism of phobia, whereby hidden feelings are projected onto an external object, seems to become fact, as if the dream world is taking hold of the real world, and fantasy commanding reality. The creatures' violence is an explosive enactment of something forbidden.

The British psychoanalyst Adam Phillips argued in 1998 that phobias vivify the world around us, lending it meaning and drama. A phobia is 'an unconscious estrangement technique', he wrote, 'a way of making ordinary places and things extremely charged'. Phillips used a bird to illustrate his point: 'To be petrified by a pigeon,' he said, 'is a way of making it new.' Hitchcock effects just such transformations, saturating his films with para-noia, uncertainty, an electrifying alienation.

☞ *See also: ovophobia, pteronophobia, zoophobia*

OSMOPHOBIA

Osmophobia, from the Greek *osmē*, is an aversion to certain smells. According to a survey of 2017, more than half of people who experience migraines are affected by this condition. The odours they cite as most offensive are perfume (reported in 88 per cent of cases), followed by cigarette smoke (62 per cent) and food (54 per cent).

Some people become osmophobic in the aftermath of a Covid-19 infection, having developed an anosmia – a distortion in their sense of smell – that renders particular scents repulsive. 'Wine smells like sewage,' wrote a woman in the Covid-19 Smell and Taste Loss Facebook group in 2021. 'Prosecco is even worse.' Another member of the group was unnerved to detect a foul smell when she was close to her boyfriend. 'What if I stink?' she wondered. 'Is that roadkill smell me or him?' A third contributor confidently attributed the off-putting aroma to her partner. 'His natural odour used to make me want him,' she said. 'Now it makes me vom.'

☞ *See also: emetophobia, phonophobia*

OVOPHOBIA

Alfred Hitchcock claimed to suffer from ovophobia (*ovum* is Latin for egg). 'I'm frightened of eggs,' he told the Italian journalist Oriana Fallaci in 1963, soon after the release of his film *The Birds*. 'Worse than frightened – they revolt me. That white round thing without any holes, and when you break it, inside there's that yellow thing, round, without any holes... Brr!' An egg was all surface or all innards: impenetrable, horribly intact, whether whole or broken, shelled or viscous. 'Have you ever seen anything more revolting than an egg yolk breaking and spilling its yellow liquid?' he asked Fallaci. 'Blood is jolly, red. But egg yolk is yellow, revolting. I've never tasted it.' A punctured yolk seemed to bleed out its rich, gleaming fluid.

Hitchcock informed Fallaci that eggs were not his only phobia. In fact, he said, he was 'the most fearful and cowardly man' she would ever meet. He claimed to lock himself into his bedroom each night, 'as if there were a madman on the other side of the door, waiting to slit my throat'. He told her that he was frightened of policemen (when he came home late one night at the age of eleven, his father had arranged for an officer to lock him in a police cell); and also of crowds, burglars, people arguing, violence, darkness and Sundays (his parents used to put him to bed at six on a Sunday, he explained, and then go out to eat at a restaurant). He said that he was scared of his own films: 'I never go to see them. I don't know how people can bear to watch my movies.'

Hitchcock told several interviewers how much he loathed eggs but, like many of his statements, the claim was as much provocation as fact. Even in the interview with Fallaci he remarked that he enjoyed his wife Alma's soufflés, and in conversation with his biographer John Russell Taylor he mentioned that he used to eat poached eggs on toast while serving with the Royal Engineers. 'Aha!' said Taylor. 'You said you never ate eggs.' 'Well,' Hitchcock conceded, 'I suppose I did eat one or two eggs when I was very young.'

When Hitchcock had finished listing his various terrors to Fallaci, she challenged him. 'That's rather illogical, Mr Hitchcock. Come to that, your movies are illogical, too. From the logical point of view, not one of them can stand inspection.'

'Agreed,' said Hitchcock airily. 'But what is logic? There's nothing more stupid than logic.'

☞ *See also: emetophobia, ornithophobia, popcorn phobia, pteronophobia*

P

PANTOPHOBIA

In 1929 the psychoanalyst Wilhelm Stekel described a nineteen-year-old Viennese student, 'Hermann G', as a victim of 'pantophobia' (from the Greek *pan*, or 'all'). Hermann had a fear of eating meat, he told Stekel, and of going to lectures, and of standing near windows. He was afraid that he might catch syphilis by walking past a prostitute, so he tried to hold his breath when out of doors. Hermann feared himself most of all. He did not like to see a knife in case he was tempted to stab one of his sisters, and he did not like to be alone in his room in case he harmed himself. Stekel traced Hermann's anxieties to the death of his younger sister, Gretel, when he was thirteen. Hermann had always been jealous of Gretel, he confessed, and when she fell ill he had wished her dead. After her death he heard that she had once been abducted in a park by a gang of soldiers and he wondered if an infection of syphilis might have killed her. Hermann's many phobias, concluded Stekel, were rooted in his remorse about Gretel and his dread that he would be punished with the same fate.

☛ *See also: agoraphobia, hypophobia, mysophobia*

PEDIOPHOBIA

The classic psychoanalytic study of pediophobia – a terror of dolls, from the Greek *paidion*, meaning little child or toy child – is Leo Rangell's 'The Analysis of a Doll Phobia', published in 1952. In this essay Rangell described a thirty-eight-year-old Philadelphian statistician, an unhappily married man with a fear of dolls that dated from his boyhood. The statistician was afraid of 'dolls with which children play', wrote Rangell, 'of manikins, of window-dummies used for display purposes, of puppets, of pieces of sculpture, of various objets d'art in the form of figurines. An ashtray or a lamp base might be carved as a figure, a bar of soap might be fashioned in the form of a little animal. Any such object was a threat, was his enemy.' Rangell realised how close a person's fear of a particular thing was to an obsession with it: 'He in a sense becomes married to the object. In order to avoid it, his eyes seek it out.'

Rangell learned that his patient was especially scared of dolls made of porcelain, plaster or china because they might break to reveal their hollowness. The statistician was also horrified by the idea of animate dolls: 'It was particularly the moment of a figure "coming to life" or simulating movement,' wrote Rangell, 'which was the most frightening.' Rubber was bad, his patient told him, because it was smooth and flesh-like; celluloid was worse, as it could curl and twitch when wet; and wax and soap, which could mutate, melt, disappear, were the worst of all.

The statistician underwent 700 hours of psychoanalytic treatment, over three years, in which he and Rangell explored his dreams and memories. It emerged that he experienced great guilt and shame about masturbation, and Rangell concluded that for him a doll that stirred into life recalled the stirring of an erection, an exciting event that he feared would incur a terrible punishment. 'The doll which is avoided is the detached penis,' wrote Rangell, 'an unwelcome reminder of castration.' But it also represented many other things, 'in turn and simultaneously': the patient's 'stool, his body *in toto*, his mother, woman in general, the female genital, another man's (father's) penis, and the little girl's fantasised penis'. A phobic object fused multiple fears and fixations.

As the analysis progressed, the statistician set himself tests outside the consulting room. At a fur salon, he sat down next to a manikin while his wife was trying on a coat. At a local museum, he shook hands with a statue of Charlie Chaplin. At his mother-in-law's house, he stroked a sewing dummy that was kept in a closet. At home, he managed to touch the bride and groom figurines that his wife had saved from their wedding cake. He was delighted to find that his phobia was fading.

Rangell ended his paper by describing another patient, a successful puppeteer who had devoted his life to his dolls: 'making them, dressing them, playing with them, and exhibiting them'. After a performance, he would invite the audience backstage to admire his creations, 'at which time this man sits on a chair nervously biting his nails, a study in mixed feelings. In him mingle great pride and satisfaction plus gnawing anxiety lest someone cause the slightest damage to his prized possession'. For both the pediophobe and the pediophile, wrote Rangell, a doll was 'the concentrate of strong feelings and values emanating from the person's unconscious. In the one case, equilibrium is maintained by shunning this concentrated symbol; in the other, he is able to embrace and enjoy it.'

In an essay of 1906, the German psychiatrist Ernst Jentsch located the eeriness of dolls in the way that they could seem alive, like the dolls of rubber or wax that Rangell's statistician so hated. To create an uncanny literary effect, Jentsch observed, a writer need only 'leave the reader in uncertainty whether a particular figure in the story is a human being or an automaton'. A doll was frightening, he suggested, because it was ambiguous. It hovered between different categories of being.

A doll to which one person attributes life can be especially disturbing to others. In London in the 1920s, the cross-dressing millionaire speedboat racer Marion Barbara 'Joe' Carstairs had a foot-high leather doll named Lord Tod Wadley which she carried with her everywhere; she had clothes made for him in Savile Row, and an account opened for him at Coutts Bank. 'We're like one,' she would say. 'He's me and I'm him.' Carstairs bought a Bahamian island in the 1930s, and its 500 inhabitants grew accustomed to the sight of 'the Boss' bombing around on a motorbike with Wadley, like a voodoo fetish, at her side. As the doll aged, his leather face blackened and cracked. Carstairs' girlfriends grew frightened of him. 'He looks so lively,' said one, 'like something dead.'

In 1970 the Japanese roboticist Masahiro Mori formulated a theory about the fear of dolls: the more life-like they were, he argued, the more appealing to humans they became, until the point at which they became too life-like and hence highly disturbing. Mori plotted a graph to show the moment at which the distinction blurred between the human and non-human, and our attraction for humanoid figures turned suddenly to repulsion – he named the phenomenon the 'Uncanny Valley', in reference to the abrupt dip of the graph. When Mori proposed this theory, humanoid robots had not yet been designed: his intuition was based on his dislike of dolls and prosthetic hands. 'Since I was a child, I have never liked looking at wax figures,' Mori said. 'They looked somewhat creepy to me. At that time, electronic prosthetic hands were being developed, and they triggered in me the same kind of sensation.'

In an unsettling instance of aversion therapy for pediophobia, two Indian psychiatrists reported in 2013 on the treatment of 'Miss A', a girl of twelve. This child, her mother explained to a therapist at the local psychiatric clinic, was not scared of all dolls but of one in particular: a sparkling-eyed figure kept in a glass case in the family home in Gujarat. When she saw this doll, Miss A would scream and run away crying. The therapist asked the mother to bring her daughter to the clinic for a single session of aversion therapy, and secretly to bring the doll along too.

After interviewing Miss A at the clinic, the therapist told her to shut her eyes, then pulled the doll from a drawer and placed it on the girl's back. The child, guessing the identity of the object, began to scream. The therapist reminded her that under no circumstance could she leave the room. The girl continued to scream, then started to cry. After fifteen minutes she asked if she could open her eyes. 'I am no longer afraid of the doll!' she said. She looked straight at the doll's glittering eyes. 'I fail to understand,' she declared, 'why I was so scared of the doll.' Smiling, she caught the doll when the therapist threw it to her and, still smiling, she threw it back again. Five minutes later she was returned to her mother, apparently cured.

A year afterwards, Miss A claimed still to be free of her fear. The authors of the paper concluded: 'Exposure-based treatments in which patients are systematically confronted with their feared objects are highly effective.' They seem not to have asked Miss A whether her fear of the doll had been replaced with any new terrors – of therapists, perhaps.

☛ *See also: coulrophobia*

PHONOPHOBIA

In Pahang, Malaysia, in 2010 a twelve-year-old girl was referred to the International Islamic Hospital's Ear, Nose and Throat department with a fear of noises. She had developed the sensitivity, her parents said, after hearing the explosions of firecrackers at a Chinese New Year celebration. Since then, she had reacted to ordinary noises as if they were incredibly loud, and she reported that the intense sounds in her head were followed by a nasty buzzing. She found the rustle of a plastic bag almost unbearable, let alone the bang of a balloon. At such noises, her heart would race, she would shiver, sweat and cry. Things had become so bad that she was refusing to attend classes or social events.

Having checked that the girl did not have a physiological sensitivity to noise, the doctors diagnosed phonophobia (*phonē*, in Greek, means voice or sound). They surmised that her obsessive fear had been generated unconsciously as a form of self-protection: her shock at the fireworks had exacerbated her natural fear of the sudden loud noises that can herald danger. The psychologists treated the girl with twice-weekly sessions, which included 'psycho-education' (for her and her parents), relaxation techniques and gradual desensitisation by exposure. After three months of therapy, the girl was able to visit a restaurant with her family, and after six months she could withstand the fizzes, cracks and bangs of a fireworks display.

Some people feel panic and rage when they hear noises such as slurping, chewing, sniffing or the rustle of crisp packets. A study of 2017 suggested that this form of anger-generating phono-phobia – known as misophonia, or a hatred of sounds – is caused by overactivity in the anterior insular cortex, a part of the brain that connects our senses to our emotions. After the Covid-19 restrictions, some people found that their noise sensitivities had been heightened even further. In the summer of 2021, for instance, the police were called to intervene in a violent altercation that had broken out when a resident of Bexhill, East Sussex, accused a neighbour of eating too loudly.

☛ *See also: brontophobia, globophobia, osmophobia, sedatephobia, telephonophobia*

PLUTOMANIA

In the seventeenth century the term plutomania – from the Greek *ploutos*, or wealth – was used to describe the reckless pursuit of riches. The Scottish writer Sir Thomas Urquhart lamented the plutomanes of his era: 'So madly they hale after money, and the trash of this world.' In 1894 the word was used in the American journal *The Forum* to describe the delusion of possessing a fortune: a hallucination of wealth. And in 1930, a different sort of 'Plutomania' swept America when Clyde Tombaugh, a young astronomer at the Lowell Observatory in Arizona, spotted a ninth planet in the solar system (an eleven-year-old British schoolgirl was awarded £5 for her suggestion that it be named Pluto, after the Roman god of the underworld).

The US went crazy for the new planet: thousands visited the Pluto show at the American Museum of Natural History in New York, while the press clamoured for interviews with Tombaugh and printed diagrams to help readers find the planet in the night sky. In 1931 Walt Disney Pictures gave the name Pluto to Mickey Mouse's pet dog, which had first appeared in 1930 as Minnie's dog Rover.

Plutomania in both of its older senses – the frenzied pursuit of riches, delusions of fabulous wealth – had contributed to the catastrophic crash on Wall Street in 1929. As the country slid into economic depression, the new Plutomania served as a distraction from the hardship to come.

☞ *See also: Beatlemania, megalomania, monomania, tulipomania*

PNIGOPHOBIA

A pnigophobe (from the Greek *pnigo*, to choke) is afraid of choking on pills, fluids or food. Individuals usually develop the disorder suddenly, after witnessing or experiencing an episode of choking.

In 1994 the American psychophysiologist Richard McNally analysed twenty-five case reports of choking phobia. An eight-year-old girl choked on a French fry during a car journey and refused solid food for the next three months, losing 8lbs. A ten-year-old boy lost 10lbs after choking on a staple. A nine-year-old girl lost more than a stone after choking on a piece of popcorn. She suffered from nightmares of choking, refused to brush her teeth in case she choked on a bristle, and slept with her head propped up on a pillow in case she choked on a loose tooth. A twenty-six-year-old woman developed pnigophobia when she was caught up in a gun battle in a restaurant in Southeast Asia in the 1970s – she said that her throat now constricted whenever she tried to eat in public.

McNally himself treated a thirty-year-old man, John, who became pnigophobic when he choked on a piece of fish at the age of sixteen, two years after his best friend had died while choking on a hot dog. John avoided solid food when he could, especially if he felt a tickling sensation, like a caught hair, in his throat, and he spent ages chewing anything that he did eat. He found that his condition waxed and waned over the years, becoming more acute when he was anxious or depressed. By the time that he consulted McNally, his weight had dropped from 13 to 10 stone.

Under McNally's care, John tried to reduce the number of chews that he gave each bite of food, with McNally sometimes eating alongside him to help him regulate his chewing. John started by masticating each bite ninety times and worked his way down (in steps of ten) to twenty. McNally persuaded John gradually to try the foods he feared, starting with bread (sessions one and two) and culminating in a bacon, lettuce and tomato sandwich (session six). At a six-month follow-up, John reported that he was now able to tackle hamburgers.

Most recorded cases of choking phobia, McNally observed, had been successfully treated with this kind of graduated exposure therapy and, sometimes, with anti-anxiety medication. In 1992 the Swedish psychologist Lars-Göran Öst used cognitive therapy on a sixty-eight-year-old woman who could not drink liquid – she prevented herself from becoming completely dehydrated by eating biscuits soaked in tea. The woman was afraid that if fluid leaked down her windpipe, she would suffocate. She believed that she would be unable to get rid of the liquid by coughing and that even a short spell without oxygen would kill her. First, Öst asked her to hold her breath for increasing periods of time, so that she would realise that she was wrong to think that people could not survive without oxygen for longer than thirty seconds. Next, he asked her to push a pen out of a paper tube by coughing into the cylinder, and then to expel water from her windpipe with coughs. 'These demonstrations,' said McNally, 'eliminated her misconceptions and abolished her choking phobia.' Correcting the woman's false beliefs about her physiology seemed to have relieved her of her fear.

☞ See also: claustrophobia, emetophobia, odontophobia, popcorn
   phobia

POGONOPHOBIA

The irascible British television presenter Jeremy Paxman accused the BBC of pogonophobia – from the Greek *pōgōn*, a beard – after he appeared on screen unshaven in 2013. He claimed that the corporation was as averse to facial hair as the dictator Enver Hoxha, who banned beards in Albania in 1967.

The first use of the satirical term pogonophobia, meaning a distaste for beards, seems to have been in a Presbyterian journal in 1851. For most of the previous century, facial hair had been shunned by the British and American establishments as lower-class and unhygienic. An 'unshorn chin', according to *The Toilette of Health, Beauty and Fashion* (1834), 'has a degenerating aspect, and is only, if at all, excusable in the lowest labourer and mechanic'. Early cave paintings indicate that even our Neanderthal ancestors removed their beards, perhaps to get rid of parasites, using clamshells as tweezers or flints as razors.

In the late 1850s facial hair became fashionable in Britain, thanks to the soldiers who returned from the Crimean War sporting the giant beards and moustaches that they had grown as protection against the cold. But by the early twentieth century clean-shaven faces were coming back into fashion, and beards were once again reviled. In Britain and the United States many public and private organisations, from Disneyland to the New York Police Department, banned employees from wearing beards. The United Parcel Service lifted its veto only in 2020.

The children's author Roald Dahl loathed beards, and in his books depicted bearded men as filthy louts. Mr Twit in *The Twits* (1980) has a huge dark beard matted with old cornflakes and scraps of Stilton and sardines. 'By sticking out his tongue and curling it sideways to explore the hairy jungle around his mouth,' wrote Dahl, 'he was always able to find a tasty morsel here and there to nibble on.' Beards were 'hairy smoke-screens behind which to hide', said Dahl in an essay on the subject. 'The whole business is disgusting.'

☛ *See also: doraphobia, mysophobia, trichomania, trichotillomania*

POPCORN PHOBIA

The musician and game designer Fisher Wagg told the podcast 'Pantophobia' in 2016 that he had a phobia of popcorn. The sight of it invoked 'anguish' in him, he said. Once, he recalled, he had watched a cartoon animation in which maggots 'danced around inside of a corpse', a sight to which he had no emotional reaction until the perspective changed and the maggots suddenly looked to him like a giant piece of live popcorn, bloating and coiling. For Wagg, the idea of this light and squeaky snack food was scarier than that of maggots feasting on an opened body.

Wagg's response seems almost comically topsy-turvy, but it offers a clue to the workings of phobia. When a piece of corn pops, the kernel puffs from the split husk and billows outwards, expanding to tens of times its original size: the inside comes out, the interior engulfs the exterior, the innards and the skin swap places. In *Purity and Danger* (1966) the British anthropologist Mary Douglas argued that disgust is provoked by 'matter that is out of place'. For most of us, maggots writhing in a sea of human flesh elicit this reaction. For Wagg, a popped piece of corn was a similar and worse transgression: it not only breached but overwhelmed and obliterated its own boundaries.

To demonstrate his phobia, Wagg recorded his thoughts as he watched slow-motion footage of popcorn popping. 'I hate that they're wet,' he says. 'It explodes as this great white thing, like the carapace of a cricket or something ... you can see it flipped inside-out.' He falls silent as he watches the white matter continue to envelop itself. 'Yeah, no, that's bad,' he says quietly, turning off the tape.

☞ See also: *bambakomallophobia, entomophobia, koumpounophobia, pnigophobia*

PTERONOPHOBIA

Several of the children interviewed for Granville Stanley Hall's survey of fears in 1897 confessed to being scared of feathers. Hall named the fear pteronophobia, from the Greek word for feather, *pteron*. A few of his subjects had become fearful after seeing a downy plume escape a pillow or quilt, he reported, and one had been disciplined with feathers. 'The nurse would keep me in a room by putting a feather in the keyhole,' recalled the child. 'If I wanted to come in, and a feather was on the door, I would just stand and yell.' A woman reported that her three-year-old daughter had 'great awe of the feather duster'.

Hall speculated that while some children recoiled from a feather's soft tickle, others were disturbed by its apparent vitality, the way that it seemed to lift itself up to dance through the air.

☛ *See also: doraphobia, ornithophobia*

PUBLIC URINATION PHOBIA

In public bathrooms, some people find that their urethral sphincters tighten so much that they cannot urinate, a psychogenic condition known as paruresis or shy bladder syndrome. Among the specific social phobias, it is thought to be second in prevalence only to glossophobia, the fear of public speaking. People with this condition may find themselves unable to provide urine for drug tests. Others are so worried by the prospect of urinating in public facilities that they feel compelled to stay home. At its worst, the phobia causes physical damage (kidney stones, urinary tract infections) and requires medical intervention with a catheter.

The first survey of paruresis, in 1954, found that 14 per cent of college students had experienced the phenomenon at least once. Since then, estimates of its prevalence have ranged from 2.8 to 16.4 per cent. The disorder is more common in men than women, which may reflect differences in physiology (men become more urine-retentive as they age, whereas women become more incontinent) as well as in the different levels of privacy afforded by public lavatories (most men's bathrooms are fitted with standing urinals, and women's with closed cubicles). Some people date their phobia to a humiliating experience of being heard or watched when urinating, but many are mystified by why they find themselves frozen in this way.

While the standard treatments for the phobia are cognitive-behavioural and desensitisation therapies, some people report that counting backwards can help to solve the problem. Another technique, described on the International Paruresis Association website, is to exhale about 75 per cent of one's breath for 45 seconds, pinching the bridge of the nose if necessary, which may encourage the pelvic floor to drop and the stream to flow.

☛ *See also: erythrophobia, gelotophobia, mysophobia, social phobia*

PYROMANIA

The compulsion to set fires was given the name pyromania, from the Greek *pyr* (fire), by Charles Chrétien Henri Marc in 1833. Marc described the actions of several servant girls, aged between twelve and sixteen, who had set fires in the premises of their masters and mistresses, and a woman who had set fire to a house in which her husband met his lover.

In 1838 Jean-Étienne Esquirol added to Marc's list the case of a thirteen-year-old servant in Barkingside, Essex, who in October 1833 had set fire to the bed of the farmer for whom she worked. When she was brought before the local magistrate, Jane Walls explained her motive. 'I did not think that I was doing mischief,' she said. 'I wished to see if by bringing a lighted candle near the bed curtain I should set it on fire. I was curious to witness the effect of the flame, and supposed that it would be more beautiful than coals of fire or a faggot burns in the fireplace.' She said that she had no ill will towards her master and had immediately told him that she had set fire to his bed. She regretted her action now that she realised that she might be sentenced to death: 'Had I known that I should be hung for having kindled a bonfire, I should not have done it.'

The farmer testified that Jane Walls seemed sane – she had been a steady and attentive nursemaid to his children, he said – but her lawyer argued that she had been deranged by fever the previous February, and had been giddy and distracted again when her father died in September. The magistrate ruled that Walls should not be charged with arson, a capital crime, but instead sent for trial on the lesser charge of committing a misdemeanour.

Many of the pyromaniac servant girls interviewed by Marc confessed to having been unhappy in their work. They had little control over their circumstances, but they handled fire every day – in hearths, lamps, candles, stoves, ranges – and it was the work of a moment to transform a single flame into a conflagration. One fifteen-year-old told Marc that a spirit, constantly by her side, had tempted her to burn down the house in which she worked, but also admitted that she longed to return to her own home. In Germany, a fourteen-year-old who twice lit fires in the house of her employer explained that she had been suffering from 'unbearable nostalgia' and was desperate to see her parents. She was put to death.

Some people tried for arson in the nineteenth century argued that they suffered from an insane compulsion to set fires, but such pleas were rarely successful. In 1858, for instance, a judge rejected the claim that an employee of the New York State Lunatic Asylum was in the grip of pyromania when he set fire to the institution's central building and barn. 'The existence of the impulsive mania,' observed the judge, 'could only be proved by the commission of the acts which it sought to excuse, which would be no evidence at all.' By the late nineteenth century, most psychiatrists, too, had turned against the idea of pyromania as a distinct mental disorder.

The diagnosis was revived in the twentieth century, when psychoanalysts such as Wilhelm Stekel argued that only unconscious drives and passions could account for some acts of fire-setting. In 1932 Freud described flames as representations of sexual desire: 'the warmth radiated by fire,' he wrote, 'evokes the same kind of flow as accompanies the state of sexual excitation, and the form and motion of the flame suggest the phallus in action'. The dousing of a fire, he said, evoked the erotic pleasure of urination. Many fires are set for nefarious reasons – to collect insurance, to punish a debtor, to cover up another crime – or as forms of protest. But psychoanalysts point out that an apparent motive may mask a compulsion, just as a claim of compulsion may mask a criminal act.

In 1957 the US Court of Appeals heard an appeal against the conviction of Thomas Briscoe, a married man who had set a fire in a vacant house in Washington DC. Briscoe confessed to having lit about a hundred fires since he was twelve. He often woke in the night feeling a strong sexual urge, he said, which could be satisfied only if he left his house, set fire to a building, sounded the alarm, and watched firemen put out the blaze. The judges upheld the appeal, accepting that Briscoe might suffer from pyromania and ruling that he could enter a 'not guilty by reason of insanity' plea if his case were retried.

The American Psychiatric Association defines pyromania as an impulse-control disorder that should be diagnosed only where fire-setting is recurrent, not explicable by another condition, preceded by tension or arousal, followed by relief or pleasure, and driven by a fascination with fire rather than a desire for revenge or for monetary gain. In 1951 Nolan Lewis and Helen Yarnell analysed the records of almost 1,200 men who had deliberately set fires, and found that only about 4 per cent conformed to the psychiatric definition of 'true pyromania'. 'These offenders are able to give a classical description of the irresistible impulse,' they explained. 'They describe the mounting tension, the restlessness, the urge for motion, the conversion symptoms such as headaches, palpitations, ringing in the ears, and the gradual merging of their identity into a state of unreality; then the fires are set.'

An American woman detailed similar sensations in an anonymous account of her pyromania in 2001. She had had a difficult childhood, she said: an older stepbrother had sexually abused her when she was about ten, and her mother suffered from alcoholism and bipolar disorder. 'Fire became a part of my vocabulary in my preschool days,' she recalled. 'During the summers our home would be evacuated because the local mountains were ablaze. I would watch in awe.' She became obsessed with fires: lighting them, reading about them, watching movies about them, listening to songs about them, discussing them, smelling them. She was enthralled by a fire's leap and light and power. She set fires, she said, when she felt empty or when she sensed that anxiety was taking her over. 'I may feel abandoned, lonely or bored,' she wrote. 'I sometimes experience severe headaches, a rapid heartbeat, uncontrollable motor movements in my hands, and tingling pain in my right arm.' The crackle and heat of a fire seemed to burn away her tension.

As a student at the University of California in the spring of 1993, the young woman was caught setting several fires on campus. She was committed to a psychiatric ward but discharged in the summer to take up an internship with a congressional representa-tive in Washington DC. In the eight years since, she had been admitted to hospital another thirty-three times, and variously diagnosed with psychosis, depression, obsessive-compulsive and borderline personality disorders. Her inner world was still lit by fire. 'My dreams are about fires that I have set, want to set, or wish I had set,' she wrote. And in her waking hours, she continued to pursue her craving for flames. She felt sadness and anguish when one of her fires was put out, she said, and a yearning to set another fire.

☛ See also: dipsomania, homicidal monomania, kleptomania, monomania, nymphomania, oniomania, trichotillomania

SEDATEPHOBIA

The fear of silence, sometimes described as sedatephobia (*sedatus* is 'calmed' in Latin), is becoming more prevalent as the world grows noisier. City dwellers are accustomed to a background buzz – the rush and beep of the street, the pinging of phones, the hum of a fridge, the burble of digitised music and chatter. Silence can feel unsettling, even unbearable. Some of us panic when we try to sleep in a noiseless room. Others are set on edge by the peace of a country lane.

In 2012 Bruce Fell, a lecturer at Charles Sturt University in Australia, reported that many of his students struggled to tolerate silence. Over six years, he had asked 580 of them to complete questionnaires on the subject. One wrote: 'I actually began doing this assignment in the library and had to return to my room minutes later to get my iPod as I found the library was so quiet that I couldn't concentrate properly!' Fell believed that many of them had been conditioned by the constant noise of televisions in their childhood homes, and that new technologies had made it all the easier to shut out the quiet. An undergraduate told him that when she returned to her family farm, she found it hard to walk down to a nearby dam without listening to music on her head-phones. Fell asked the students to spend an hour either reading, walking or just sitting in silence. Most of them found this difficult. 'The lack of noise made me uncomfortable,' said one. 'It actually seemed foreboding.' For this student, silence was an ominous pause, a state of suspense, a prelude to danger.

An experiment of 2013 tested the effects of different sounds on the brains of mice. The researchers divided the mice into four groups and exposed one group to white noise for two hours a day; one to the cries of baby mice; one to Mozart piano music; and one to silence. For the rest of the time the mice heard the ambient sounds of the laboratory. The researchers discovered that the mice exposed to silence developed more brain cells than the other groups. They hypothesised that the unusual quiet acted as an alarm, a kind of 'good stress' in which the mice – like the uneasy Australian student – were tensely awaiting a noise. 'The alert elicited by such unnatural silence,' write the brain scientists, 'might stimulate neurogenesis as preparation for future cognitive challenges.' An unfamiliar silence, by generating a state of nervous attention, expanded the mice's minds.

☛ *See also: hypnophobia, nomophobia, nyctophobia, phonophobia*

SIDERODROMOPHOBIA

In 1879 the German physician Johannes Rigler gave the name siderodromophobia to a new form of illness suffered by railway workers – the word was a translation of the German *Eisenbahnangst*, or 'iron-road-angst', into the Greek *sideros* (iron) and *dromos* (track) and *phobia* (fear). According to Rigler, the violent jolts of train travel could bring on physical and mental breakdown. When George Miller Beard introduced the term to an English-speaking readership, he explained: 'This is a form of intense spinal irritation coupled with a hysterical condition, and morbid disinclination for work.' He attributed the illness to the 'perpetual jarring, shaking, and noise' of railway travel.

The diagnosis of siderodromophobia, in passengers as well as railway employees, reflected a rising anxiety about the effects of industrialisation. Many believed that it was dangerous for the human body to be moved at the speed of a train. On a railway journey, observed Malcolm Alexander Morris in *The Book of Health* (1884), 'the man, for the time being, becomes a part of the machine in which he has placed himself, being jarred by the self-same movement, and receiving impressions upon nerves of skin and muscle'. Siderodromophobia was understood as an illness caused by new technology, much as shellshock would be in the First World War. The vibration of a railway carriage, like the blast of a bomb, could reverberate through the body and the mind.

Rigler's term was also used to describe a passenger's dread of train travel, a phobia from which Sigmund Freud said that he suffered in his thirties and early forties. In a letter to his friend Wilhelm Fliess in 1897, Freud complained that daily press reports of train accidents were fuelling his anxiety about an upcoming journey. He wondered if his railway phobia had begun on an overnight train trip from Leipzig to Vienna that he made with his mother when he was two. 'We must have spent the night together,' he wrote, 'and there must have been the occasion of seeing her *nudam*.' In an early formulation of the Oedipus complex, he speculated that his phobia was a displacement onto the train both of his excitement at the sight of his naked mother – 'my libido was stirred up towards *matrem*' – and his corresponding fear that his father would punish him for his desire.

In 'Three Essays on Sexuality', Freud argued that boys were sexually aroused by the pounding, juddering motion of railway travel, its 'rhythmic mechanical agitation of the body'. Those who repressed the fantasies associated with these sensations might, like him, acquire a phobia of trains. Instead of inducing excitement, the tremble of the locomotive would bring on nausea, anxiety and dread.

☞ See also: *aerophobia, claustrophobia, ergophobia, phonophobia*

SOCIAL PHOBIA

Social phobia, also known as social anxiety disorder, is a fear of being scrutinised or judged by others. The physical symptoms include sweating, stuttering, trembling, a feeling of queasiness and a racing heart. People with this condition may dread particular situations, such as being in crowded or empty spaces (agoraphobia), blushing (erythrophobia), public speaking (glossophobia) or urinating in public lavatories.

The condition was originally identified by the American psychiatrist George Miller Beard in 1880 as 'anthropophobia', an 'aversion to society, a fear of seeing, encountering, or mingling with a multitude, or of meeting anyone besides ourselves'. This form of morbid fear, said Beard, 'is often accompanied with turning away of the eyes or hanging down of the head'. In France in 1903, Pierre Janet named the syndrome *phobie des situations sociales*.

Social phobia was first listed as a disorder in the *Diagnostic and Statistical Manual 3* in 1980, an inclusion that enabled those with the condition to claim the costs of medication from insurance companies. This created a boom in diagnosis and in the prescription of anti-anxiety drugs. A survey of 1994 found that 13.3 per cent of Americans were afflicted by the phobia at some point in their lives, making it the country's most common anxiety disorder – and second only to depression and alcoholism as a psychiatric condition. There seems to be a genetic component to the trait. The 10 to 15 per cent of the population who show behavioural inhibition as infants – being introspective and cautious – are more likely to become socially phobic. But the phobia can be triggered or reinforced by highly protective or highly critical parents, or by a traumatic experience such as being bullied. According to a study in *The Lancet* in 2008, half of people who develop the disorder do so by the age of eleven, and 80 per cent by the time that they are twenty. As with most phobias, avoidance of the phobic objects – in this case, people – entrenches the fear. Some socially phobic people respond well to cognitive behavioural therapy, which can tackle their negative, inaccurate impressions of others' judgements, as well as their tendencies to brood on the past and to worry about the future.

In the West, introversion is often seen as a weakness, but individuals with reserved temperaments are valued more highly in some other cultures: a study in China in 1995 found that inhibited schoolchildren were the most likely to be trusted by their peers and their teachers with positions of responsibility and power, and no more likely to develop depression than their classmates. But a society that values restraint can also generate even more crippling manifestations of shyness. In the 1920s the Japanese psychiatrist

Shoma Morita identified a syndrome he named *taijin-kyōfu*, or 'fear in relation to others'. Those affected by this condition are extremely worried that they might offend other people by making eye contact with them, by blushing, exuding unpleasant smells, grimacing or simply by being unattractive. It is not so much the judgment of others that they fear, but the sense that just by existing they inflict pain.

In *Shyness: How Normal Behavior Became a Sickness* (2007), Christopher Lane describes how pharmaceutical companies helped to persuade the American Psychiatric Association to include social phobia in the *DSM* of 1980. He argues that the diagnosis in many cases turned a personality trait into an illness, pathologising people who were reserved, private or quiet. 'Over the course of six years,' he writes, 'a small group of self-selecting American psychiatrists built a sweeping new consensus: shyness and a host of comparable traits were anxiety and personality disorders. And they stemmed not from psychological conflicts or social tensions, but rather from a chemical imbalance or faulty neurotransmitters in the brain.' Lane believes that there is a great cost to medicalising our quirks, eccentricities and ordinary feelings. 'The sad consequence,' he says, 'is a vast, perhaps irrecoverable, loss of emotional range, an impoverishment of human experience.'

☞ *See also: agoraphobia, erythrophobia, gelotophobia, glossophobia, haphephobia, lypemania, public urination phobia, syllogomania*

SYLLOGOMANIA

Syllogomania, from the Greek *syllogē*, or 'collecting', is an impulse to hoard things that – according to a study in 2008 – afflicts 2 to 5 per cent of the population. The term seems first to have been used in the early 1960s, when studies of hoarding began to appear in British medical journals, but the prevalence of the condition became apparent only in the 1990s.

Long before this, in the first decades of the twentieth century, two rich New Yorkers accumulated 170 tons of objects in their three-storey Fifth Avenue brownstone home. Langley Collyer, an engineering graduate and concert pianist, constructed a maze of tunnels inside the house in which he lived with his blind brother Homer, a former admiralty lawyer. Embedded in Langley's wall-high stacks of books and newspapers were several grand pianos, an X-ray machine, the preserved remains of a two-headed foetus, car parts, tin cans, a canoe, a chandelier. The brothers stopped using the telephone in the 1910s, gas in the 1920s and electricity in the 1930s. Langley fed Homer a hundred oranges a day, in an attempt to cure his blindness, and claimed to be saving the newspapers for him to read when he recovered his sight. After neighbours raised the alarm in 1947, police broke into the house to find Langley crushed to death in his labyrinth by a booby trap of his own devising. His corpse had been gnawed by rats. Ten feet away they found the body of Homer, who had starved to death once his brother stopped feeding him.

For years afterwards, American parents would warn their children that if they didn't tidy their rooms they would end up like the Collyer brothers. But E. L. Doctorow's novel *Homer & Langley* (2009) depicted the Collyers' hoarding more romantically, as a kind of quest. The brothers were 'emigrants', wrote Doctorow, who when they constructed their kingdom of rubble 'were leaving this country, and going into the country of their home'.

In the year of the Collyers' deaths, the German sociologist Erich Fromm argued that individuals defined themselves either by 'having' or by 'being', by their possessions or their experiences. Those with a 'hoarding orientation', he wrote in *Man for Himself*, were suspicious, withdrawn types who invested their emotions in things rather than people. The psychoanalyst Donald Winnicott proposed in 1951 that as infants we all invest emotion in 'transitional objects', such as soft toys and blankets, which stand in for a consoling parent until we learn to soothe

ourselves. Perhaps hoarders fail ever to internalise the nurturing aspects of a parent, and continue to endow the things around them with this caretaking role. Many hoarders' homes are so thickly lined with stuff that they resemble nests, cocoons, caves, bunkers – a hoarder, far from feeling trapped by a confined space, can feel cradled. And for those who have undergone a traumatic experience, objects can be literal shields against harm: they block the path of an intruder.

In *Stuff: Compulsive Hoarding and the Meaning of Things* (2010), Randy O. Frost and Gail Steketee observe that hoarders' objects often act as extensions of themselves. 'My body and my house are kind of the same thing,' a fifty-three-year-old woman called Irene told Frost. 'I take things into them for solace.' Irene was lively and sociable, a part-time estate agent and a mother of two children, but her hoarding, by her own account, had driven away her husband, and left her too ashamed to invite friends to visit. Her objects were integral to her identity. 'Having, keeping and preserving are part of who I am,' she said. 'If I throw too much away, there'll be nothing left of me.'

When Frost visited her house, Irene led him on 'goat paths' through the rooms, which were piled high with clothes, books, newspapers, bags and baskets and boxes. The surfaces were strewn with photographs, leaflets, coupons, pens and pencils, bottles of pills, scraps of paper scrawled with notes and phone numbers. Like many hoarders, Irene kept things just in case they came in useful. Frost realised that her objects stood in for her memory, like a three-dimensional inventory of her past and her imagined future. Hoarders dwell in a realm of possibility, he observes, surrounded by options that they cannot bear to close down. Everything is provisional. For a hoarder, writes Frost, 'the fear of losing an opportunity is greater than the reward of taking advantage of one'.

Frost interviewed two rich middle-aged hoteliers, Alvin and Jerry, who described themselves to him as 'the modern-day Collyer brothers'. The pair, both in rumpled suits and bow ties, showed him round the hotel in which they lived. Each brother had a penthouse suite packed with art and antiques, and scattered with business cards, clothes and clutter. These suites had become too full for habitation, so the brothers had moved into other apartments in the hotel, which were quickly filling up; Jerry slept on the floor when his bed was overrun.

Jerry had remarkable recall of the location of every object in his rooms. 'Everything here has a story,' he said, 'and I remember them all. If I get rid of any of it, the story would be lost.' When Alvin showed Frost his belongings, each sparked a new memory. 'It's like a language,' he said. 'The things speak out.' Several of Frost's interviewees shared this tendency to anthropomorphise objects. A retired gallery owner said that he was becoming engulfed by his collections of suits, shirts and wingtip shoes. 'They seem to be controlling me,' he said. 'It's getting a bit dangerous; they trip me and fall on me and make me late.'

Alvin and Jerry gave rambling answers to Frost's questions, and admitted that they sometimes got lost in the branching paths of their own thoughts: 'Everything is interesting,' said Alvin, 'like it's attached to something else.' Frost and Steketee argue that many hoarders have symptoms of attention deficit hyperactivity disorder (ADHD): they are loquacious, forgetful, easily distracted. These traits make it difficult to manage possessions, to reach decisions, to complete a task or carry out a plan.

Frost, Steketee and others have found evidence of a predisposition to hoard. In 2010 the forensic psychiatrist Kenneth J. Weiss wrote that hoarding may be an adaptive trait that has 'gone haywire', a rogue offshoot of our innate impulse to gather goods. The animal behaviourist Konrad Lorenz hypothesises that the habit is an enactment of a long-dormant 'fixed action pattern', like nut-gathering in squirrels and nest-building in birds. Geneticists have discovered similar configurations of genes (on chromosome 14) in families with two or more hoarders, while neuroscientists have shown that hoarders sometimes have damage to the front section of the frontal lobes, which controls planning and organisation, and lower metabolic rates in the anterior cingulate cortex, which plays a part in motivation, focus and decision-making. But these neurological observations do not prove that some people are destined to hoard – the different patterns in the brain may reflect rather than drive behaviour. Frost and Steketee speculate that hoarders may inherit a trait or traits conducive to hoarding – an intense perceptual sensitivity to detail, perhaps, or a quirk in the way that they retrieve memories – but that the hoarding behaviour develops only if they also undergo emotionally damaging experiences.

Though hoarding was recognised as a distinct mental illness in 2013, when it was included in the American Psychiatric Association's *Diagnostic and Statistical Manual 5*, some argue that it is an eccentric behaviour rather than a disease. As the sociologist Allan V. Horwitz observes, 'socially deviant actions in themselves – whether murder, collecting trash, or going naked – are not signs of mental disorder'. Our horror at hoarding is part of a 'moral panic', suggests Horwitz, a fascination with something that we fear in our society and ourselves. In some times and places, gathering goods is a sign of thrift and good sense – a guard against future scarcity – and discarding resources is considered reckless, wasteful, even immoral. But in affluent societies at the close of the twentieth century, things had become so much easier and cheaper to produce and acquire that some people felt overwhelmed by stuff. Designers started to promote a modernist aesthetic, favouring light and space, clean lines and clear surfaces over the elaborate and the fiddly; in 1996 the Swedish furniture store IKEA urged the British public to 'chuck out your chintz'; the value of antique objects plummeted. Television networks commissioned a string of documentaries about clutter – *Hoarders*, *The Hoarder Next Door*, *Hot Mess House*, *Tidying Up with Marie Kondo*.

In *The Hoarders* (2014), Scott Herring argues that hoarders remind us of our culture's 'redundabundance', the 'unrestricted desire and ability to obtain more and more of what you already have too much of'. Scenes of hoarding dramatically stage our own dysfunctional relationships with objects, all the pointless things after which we hanker and the yearnings that we expect them to satisfy. If compulsive shopping is an excessive embrace of consumer culture, then the compulsive keeping of things is a malfunction or parody of that culture, in which the consumers fail to consume. Possessions begin to look oppressive, like captors or burdens rather than booty.

In Russia, syllogomania is referred to as 'Plyushkin Syndrome', after the rich miser and landowner in Nikolai Gogol's *Dead Souls* (1842). Plyushkin hoards not only his own belongings but any junk he finds scattered about his estate. The narrator warns: 'As you pass from the tender years of youth into harsh and embittered manhood, make sure you take with you on your journey all the human emotions! Don't leave them on the road, for you will not pick them up afterwards!' Plyushkin has got things back to front, suggests Gogol: while greedily gathering up objects, he has been unwittingly shedding the stuff of his humanity, leaving it strewn like litter along the road.

Plyushkin's English counterpart is the illiterate rag and bottle merchant Krook in Charles Dickens's *Bleak House* (1853). Krook hoards sacks of women's hair, and old documents that he cannot read. 'All's fish that comes to my net,' he says. 'And I can't bear to part with anything I once lay hold of.' Halfway through the novel, which is itself prodigiously stuffed with matter, the gin-soaked Krook spontaneously combusts amid the clutter in the back of his shop, leaving only soot, grease and his stash of unread treasure behind him.

In the early 1990s, as she completed her research for a book about Sylvia Plath, the American author Janet Malcolm found herself deeply unsettled by an interviewee's chaotic house, 'a depository of bizarre clutter and disorder' in the east England market town of Bedford. 'Along the walls and on the floor and on every surface hundreds, perhaps thousands, of objects were piled,' writes Malcolm in *The Silent Woman* (1994), 'as if the place were a secondhand shop into which the contents of ten other second-hand shops had been hurriedly crammed, and over everything there was a film of dust: not ordinary transient dust but dust that itself was overlaid with dust – dust that through the years had acquired a kind of objecthood, a sort of immanence'.

After her visit, she wondered if she was so disturbed by the chaos of the house because it was a metaphor for the problem that she faced in writing her book. To tell a story about Plath, Malcolm would need to select stories from the huge, confused jumble of information that she had gathered, throwing out much of what she knew in order to 'make a space where a few ideas and images and feelings may be so arranged that a reader will want to linger a while among them, rather than to flee'. But for the biographer, as for the hoarder, to discard material is a process of falsification. The house was so troubling to Malcolm because it reminded her of the reality that she was about to betray. Its hoard was 'unmediated actuality, in all its multiplicity, randomness, inconsistency, redundancy, *authenticity*', she writes: 'a monstrous allegory of truth'. The story that she would tell would be more elegant, more pleasing, and less true.

☞ *See also: aboulomania, monomania, mysophobia, nomophobia, oniomania, social phobia*

T

TAPHEPHOBIA

The Italian psychiatrist Enrico Morselli coined the term taphephobia – from the Greek *taphe*, or grave – to diagnose a patient who so feared premature burial that he stipulated in his will that his coffin be equipped with a candle, food, drink and an air hole. 'He has heard or read terrible stories of people being in a state of apparent death, and he fears that the same might happen to him,' wrote Morselli in 1891. It was a situation 'he feels powerless to avoid or prevent, especially since at that moment he would be unconscious, or, even if he were conscious, he would be unable to move himself, or by any sign or action or word to inform the people that he was not yet dead, but still alive'.

Live burial was once a real danger, as Jan Bondeson shows in *Buried Alive* (2001). People were occasionally buried alive as a punishment: vestal virgins who broke their vows of chastity in ancient Rome, murderers who refused to repent in medieval Italy, women who killed their husbands in seventeenth-century Russia. Many more were accidentally buried after being too hastily pronounced dead. In the eighteenth century, several coffins were dug up and opened to reveal cadavers with ripped nails, torn knees and bloodied elbows. In 'Treatise Concerning the Screaming and Chewing of Corpses in their Graves' (1734), Michael Ranft tried to ascribe such injuries to supernatural interference, but most saw them as horrifying proof of premature interments.

Taphephobia became rampant in Germany. As Bondeson details, Duke Ferdinand of Brunswick ordered a custom-made coffin in 1792, with a window, an air hole, and a lock that could be opened from within; the keys were tucked into a pocket of his burial shroud. A German pastor, meanwhile, proposed that ropes from the church bells be fed into each coffin in his churchyard. Dozens of variations on these 'security coffins' were produced in Germany in the years that followed, fitted with hammers, firecrackers and sirens.

The phobia intensified in the nineteenth century. 'The danger of premature burial,' writes Bondeson, 'had become one of the most-feared perils of everyday life, and a torrent of pamphlets and academic theses were dedicated to this subject by writers all over Europe.' Essayists argued that catalepsy and coma were often mistaken for death. Some claimed that more than a tenth of humanity was buried alive.

Edgar Allan Poe's short story 'The Premature Burial' (1844) evoked the terrors of the taphephobe. 'I writhed,' says the narrator, 'and made spasmodic exertions to force open the lid: it would not move. I felt my wrists for the bell-rope: it was not to be found.' He describes the 'stifling fumes of the damp earth ... the rigid embrace of the narrow house – the blackness of the absolute Night – the silence like a sea that overwhelms – the unseen but palpable presence of the Conquerer Worm – these things ... carry into the heart, which still palpitates, a degree of appalling and intolerable horror from which the most daring imagination must recoil.'

In Britain, the anxiety was exacerbated by the hurried burials of cholera victims in the epidemic of 1831–2. Further security coffins were designed, a few furnished with compartments for wine as well as food. Some taphephobes made sure that they would never be buried at all. The Swedish chemist Alfred Nobel, the inventor of dynamite, specified that his veins should be emptied when he died, and his bloodless corpse then burnt. Others took precautions to ensure that they were dead before being buried. The composer Frédéric Chopin left instructions that his body be cut open prior to burial. Hans Christian Andersen, the fairytale writer, left a note by his bedside each night to say that he was not dead but sleeping.

The fear was categorised as a phobia only when the danger of live burial receded in the late nineteenth century: medical advances made it easier to be sure whether a person was alive or dead. There are still taphephobes – in the early years of the twenty-first century, the Brazilian entrepreneur Freud de Melo built himself a crypt equipped with air vents, a fruit pantry, a television and megaphones. And there are still brushes with premature interment – in Massachusetts in 2001 an undertaker heard gurgling from a body bag and realised that the thirty-nine-year-old woman whom he was about to bury was recovering from her apparently fatal drug overdose.

☞ See also: *claustrophobia, nyctophobia*

TELEPHONOPHOBIA

Doctors at a Parisian hospital made the first diagnosis of *téléphonophobie* in 1913. Their patient, 'Madame X', was seized by a kind of anguished terror when she heard a telephone ring, they observed, and upon answering a call she froze and became almost incapable of speech. A Welsh newspaper expressed sympathy with her plight. 'If you come to think of it, practically every user of the telephone suffers from that complaint,' noted the *Merthyr Express*. 'It is a horribly prevalent disease, this "telephonophobia".'

In the early years of the telephone, some people feared that the device would electrocute them, as it did Robert Graves when he was serving in the Great War. The poet was taking a call from a fellow officer when lightning struck the line, giving him such a severe shock that he was spun round. For more than a decade afterwards, he said, he would stammer and sweat if he had to use a phone. George V's widow, Queen Mary, who was born in 1867, remained telephonophobic to the end – shortly before her death in 1953 her older son, the Duke of Windsor, told the press that she had never taken a call.

The telephone could seem a sinister, intrusive device. It 'rang peremptorily and without warning in the depths of the bourgeois home', observes the literary scholar David Trotter, 'turning it inside out'. Its commanding ring was an assault on privacy, at once abrupt and unrelenting. In Prague in the 1910s, Franz Kafka developed a terror of the phone, which seemed to him almost supernatural in its capacity to sever voices from bodies. In Kafka's short story 'My Neighbour', written in 1917, a young business-man imagines that a rival can hear his phone calls through the wall, as if the device has dissolved physical barriers altogether.

Now that we have so many alternative ways of communicating remotely, the fear of making and receiving telephone calls has returned. In 2013 a survey of 2,500 18-to-24-year-old British office workers found that 94 per cent of them would rather send an email than make a phone call, 40 per cent felt nervous making a call, and 5 per cent were 'terrified' by the idea of doing so. By 2019 the situation seemed to have worsened: in a survey of 500 British office workers of all ages, 62 per cent were anxious about phone calls. Some were scared that, without the chance to prepare a response, they would sound stupid or strange; others were afraid of being unable to understand the caller; others of being over-heard – in an open-plan office, not only the person at the other end of the line is appraising your words, but your colleagues, too, can listen and judge. The most telephonophobic respondents to the survey were the youngest: 76 per cent of millennials (those born in the 1980s and 1990s) said that they felt anxious when a telephone rang.

In an article in the *Guardian* in 2016, Daisy Buchanan explained that she and her friends were not only less accustomed to phone calls than older people, but more sensitive to their effect on others. 'The millennial attitude to phone calls is actually about manners,' she wrote. 'We've grown up with so many methods of communication available to us, and we've gravitated towards the least intrusive ones because we know how it feels to be digitally prodded on a range of different channels.' An unscheduled phone call can seem aggressive and insistent, as it did a century ago: an unacceptably demanding form of address.

☛ *See also: glossophobia, nomophobia, social phobia*

TETRAPHOBIA

An irrational fear of the number four (*tessares* in Ancient Greek) is common in East Asian countries, because in several languages (among them Mandarin, Cantonese, Korean and Japanese) the sound of the word 'four' is very similar to the sound of the word 'death'.

Many buildings in East Asia skip all floor and room numbers that include four: 4, 14, 24, 34 and so on. Some Hong Kong hotels jump from floor 39 to floor 50. In Taiwan, South Korea and China the numbers of ships and aircraft rarely end in a four, and many Chinese and Japanese restaurants all over the world avoid the number. Certain combinations are considered especially unlucky: 514 in Mandarin sounds like 'I want to die', 748 like 'go die' and 74 like 'will die in anger' or 'already dead'.

For many people the fear of the number four is a mild superstition, but for a few it becomes a fixation. As a girl in Hong Kong, the actor Jo Chim was amused by her father's tetraphobia, but as she grew older she became phobic herself. At first it was a quirk

– she would avoid sitting in the fourth row at a theatre, make sure that her phone number did not feature a four. But when she became pregnant with her first child, having experienced difficulties in conceiving, the phobia took over. Her pregnancy seemed so arbitrary, so mysteriously granted, that it felt safest not to tempt fate. 'The supermarket was rife with challenges,' she recalls in her blog. 'God forbid I would ever buy 4 items. Never checkout number 4, naturally ... I'd watch the cashier display like a hawk. Whenever the total came to anything with 4 in it, my heart would quicken and my palms start sweating. I'd instantly grab an extra pack of gum, chips, batteries, whatever I could, and lay it on the belt just to make the total round up.'

In an analysis of all deaths in the US between 1973 and 1998, published in the *British Medical Journal* in 2001, a team of researchers in San Diego showed that Asian-Americans were 13 per cent more likely to die of heart failure on the fourth day of the month than on any other day, a peak that was not followed by a compensatory drop in cardiac arrests in the days that followed. In California, where more than 40 per cent of Asian-Americans were then based, the effect was even more pronounced: the fourth of the month saw a 27 per cent increase in fatal heart attacks among this group. The paper's authors speculated that the size of the Chinese and Japanese communities in California reinforced the power of their tetraphobia.

The researchers titled their paper 'The *Hound of the Baskervilles* Effect: a Natural Experiment on the Influence of Psychological Stress on the Timing of Death'. The solution to Arthur Conan Doyle's mystery of 1902, they pointed out, depends on the idea that fright can cause a deadly heart attack. The hypothesis is extremely difficult to test, because the dead cannot report back on their final feelings, but the *BMJ* analysis of the effects of tetraphobia seemed to confirm that fear could be fatal.

☞ *See also: arithmomania, triskaidekaphobia*

THALASSOPHOBIA

Thalassophobia, from the Greek *thalassa*, or sea, is an intense fear of large bodies of water. It is natural to be afraid of the ocean, because it can be dangerous – we might be caught in a riptide or a tsunami or a storm, stung by jellyfish, mauled by sharks. These fears are expressed in films such as *The Poseidon Adventure* (1972), *Jaws* (1975) and *Titanic* (1997), and in the many myths of deep-sea monsters. The Greeks were terrified by Scylla, Charybdis and Hydra, the Norse by the Kraken, and the Japanese by Kappa; Icelandic and Celtic sailors were warned of the Selkies, Peruvians of Yacumama and Polynesians of Taniwha. Such creatures rear up from the depths to devour us. 'The thing slid into view above the dark waters,' says the shipwrecked narrator of H. P. Lovecraft's short story 'Dagon' (1919). 'Vast, Polyphemus-like, and loathsome, it darted like a stupendous monster of nightmares.'

In the *Journal of Marine Science* in 2020, a group of biologists warned that thalassophobia poses a threat to the planet. Our fear of the deep sea, they claim, stops us from fighting to preserve it. The layer of ocean that lies more than 20,000 feet below the surface – named the 'hadal zone', after Hades, the ruler of the Greek underworld – is disproportionately harmed by trawling and mining, by the dumping of plastics, sewage and radioactive waste. The marine biologists argue that television documentaries exaggerate the weirdness and mystery of these depths, estranging us from a seascape that we need to love. In an episode about the deep ocean in the BBC series *Blue Planet*, for instance, David Attenborough describes an 'alien' world, 'a sea of eternal gloom' and 'perpetual darkness' – 'a giant black void' inhabited by 'strange creatures' that live 'beyond the normal rules of time'. This ominous and 'erroneous' characterisation, say the biologists, conjures up an 'unfamiliar, miserable, unforgiving, and off-world environment'. Deep-sea creatures are not monsters, they insist: the hatchetfish, the fangtooth and the dragonfish look freakish to us only because they have evolved specialist attributes, such as giant eyes and jaws and teeth, to help them survive in black and twilit places. And there are prettier, more delicate species down there too: red-legged prawns and translucent pink snailfish flicker in the gloaming; feathery sea lilies sway in the dark of the ocean floor. The marine biologists argue that we should be doing all we can to protect this watery wonderland, the largest and perhaps the most important habitat on earth.

☞ *See also: ablutophobia, aquaphobia, fykiaphobia, hydrophobia, kayak phobia, nyctophobia*

TOKOPHOBIA

Six per cent of pregnant women are pathologically afraid of giving birth, according to a survey of 2001, and 14 per cent of all women are terrified enough to avoid or postpone or terminate a pregnancy, even when they want a child. The word tokophobia – from the Greek *tokos*, birth – was coined by Kristina Hofberg in the *British Journal of Psychiatry* in 2000, but its symptoms had been described by the French psychiatrist Louis-Victor Marcé in 1858. He identified two categories of women who suffered from an extreme fear of childbirth. There were those who were pregnant for the first time, he said, in whom 'the expectation of unknown pain preoccupies them beyond all measure, and throws them into a state of inexpressible anxiety'. And there were those who were already mothers, whose dread was informed by their memories of giving birth.

In 1978 the French doctors Monique Bydlowski and Anne Raoul-Duval published an influential study of ten women who had endured long, painful deliveries and afterwards suffered nightmares and a terror of falling pregnant again. 'Parturition,' they concluded, 'especially the first, can, by its obligatory violence and confrontation with an imminent and lonely death put the mother under extreme stress.' For women who have not given birth, the fear can be triggered by another traumatic event, such as a sexual assault, or by disturbing images and stories. The English actor Helen Mirren vowed never to have children after watching a graphic film about childbirth at her convent school. 'I swear it traumatised me to this day,' she said in 2007. 'I haven't had children and now I can't look at anything to do with childbirth. It absolutely disgusts me.'

Some women do not fear only the process of giving birth, with its real dangers to the mother and child, but also what might emerge from their bodies. In Roman Polanski's film *Rosemary's Baby* (1968), a young wife comes to believe that she has been impregnated by the Devil. She feels sharp pains in her belly as her pregnancy progresses, and she dreads the being that is growing inside her. Rosemary is sedated as she goes into labour. When she comes round she seeks out her baby's cradle, lifts the canopy, and starts back in horror from the creature she has brought forth.

☛ *See also: blood-injection-injury phobia, demonomania, emetophobia, mysophobia*

TRICHOMANIA

The first known use of 'trichomaniac', meaning a person with a passion for hair (*thrix* in Greek), is in an essay of 1949 by the English poet Robert Graves. In *The Common Asphodel*, Graves declared that the seventeenth-century poet John Milton was a trichomaniac. At Christ's College, Cambridge, said Graves, Milton's luxuriant hair earned him the mocking nickname 'Our Lady of Christ's', and in his verse he liked to linger on 'ringlets, mazes, curious knots, Gordian twines and quaint curves'.

In Milton's day – when neatly shorn, close-shaven Roundheads went to war with loose-locked, moustachioed Cavaliers – hair was highly charged with moral, religious, sexual and political meanings. Long, free-flowing hair could be a symbol of innocence, or of hedonism, dandyism, elitism, femininity, foreignness, sensuality. Cropped hair represented discipline, manliness and restraint. In *Paradise Lost*, Milton evokes the prelapsarian freedom of the Garden of Eden through Adam's curling 'hyacinthine locks' and foreshadows the Fall in Eve's 'dishevelled', 'wanton ringlets'.

Graves identified the second-century author Apuleius as another hair fanatic. In *Metamorphoses*, the Roman poet lovingly describes hair bunched up high on women's heads and curling down their backs, the colour of gold or honey, or as 'black as a raven's wing and suddenly taking on the pale bluish tints of a dove's neck-feathers'.

The heyday of trichomania was the nineteenth century, when the Pre-Raphaelite painters revelled in their muses' dense, ensnaring cascades of hair. In *Psychopathia Sexualis*, Richard von Krafft-Ebing detailed cases of individuals so obsessed with hair that they committed deviant acts. A man in his thirties longed to suck thick black hair, and when out walking would impulsively press his lips to the heads of dark-haired girls. A forty-year-old locksmith was arrested in 1889 at the Trocadéro concert hall in Paris with a pair of shears in his pocket and a sheaf of hair in his hand. He confessed to having chopped off a young lady's locks that evening, and explained that he could reach orgasm only by combing or fondling or smothering himself in women's tresses. When the police searched his home, sixty-five more hanks of hair were found, sealed in separate packets, and an assortment of pins and ribbons.

In Charles Baudelaire's 'A Hemisphere in Her Hair' (1857), the poet buries his face in his lover's locks:

> *In the ardent hearth of your hair, I breathe the odor of tobacco mixed with opium and sugar; in the night of your hair, I see the infinity of tropical azur resplendent; on the downy shores of your hair I get drunk on the combined odors of tar, of musk, and of coconut oil.*

'Let me bite into your heavy black tresses for a long time,' he pleads. 'When I nibble at your elastic hair it seems to me that I am eating memories.'

☛ *See also: pogonophobia, trichotillomania*

TRICHOTILLOMANIA

In 1906 the psychiatrist Pierre Janet was startled when a woman aged twenty-four visited his surgery and lifted a blonde wig from her head. 'Upon her uncovered skull there are but a few rare locks of short hair,' he wrote, 'separated by large, absolutely bald spots.' At first he thought it a dramatic case of alopecia, but the young woman told him otherwise. For the past eighteen months, she said, she had been plucking out her hairs and eating them. It began when she was sent from her rural home to be a servant to a family in Paris; her employers were demanding and scornful, she said, and she became very homesick. Janet observed that his patient was otherwise quite rational and well-balanced; she was just regularly seized with the 'singular desire' to pull out a hair 'and feel the little pain resulting from it'.

The term *trichotillomanie* (*thrix*, for hair, plus *tillein*, to pull) was coined in 1889 by the dermatologist François Hallopeau to diagnose a patient who was ripping tufts from his scalp. As a figure of speech, to 'tear one's hair out' is an expression of frustration, but in practice the activity is more often systematic than impulsive, methodical rather than furious. A trichotillomane nips hairs one by one from the scalp, eyelashes or eyebrows and, occasionally, the pubic area.

Trichotillomania is thought to affect about 2 per cent of the population. The behaviour is especially widespread among children, who are seven times more likely than adults to pull out their hair, and it is nine times more prevalent in women than men. Sometimes hair-plucking is an unconscious activity, carried out automatically while watching television or daydreaming; and sometimes it is focused and deliberate. 'A hair is located which "does not feel right" (too wiry, kinky, crooked, straight or otherwise different),' explains the *Journal of Child Psychology and Psychiatry*. 'The hair is then plucked and examined, and the root or the entire hair sometimes eaten. Hairs may be piled before being discarded. Hair-pulling sessions vary from four or five hours in which several hundred hairs are pulled to brief episodes in which only a few hairs are pulled at a time, but which re-occur dozens of times each day.'

Some studies report that individuals with this and other body-focused repetitive disorders are unusually responsive to sounds and textures: their hair-pulling serves as a distraction from overwhelming external stimuli. Others suggest that trichotillomania is a pathological variant of our instinct to groom ourselves, a behaviour designed to protect us from parasites and infections. And others argue that obsessive hair-pulling develops as a self-protective ritual, to deal with separation anxiety or trauma, or as a displacement of the erotic drive. The disorder can be treated with drugs that alter brain function, such as selective serotonin reuptake inhibitors, or with habit-reversal techniques, whereby the trichotillomane is taught to identify triggers for an episode of hair-pulling and to develop a substitute response, such as fist-clenching.

Many manias and phobias are acquired by imitation, but trichotillomania is a private, shame-inducing activity. Its effects are often disguised – by wigs or hats, make-up or spectacles. As Jemima Khan learnt when she interviewed trichotillomanes at a London clinic in 2009, hair-pluckers go to great lengths to hide their habit. One avoided walking near double-decker buses for fear that the bald spots on her scalp might be seen from above; another was wary of walking up stairs, of overhead security mirrors in shops, of swimming, of rain; another would not spend the night with her boyfriend.

In 1989 an American woman in her thirties was overjoyed to discover that there was a name for her condition and that she was not alone in feeling compelled to pull out her hair. She agreed to speak about the disorder on a Seattle radio show, where she mentioned that she had just set up a telephone helpline. When she got home there were 600 messages on her answering machine. 'People were crying and sobbing and begging for help,' she said. Over the next week she called everyone back. 'It was the best therapy I ever had,' she recalled, 'because I heard my life coming out of other people's mouths.'

In some times and places, the practice has been socially sanctioned. In ancient Greece and Egypt, women pulled hair from their heads as a mourning rite. In India, Jain monks still perform *kaya klesh*, a two-hour procedure in which they demonstrate their capacity to detach from pain by removing every strand of hair from their faces and their scalps. All of the trichotillomaniac respondents to a survey in *Medical Anthropology* in 2018 rejected the description of their condition as 'self-harm'. Rather, they emphasised the pleasure and relief that hair-plucking gave them. As Pierre Janet wrote in his paper of 1906, 'the act once performed, the patient experiences a joy, a peculiar satisfaction, and for a time he seems freed from the fatigue and the various painful sensations he constantly suffered before'.

☛ *See also: dermatillomania, monomania, onychotillomania, pogonophobia, trichomania*

TRISKAIDEKAPHOBIA

The irrational fear of the number thirteen (*treiskaideka* in Ancient Greek) is widespread in the West. It may originate in the story of Loki, the trickster god of Norse mythology, who was so angry to be excluded from a dinner party for twelve gods at Valhalla that he gatecrashed the event, becoming the thirteenth at the table, and cursed the earth with darkness. Thirteen may also strike us as an awkward number because it is not neatly divisible, and because we group many things in dozens (times tables, apostles, months of the year, hours in the day, signs of the Zodiac, eggs).

'The number 13 never fails to trace that old icy finger up and down my spine,' confessed the novelist Stephen King. 'When I'm writing, I'll never stop work if the page number is 13 or a multiple of 13; I'll just keep on typing till I get to a safe number.' To accommodate triskaidekaphobes, hotels and blocks of flats routinely omit rooms and floors numbered thirteen; airlines skip the row 13 on planes; terraces of houses jump from 12 to 14 by way of 12a. On Friday 13th, people avoid making large financial transactions or getting married. In 2004 the Stress Management Center and Phobia Institute in North Carolina estimated that the US lost more than $800 million a year because employees refused to work or fly on that day (the institute's director gave the phobia of Friday 13th its own name: paraskevidekatriaphobia, *Paraskevi* being Friday in Modern Greek).

Though some hospitals choose not to assign the number thirteen to any of their wards or beds, the Southmead Hospital in Bristol decided to ignore the superstition when it opened its Brunel Building in 2014. Two of the hospital's doctors took the opportunity to compare the outcomes of patients in different beds in the new intensive-care unit between 2015 and 2017. They found no statistically significant variation between the death rates of patients in Bed 13 and those in Beds 14 to 24. If anything, they said, patients who occupied Bed 13 fared slightly better. The results were published in the *Journal of Critical Care* in 2018 under the title 'Admission to Bed 13 in the ICU Does Not Reduce the Chance of Survival'.

'We hope that our data will reassure patients, their families, and indeed staff members who may have this phobia,' write the doctors, optimistically, 'and encourage a less superstitious and a more sensible approach to the numbering of hospital wards and beds.'

☞ *See also: arithmomania, tetraphobia*

TRYPOPHOBIA

Trypophobia, an aversion to clusters of holes or bumps, emerged as a phenomenon in 2003, when an image of a seemingly maggot-infested female breast was circulated on the internet. Those who reacted most strongly to the picture – with feelings of nausea and panic – learnt that they shared a horror of such patterns. Some created online discussion and support groups, and in 2005 one participant ('Louise' in Ireland) invented the word trypophobia (from the Greek *trupē*, or hole) to describe the trait. The original internet meme turned out to be a composite of a lotus-seed pod and a woman's breast, but this made it no less repulsive to true trypophobes. The phobia can be provoked by any conglomeration of rough circular shapes: in sponges, barnacles, crumpets, soap suds, honeycombs, Swiss cheese, pomegranates, a bubbling hot drink, the pitted back of the Surinam toad. 'I can't even look at little holes,' said the model and reality television star Kendall Jenner in a blog post of 2016. 'It gives me the worst anxiety. Who knows what's in there???'

To begin with, the phobia was dismissed as a creation of the internet. It seemed to be an emotionally contagious condition, a psychogenic anxiety transmitted by suggestion alone. Many of the online trypophobia forums were studded with images of holes, which seemed designed to cultivate rather than relieve the condition. But some users of these sites explained that they were attempting a kind of exposure therapy, trying to desensitise themselves through repetition and familiarity. Others spoke of a desire to crush holey surfaces, admitting to a longing to touch as well as to eliminate the objects of their repulsion.

Some scientists speculate that trypophobia is an evolutionary adaptation designed to protect us from pathogens: irregular holey patterns are reminiscent of sores, cysts and blisters, a rash or a fungus, the pimples and pustules of infectious diseases such as smallpox. According to a study in Amsterdam in 2018, most of us have a dislike of 'disease-relevant cluster stimuli', and trypophobes extend the aversion to other spongy or pocked surfaces. In open-ended questions about looking at groups of holes, the trypophobes often reported sensations on the skin, such as itching and crawling. 'These findings,' conclude the researchers, 'support the proposal that individuals with trypophobia primarily perceive cluster stimuli as cues to ectoparasites and skin-transmitted pathogens.'

Often, a trypophobic response doesn't interfere with a person's normal routine, and is more a discomfort or unease than a phobia, but for a few it is a powerful, disabling aversion, capable of setting off panic attacks. 'I cry uncontrollably and breathe faster,' said a nineteen-year-old in Ohio, who was horrified by everything from peach pits to cheese graters. 'My heart and mind races. My chest gets tight, and I just want everything to stop. In that moment, I would give my left leg for it to stop. I want to run away as fast as possible, but it's in my mind, and unfortunately, you can't run from your own thoughts.'

☛ *See also: acarophobia, koumpounophobia, mysophobia*

TULIPOMANIA

Nations, like individuals, can go crazy, wrote the Scottish journalist Charles Mackay in *Extraordinary Popular Delusions and the Madness of Crowds* (1841): 'We find that whole communities suddenly fix their minds upon one object, and go mad in its pursuit; that millions of people become simultaneously impressed with one delusion, and run after it.' As an example, Mackay gave the Dutch 'tulipomania' of 1634 to 1637, in which the price of tulip bulbs soared and then abruptly fell, ruining the lives of many speculators.

Tulips were brought to Western Europe from Turkey in the mid-sixteenth century – 'tulip' was a Persian and Turkish word for 'turban', the shape of the flower's head – and they became a symbol of status during the Dutch Golden Age, when the Netherlands was as prosperous a nation as any on earth. The most prized tulips had richly coloured petals streaked with feathery flares of yellow or white. Since these grew from broken bulbs, they were the slowest and riskiest to cultivate.

Tulip traders created a futures market by drawing up contracts in the spring and summer for the purchase of bulbs that would be gathered at the end of the season. By 1636 some contracts were said to be changing hands ten times a day. They attained extraordinary prices. A single Viceroy tulip, according to a contemporary writer, was traded for four fat oxen, eight fat pigs, twelve fat sheep, two hogsheads of wine, four tuns of beer, two tuns of butter, 1,000 pounds of cheese, a bed, a suit of clothes, a silver cup and a large quantity of wheat and rye. Mackay recounted a possibly apocryphal anecdote about a hungry sailor who filched a tulip bulb from a merchant's counter, thinking it an onion, and was found by the side of his ship happily munching on the bulb with a herring for breakfast; the tulip if sold, said Mackay, could have fed the vessel's entire crew for a year.

Mackay claimed that the rage to possess tulips became so great that 'the ordinary industry of the country was neglected, and the population, even to its lowest dregs, embarked on the tulip trade ... Nobles, citizens, farmers, mechanics, sea-men, footmen, maid-servants, even chimney-sweeps and old clothes-women, dabbled in tulips. People of all grades converted their property into cash, and invested it in flowers.' Everyone imagined that the passion for tulips would last for ever, he wrote, but at the beginning of 1637 confidence in the market began to falter and in February it collapsed. The Dutch government failed to find a remedy, said Mackay, and many merchants were reduced almost to beggary.

Mackay has been charged with overstating the extent of tulipomania. The historian Anne Goldgar, having examined contracts of the period, argues that the tulip market was small and the impact of the crash limited. She could not find a single person who was bankrupted by tulips. The mania about the mania, she says, was whipped up by Dutch Calvinist pamphleteers, who depicted the tulip craze as proof of the evils of speculation. But she agrees that the episode was influential: 'Even though the financial crisis affected very few, the shock of tulipmania was considerable. A whole network of values was thrown into doubt.' The lust for tulips became a symbol of hubris, greed and capitalist hysteria.

☛ *See also: bibliomania, plutomania*

XENOPHOBIA

In the 1880s 'xenophobia' was a synonym for 'agoraphobia', the fear of open or public spaces – *xenos* means 'foreign' or 'strange' in Greek – and it was not until the early 1900s that the word came to mean an antipathy to people of a different race, nationality or creed. Specific forms of xenophobia are Islamophobia (from the French *Islamophobie*, in use since the 1870s but widespread in the West only since the 1990s), Judeophobia (used as early as 1847 to describe anti-Semitism) and Sinophobia (apparently first used in a book on the opium trade in 1876, to mean an aversion to Chinese people and culture). In 1923 *The New York Times* described the Ku Klux Klan's attitude to Black Americans as xenophobia, 'a disease more dangerous to a free people than a physical plague'.

Psychoanalysts argue that xenophobia springs from a fear of our own impulses. 'Other people are identified with that part of ourselves of which we disapprove,' wrote Joost Meerloo, a Dutch Jew who fled the Nazis in 1942, 'and thus hatred for the object of our identification grows within us; in fact, it becomes the personification of our fear even though it may be only a symbolic scapegoat … Much hatred and persecution of minorities can be traced to unanalysed, unexplained fear.'

Like other phobias, such prejudices can become physiological aversions. Recent work in social psychology shows that cultural stereotypes embed themselves in the brain. 'Repeatedly associating a token of an out-group type with negative affect will tag all members of the type with a negative somatic marker,' writes the philosopher Stephen T. Asma. 'The amygdala system does this nefarious work.' In experiments at New York University in 2013, David Amodio tracked these subconscious reactions to racial difference. But Amodio points out that people can retrain their anti-social impulses, using the reflective powers of the complex frontal cortex to modify irrational conditioned fears. 'The human mind is extremely adept at control and regulation,' writes Amodio, 'and the fact that we have these biases should really be seen as an opportunity for us to be aware and to do something about them.'

The British educational consultant Robin Richardson popularised the term Islamophobia in a report on anti-Muslim feeling that he wrote in 1997, but fifteen years later he cautioned against using the word. Describing racism and nationalism as phobic can backfire, he argued in 2012, by seeming to naturalise and justify divisions between people, and it can shut down debate. 'To accuse someone of being insane or irrational is to be abusive and, not surprisingly, to make them defensive and defiant,' writes Richardson. 'Reflective dialogue with them is then all but impossible.' A better approach, he suggests, is to think of racist and nationalist feelings not as aversions or diseases but as manifestations of anxiety.

☛ *See also: homophobia*

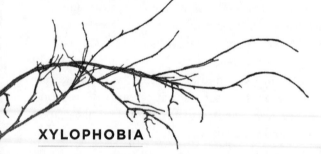

XYLOPHOBIA

The word xylophobia, meaning an intense fear of forests, is formed from the Ancient Greek word *xylon*, or wood. The fear infuses fairy tales such as 'Hansel and Gretel' and 'Little Red Riding Hood', and horror films such as *The Evil Dead* (1981) and *The Blair Witch Project* (1999). A forest can harbour boars and bears and wolves, witches and wild men. It is a place in which we lose our bearings and become lost, perhaps never to return.

In his essay 'Fear and Loathing on the Eastern Front', David Alegre Lorenz documents the terror that the dense, north-central

Soviet forests aroused in the French, Walloon and Spanish volunteers who fought with Germany's armed forces in the Second World War. As the soldiers advanced on the Soviet Union in 1941, the forest floor rose thick about them and the tree canopy closed over their heads. The Spanish fascist leader Dionisio Ridruejo described 'a forest full of puddles, heavy aroma; dark, with great fir trees that make it even blacker'.

The volunteers sensed that Soviet partisans were hidden in the trees – 'We are being observed,' wrote a Frenchman in Belarus, 'a disagreeable sensation, to shave knowing that a hundred metres away someone is watching you, rifle in hand' – and some feared that supernatural forces were at work. 'The forest evokes the Devil,' wrote one Spanish soldier, while another even as he left the woods felt pursued by 'the ghost from those forests crossing the lines and plunging itself into the backs of the rearguard, those partisan lairs, those forests that squealed on you.'

'The forest is rotting with partisans,' said a Walloon volunteer in 1943. 'This muck, this rain, these fir trees, give one the impression of fighting against ghosts that emerge from the fog ... Russia is setting a trap for us.' The forest, it seemed, was in league with the enemy.

Lorenz argues that a fear of the primeval forest had long permeated Western perceptions of Russia, and was revived by the fighting on the Eastern Front. The forests of the Soviet Union, he writes, 'came to incarnate the myth of Russia and the "Savage East".' An advertisement in Ronald Reagan's electoral campaign of 1984 invoked anti-Soviet sentiment with the slogan: 'There's a bear in the woods,' beneath an image of a huge bear, a traditional symbol of Russia, pushing through a dark thicket of trees.

☛ *See also: claustrophobia, nyctophobia, thalassophobia*

ZOOPHOBIA

Zoophobia – from the Greek *zōion,* or living creature – is an excessive fear of animals, whether a particular animal or animals in general. Animal fears are surprisingly consistent across the globe. According to a study of 1998, the people of the UK, the US, South Korea, the Netherlands and India showed very similar levels of fear towards the same animals, with the citizens of Japan and Hong Kong reporting only slightly higher rates. The most feared predators included the tiger, alligator, crocodile, bear, wolf, shark, lion and snake. Of these, only the snake is a common object of phobia – that is, of excessive or irrational fear. We are much more likely to be irrationally afraid of the creatures that elicit disgust-related fear, of which the top seven are the cockroach, spider, worm, leech, bat, lizard and rat.

Nine out of ten zoophobes show significant improvement if they submit first to systematic desensitisation therapy, in which they engage in controlled visualisations of the object of their phobia, and then live exposure, in which they directly confront the dreaded creature. But most zoophobic people avoid (or drop out of) treatments of this kind, so in 2018 a team of neuroscientists from Japan, Hong Kong and the US tried an alternative: a therapy for zoophobia that bypasses the conscious mind.

To start with, the researchers used the new technique of 'hyper-alignment decoding' of functional magnetic resonance imaging (fMRI), to identify the brain patterns associated with particular animals in a group of non-phobic people. Armed with these codes, the scientists used the fMRI scanner to monitor the brains of seventeen individuals who each had a phobia of at least two animals. Each participant was shown a grey disc, which grew larger whenever the activity in his or her ventral cortex matched the pattern of code corresponding to one of those two animals. As an incentive for the subjects to dwell on whatever they were thinking about at those moments, the researchers told them that the bigger the disc, the greater the financial reward they would receive for taking part in the study.

The participants were not consciously thinking of their feared animals when the code was spotted. Even after five sessions, they could not tell which animals had been targeted by the scanner. Nonetheless, their phobia of the targeted creatures, as measured by bodily responses such as skin conductivity, had reduced significantly, while their fear of the control animals remained intact.

'This study provides evidence,' say the researchers, 'that physiological fear responses to specific, subclinical, naturally occurring fears can be reduced unconsciously with hyperalignment decoders, completely outside the awareness of human subjects.' The zoophobes had learned to associate their once-feared animals with reward, while not knowing that the creatures had even crossed their minds.

☛ *See also: acarophobia, ailurophobia, arachnophobia, batrachophobia, cynophobia, entomophobia, hippophobia, musophobia, ophidiophobia*

SOURCES

INTRODUCTION

American Psychiatric Association, *Diagnostic and Statistical Manual 5* (Washington DC, 2013)

Stephen T. Asma, 'Monsters on the Brain: An Evolutionary Epistemology of Horror', *Social Research,* Vol. 81, No. 4 (2014)

George Miller Beard, *A Practical Treatise on Nervous Exhaustion (Neurasthenia): Its Symptoms, Nature, Sequences, Treatment* (New York, 1880)

Joanna Bourke, *Fear: A Cultural History* (London, 2005)

S. E. Cassin, J. H. Riskind, and N. A. Rector, 'Phobias', in V. S. Ramachandran (ed.), *Encyclopedia of Human Behaviour* (Amsterdam, 2012)

Graham C. L. Davey (ed.), *Phobias: A Handbook of Theory, Research and Treatment* (Chichester and New York, 1997)

William W. Eaton, O. Joseph Bienvenu, and Beyon Miloyan, 'Specific Phobias', *The Lancet Psychiatry*, Vol. 5, No. 8 (2018)

Jean-Étienne Esquirol, *Mental Maladies: A Treatise on Insanity*, trans. E. K. Hunt (London, 1845)

Hilary Evans and Robert Bartholomew, *Outbreak! The Encyclopedia of Extraordinary Social Behavior* (San Antonio, Texas, 2009)

Sigmund Freud, *New Introductory Lectures on Psychoanalysis*, trans. James Strachey (London, 1933)

G. Stanley Hall, 'A Study of Fears', *American Journal of Psychology*, Vol. 8, No. 2 (1897)

—'A Synthetic Genetic Study of Fear: Part 1', *American Journal of Psychology*, Vol. 25, No. 2 (1914)

—'A Synthetic Genetic Study of Fear: Part 2', *American Journal of Psychology*, Vol. 25, No. 3 (1914)

Pierre Janet, 'On the Pathogenesis of Some Impulsions', *Journal of Abnormal Psychology*, Vol. 1, No. 1 (1906)

Jeffrey A. Lockwood, *The Infested Mind: Why Humans Fear, Love and Loathe Insects* (Oxford, 2013)

Richard J. McNally, 'The Legacy of Seligman's "Phobias and Preparedness" (1971)', *Behavior Therapy*, Vol. 47, No. 5 (2015)

Isaac M. Marks and Randolph M. Nesse, 'Fear and Fitness: An Evolutionary Analysis of Anxiety Disorders', *Ethology and Sociobiology*, Vol. 15, No. 5 (1994)

Benjamin Rush, 'On the Different Species of Phobia' and 'On the Different Species of Mania', *Columbian Magazine* (1786)

—*Medical Inquiries and Observations Upon Diseases of the Mind* (Philadelphia, 1812)

Martin E. P. Seligman, 'Phobias and Preparedness', *Behavioural Therapy*, Vol. 2 (1971)

Mick Smith and Joyce Davidson, '"It Makes My Skin Crawl...", The Embodiment of Disgust in Phobias of "Nature"', *Body & Society*, Vol. 12, No. 1 (2006)

David Trotter, *The Uses of Phobia: Essays on Literature and Film* (Malden, Massachusetts, 2010)

K. J. Wardenaar et al., 'The Cross-National Epidemiology of Specific Phobia in the World Mental Health Surveys', *Psychological Medicine*, Vol. 47, No. 10 (2017)

Fritz Wittels, 'The Contribution of Benjamin Rush to Psychiatry', *Bulletin of the History of Medicine*, Vol. 20, No. 2 (1946)

ABLUTOPHOBIA

G. Stanley Hall, 'A Study of Fears', *American Journal of Psychology*, Vol. 8, No. 2 (1897)

Stephen Zdatny, 'The French Hygiene Offensive of the 1950s: A Critical Moment in the History of Manners', *The Journal of Modern History*, Vol. 84, No. 4 (2012)

ABOULOMANIA

William A. Hammond, *A Treatise on Insanity in Its Medical Relations* (New York, 1883)

Pierre Janet, 'The Fear of Action', trans. Lydiard H. Horton, *The Journal of Abnormal Psychology and Social Psychology*, Vol. 10, No. 1 (1921)

Ralph W. Reed, 'An Analysis of an Obsessive Doubt with a Paranoid Trend', *Psychoanalytic Review*, Vol. 3, No. 4 (1916)

ACAROPHOBIA

Luis Buñuel, *My Last Breath* (London, 1994)

Jeffrey A. Lockwood, *The Infested Mind: Why Humans Fear, Love and Loathe Insects* (Oxford, 2013)

William G. Waldron, 'The Entomologist and Illusions of Parasitosis', *California Medicine*, Vol. 117 (1972)

P. Weinstein and D. Delaney, 'Psychiatry and Insects: Phobias and Delusions of Insect Infestations in Humans', in J. L. Capinera (ed.), *Encyclopedia of Etymology* (Heidelberg, 2008)

ACROPHOBIA

Graham C. L. Davey, Ross Menzies, and Barbara Gallardo, 'Height Phobia and Biases in the Interpretation of Bodily Sensations: Some Links Between Acrophobia and Agoraphobia', *Behaviour Research and Therapy*, Vol. 35, No. 11 (1997)

Daniel Freeman et al., 'Automated Psychological Therapy Using Immersive Virtual Reality for Treatment of Fear of Heights: A Single-Blind, Parallel-Group, Randomised Controlled Trial', *Lancet Psychiatry*, Vol. 5, No. 8 (2018)

G. Stanley Hall, 'A Study of Fears', *American Journal of Psychology*, Vol. 8, No. 2 (1897)

—'A Synthetic Genetic Study of Fear: Part 1', *American Journal of Psychology*, Vol. 25, No. 2 (1914)

Milan Kundera, *The Book of Laughter and Forgetting*, trans. Michael Henry Helm (New York, 1980)

Isaac M. Marks and Randolph M. Nesse, 'Fear and Fitness: An Evolutionary Analysis of Anxiety Disorders', *Ethology and Sociobiology*, Vol. 15, No. 5 (1994)

Andrea Verga, 'Acrophobia', *American Journal of Psychology*, Vol. 2, No. 1 (1888)

AEROPHOBIA

Julian Barnes, *Staring at the Sun* (London, 1986)

Gerd Gigerenzer, 'Dread Risk, September 11, and Fatal Traffic Accidents', *Psychological Science*, Vol. 15, No. 4 (2004)

Erica Jong, *Fear of Flying* (New York, 1973)

Margaret Oakes and Robert Bor, 'The Psychology of Fear of Flying (Part I): A Critical Evaluation of Current Perspectives on the Nature, Prevalence and Etiology of Fear of Flying', *Travel Medicine and Infectious Disease*, Vol. 8, No. 6 (2010)

—'The Psychology of Fear of Flying (Part II): A Critical Evaluation of Current Perspectives on Approaches to Treatment', *Travel Medicine and Infectious Disease*, Vol. 8, No. 6 (2010)

David Ropeik, 'How Risky is Flying?', *Nova*, 17 October 2006

Richard Sugden, 'Fear of Flying', in Jay S. Keystone et al. (eds), *Travel Medicine* (Missouri, 2008)

AGORAPHOBIA

J. H. Boyd and T. Crump, 'Westphal's Agoraphobia', *Journal of Anxiety Disorders*, Vol. 5, No. 1 (1991)

Paul Carter, *Repressed Spaces: The Poetics of Agoraphobia* (London, 2002)

CNN Transcripts, 'Larry King Live: Interview with Macaulay Culkin', 27 May 2004

Allan Compton, 'The Psychoanalytic View of Phobias Part I: Freud's Theories of Phobias and Anxiety', *Psychoanalytic Quarterly* (1992)

Helene Deutsch, 'The Genesis of Agoraphobia', *International Journal of Psychoanalysis*, Vol. 10 (1929)

Sigmund Freud, *New Introductory Lectures on Psychoanalysis*, trans. James Strachey (London, 1933)

Joshua Holmes, 'Building Bridges and Breaking Bridges: Modernity and Agoraphobia', *Opticon 1826*, Vol. 1, No. 1 (2006)

Klaus Kuch and Richard P. Swinson, 'What Westphal Really Said', *Canadian Journal of Psychiatry*, Vol. 37, No. 2 (1992)

John Lanchester, 'Diary', *London Review of Books*, 30 August 1990

Maureen C. McHugh, 'A Feminist Approach to Agoraphobia', in *Lectures on the Psychology of Women*, 3rd edn (New York, 1994)

Kathryn Milun, *Pathologies of Modern Space: Empty Space, Urban Anxiety, and the Recovery of the Public Self* (Abingdon, 2007)

Robert Seidenberg and Karen DeCrow, *Women Who Marry Houses: Panic and Protest in Agoraphobia* (New York, 1983)

Mabel Loomis Todd (ed.), *Letters of Emily Dickinson* (Boston, 1894)

David Trotter, 'Platz Angst', *London Review of Books*, 24 July 2003

—*The Uses of Phobia: Essays on Literature and Film* (Malden, Massachusetts, 2010)

Anthony Vidler, *Warped Space: Art, Architecture and Anxiety in Modern Culture* (Cambridge, Massachusetts, 2000)

Alex Williams, 'Generation Agoraphobia', *New York Times*, 16 October 2020

AIBOHPHOBIA

Stan Kelly-Bootle, *The Devil's DP Dictionary* (New York, 1981)

AILUROPHOBIA

H. L. Freeman and D. C. Kendrick, 'A Case of Cat Phobia: Treatment by a Method Derived from Experimental Psychology', in H. J. Eysenck (ed.), *Experiments in Behaviour Therapy: Readings in Modern Methods of Treatments of Mental Disorders Derived from Learning Theory* (Oxford, 1964)

G. Stanley Hall, 'A Synthetic Genetic Study of Fear: Part 2', *American Journal of Psychology*, Vol. 25, No. 3 (1914)

Don James McLaughlin, 'Infectious Affect: The Phobic Imagination in American Literature', PhD dissertation, University of Pennsylvania, Philadelphia (2017)

Silas Weir Mitchell, 'Of Ailurophobia and the Power to be Conscious of the Cat as Near, When Unseen and Unheard', *Transactions of the Association of American Physicians*, Vol. 20 (1905)

AQUAPHOBIA

Kevin Dawson, 'Parting the Waters of Bondage: African Americans' Aquatic Heritage', *International Journal of Aquatic Research and Education*, Vol. 11, No. 1 (2018)

J. Graham and E. A. Graffan, 'Fear of Water in Children and Adults: Etiology and Familial Effects', *Behaviour Research and Therapy*, Vol. 35, No. 2 (1997)

Carol Irwin et al., 'The Legacy of Fear: Is Fear Impacting Fatal and Non-Fatal Drowning of African American Children?', *Journal of Black Studies*, Vol. 42, No. 4 (2011)

Stanley J. Rachman, *Fear and Courage: A Psychological Perspective* (San Francisco, 1978)

ARACHNOPHOBIA

Karl Abraham, 'The Spider as a Dream Symbol' (1922), *Selected Papers on Psychoanalysis* (New York, 1953)

S. Binks, D. Chan and N. Medford, 'Abolition of Lifelong Specific Phobia: A Novel Therapeutic Consequence of Left Mesial Temporal Lobectomy', *Neurocase*, Vol. 21, No. 1 (2015)

Charlie Brooker, 'Forget Religious Fanatics: The Biggest Threat We Face Today has Eight Legs and is Hiding Behind My Telly', *Guardian*, 3 September 2007

Graham C. L. Davey, 'The "Disgusting" Spider: The Role of Disease and Illness in the Perpetuation of the Fear of Spiders', *Society and Animals*, Vol. 2, No. 1 (1994)

—'Arachnophobia – the "Disgusting' Spider", *Psychology Today*, 7 July 2014

Graham C. L. Davey et al., 'A Cross-Cultural Study of Animal Fears', *Behaviour Research and Therapy*, Vol. 36, Nos 7–8 (1998)

Jenny Diski, *What I Don't Know About Animals* (London, 2010)

Tim Flannery, 'Queens of the Web', *New York Review of Books*, 1 May 2008

Jeffrey A. Lockwood, *The Infested Mind: Why Humans Fear, Love and Loathe Insects* (Oxford, 2013)

Claire Charlotte McKechnie, 'Spiders, Horror, and Animal Others in Late Victorian Empire Fiction', *Journal of Victorian Culture*, Vol. 17, No. 4 (2012)

Paul Siegel, 'The Less You See: How We Can Unconsciously Reduce Fear', *Psychology Today*, 27 August 2018

Mick Smith, Joyce Davidson and Victoria L. Henderson, 'Geographies, Spiders, Sartre and "Magical Geographies": The Emotional Transformation of Space', *Transactions of the Institute of British Geographers*, Vol. 37, No. 1 (2012)

Marieke Soeter and Merel Kindt, 'An Abrupt Transformation of Phobic Behavior After a Post-Retrieval Amnesic Agent', *Biological Psychiatry*, Vol. 78, No. 12 (2015)

George W. Wood, *Glimpses into Petland* (London, 1863)

ARITHMOMANIA

George Frederick Abbott, *Macedonian Folklore* (London, 1903)

Nikki Rayne Craig, 'The Facets of Arithmomania', www.theodysseyonline.com/facets-arithmomania, 28 June 2016

Lennard J. Davis, *Obsession: A History* (Chicago, 2008)

Gilbert King, 'The Rise and Fall of Nikola Tesla and his Tower', *Smithsonian*, 4 February 2013

Sesame Street, Episodes 539 (22 November 1973) and 1970 (23 November 1984)

Daniel Hack Tuke, 'Imperative Ideas', *Brain*, Vol. 17 (1894)

BAMBAKOMALLOPHOBIA

Chris Hall, 'Can Anything Cure My Lifelong Fear of Cotton Wool?', *Guardian*, 10 November 2019

Mario Maj et al. (eds), *Phobias* (Hoboken, New Jersey, 2004)

Crystal Ponti, 'Investigating My Lifelong Phobia of Cotton Balls', *The Cut*, 19 July 2017

Lawrence Scott, private communication, November 2021

BATRACHOPHOBIA

Bruce A. Thyer and George C. Curtis, 'The Repeated Pretest-Posttest
Single-Subject Experiment: a New Design for Empirical Clinical
Practice', *Journal of Behaviour Therapy and Experimental
Psychiatry*, Vol. 14, No. 4 (1983)

John Locke, *An Essay Concerning Human Understanding* (London,
1690)

Marta Vidal, 'Portuguese Shopkeepers Using Ceramic Frogs to "Scare
Away" Roma', *Al Jazeera*, 4 February 2019

BEATLEMANIA

Garry Berman, *We're Going to See the Beatles!: An Oral History of
Beatlemania as Told by the Fans Who Were There* (Santa Monica,
California, 2008)

Barbara Ehrenreich, Elizabeth Hess, and Gloria Jacobs, 'Beatlemania:
A Sexually Defiant Consumer Subculture?', in Ken Gelder and Sarah
Thornton (eds), *The Subcultures Reader* (London, 1997)

Lisa A. Lewis, *The Adoring Audience: Fan Culture and Popular Media*
(London and New York, 1992)

Dorian Lynskey, 'Beatlemania: "The Screamers" and Other Tales of
Fandom', *Guardian*, 29 September 2013

Nicolette Rohr, 'Yeah Yeah Yeah: The Sixties Screamscape of
Beatlemania', *Journal of Popular Music Studies*, 28 June 2017

Julia Sneeringer, 'Meeting the Beatles: What Beatlemania Can Tell Us
About West Germany in the 1960s', *The Sixties: A Journal of History,
Politics and Culture*, Vol. 6, No. 2 (2013)

Shayna Thiel-Stern, *From the Dancehall to Facebook: Teen Girls, Mass
Media, and Moral Panic in the United States, 1905–2010* (Amherst,
Massachusetts, 2014)

BIBLIOMANIA

Nicholas A. Basbanes, *A Gentle Madness: Bibliophiles, Bibliomanes, and
the Eternal Passion for Books* (New York, 1995)

Philip Connell, 'Bibliomania: Book Collecting, Cultural Politics, and
the Rise of Literary Heritage in Romantic Britain', *Representations*,
No. 71 (2000)

Jeremy B. Dibbell, 'Not Wisely', *Fine Books and Collections*, February 2009

Thomas Frognall Dibdin, *Bibliomania, or Book Madness: A Bibliographical Romance* (London, 1876)

—*Reminiscences of a Literary Life* (London, 1836)

Isaac D'Israeli, 'Of Erudition and Philosophy', *Literary Miscellanies* (London, 1801)

Gustave Flaubert, 'Bibliomanie', *Le Colibri,* 12 February 1837

Holbrook Jackson, *The Anatomy of Bibliomania* (London, 1930)

C. G. Roland, 'Bibliomania', *Journal of the American Medical Association*, Vol. 212, No. 1 (1970)

BLOOD-INJECTION-INJURY PHOBIA

H. Stefan Bracha, O. Joseph Bienvenu and William W. Eaton, 'Testing the Paleolithic-Human-Warfare Hypothesis of Blood-Injection Phobia in the Baltimore ECA Follow-up Study – Towards a More Etiologically-Based Conceptualization for DSM-V', *Journal of Affective Disorders*, Vol. 97, Nos 1–3 (2007)

Josh M. Cisler, Bunmi O. Olatunji and Jeffrey M. Lohr, 'Disgust, Fear, and the Anxiety Disorders: A Critical Review', *Clinical Psychological Review*, Vol. 29, No. 1 (2009)

James G. Hamilton, 'Needle Phobia: A Neglected Diagnosis', *Journal of Family Practice*, Vol. 41, No. 2 (1995)

L. Öst and K Hellstrom, 'Blood-Injury-Injection Phobia' in Graham C. Davey (ed.), *Phobias: A Handbook of Theory, Research and Treatment* (Chichester and New York, 1997)

John Sanford, 'Blood, Sweat and Fears: A Common Phobia's Odd Pathophysiology', *Stanford Medicine* (Spring 2013)

BRONTOPHOBIA

George Miller Beard, *A Practical Treatise on Nervous Exhaustion (Neurasthenia): Its Symptoms, Nature, Sequences, Treatment* (New York, 1880)

D. J. Enright, *The Faber Books of Fevers and Frets* (London, 1989)

G. Stanley Hall, 'A Study of Fears', *American Journal of Psychology*, Vol. 8, No. 2 (1897)

Andrée Liddell and Maureen Lyons, 'Thunderstorm Phobias', *Behavioural Research and Therapy*, Vol. 16, No. 4 (1978)

Barry Lubetkin, 'The Use of a Planetarium in the Desensitisation of a Case of Bronto- and Astra-phobia', *Behavior Therapy*, Vol. 6 (1975)

Martin E. P. Seligman, 'Phobias and Preparedness', *Behavior Therapy*, Vol. 2 (July 1971)

CHOREOMANIA

Robert Bartholomew, 'Rethinking the Dancing Mania', *Skeptical Inquirer*, Vol. 24, No. 4 (2000)

Hilary Evans and Robert Bartholomew, *Outbreak! The Encyclopedia of Extraordinary Social Behavior* (San Antonio, Texas, 2009)

Kélina Gotman, *Choreomania: Dance and Disorder* (Oxford, 2018)

J. F. C. Hecker, *The Black Death and the Dancing Mania*, trans. B. G. Babington (London, 1894)

CLAUSTROPHOBIA

Benjamin Ball, 'On Claustrophobia', *British Medical Journal*, 6 September 1879

Edgar Jones, 'Shell Shock at Maghull and the Maudsley: Models of Psychological Medicine in the UK', *Journal of the History of Medicine and Allied Sciences*, Vol. 65, No. 3 (2010)

Don James McLaughlin, 'Infectious Affect: The Phobic Imagination in American Literature', PhD dissertation, University of Pennsylvania, Philadelphia (2017)

Stanley Rachman, 'Claustrophobia', in Graham C. Davey (ed.), *Phobias: A Handbook of Theory, Research and Treatment* (Chichester and New York, 1997)

Stanley Rachman and Steven Taylor, 'Analyses of Claustrophobia', *Journal of Anxiety Disorders*, Vol. 7 (1993)

W. H. R. Rivers, 'A Case of Claustrophobia', *The Lancet*, 18 August 1917

Siegfried Sassoon, *Counter-Attack, and Other Poems* (London, 1918)

Anthony Vidler, *Warped Space: Art, Architecture and Anxiety in Modern Culture* (Cambridge, Massachusetts, 2000)

Minna Vuohelainen, 'Cribb'd, Cabined, and Confined', *Journal of Literature and Science*, Vol. 3 (2010)

COULROPHOBIA

Anon., 'No More Clowning Around – It's Too Scary', *Nursing Standard*, Vol. 22, No. 19 (2008)

Katie Gibbons, 'To Help Child Patients, Send in the Clowns', *The Times*, 17 December 2020

Stephen King, *It* (New York, 1986)

Andrew McConnell Stott, 'Clowns on the Verge of a Nervous Breakdown: The Memoirs of Joseph Grimaldi', *Journal for Early Modern Cultural Studies*, Vol. 12, No. 4 (2012)

Craig Marine, 'Johnny Depp', *San Francisco Examiner*, 17 November 1999

Linda Rodriguez McRobbie, 'The History and Psychology of Clowns Being Scary', *Smithsonian Magazine*, 31 July 2013

Benjamin Radford, *Bad Clowns* (Albuquerque, New Mexico, 2016)

CYNOPHOBIA

Emma Brazell, 'China to Recognise Dogs as Pets and Not Food', *Metro* (London), 10 April 2020

S. E. Cassin, J. H. Riskind and N. A. Rector, 'Phobias', in V. S. Ramachandran (ed.), *Encyclopedia of Human Behavior* (Amsterdam, 2012)

L. Kevin Chapman, Sarah J. Kertz, Megan M. Zurlage and Janet Woodruff-Borden, 'A Confirmatory Factor Analysis of Specific Phobia Domains in African American and Caucasian American Young Adults', *Journal of Anxiety Disorders*, Vol. 22, No. 2 (2008)

Benoit Denizet-Lewis, 'The People Who Are Scared of Dogs', *Pacific Standard*, 24 July 2014

J. Gilchrist, J. J. Sacks, D. White and M.-J. Kresnow, 'Dog Bites: Still a Problem?', *Injury Prevention*, Vol. 14, No. 5 (2008)

Marian L. MacDonald, 'Multiple Impact Behaviour Therapy in Child's Dog Phobia', *Journal of Behavior Therapy and Experimental Psychiatry*, Vol. 6, No. 4 (1975)

Julia McKinnell, 'Big (Bad) Dogs', *Maclean's*, Vol. 120, No. 34 (2007)

Solomon Northup, *Twelve Years a Slave* (New York, 1853)

Timothy O. Rentz et al., 'Active Imaginal Exposure: Examination of a New Behavioral Treatment for Cynophobia (Dog Phobia)', *Behaviour Research and Therapy*, Vol. 41, No. 11 (2003)

Shontel Stewart, 'Man's Best Friend? How Dogs Have Been Used to
    Oppress African Americans', *Michigan Journal of Race and Law*,
    Vol. 25 (2020)

DEMONOMANIA

Jean-Étienne Esquirol, *Mental Maladies: A Treatise on Insanity*, trans.
    E. K. Hunt (London, 1845)

Hilary Evans and Robert Bartholomew, *Outbreak! The Encyclopedia of
    Extraordinary Social Behavior* (San Antonio, Texas, 2009)

Ruth Harris, 'Possession on the Borders: The "Mal de Morzine" in
    Nineteenth-Century France', *Journal of Modern History*, Vol. 69,
    No. 3 (1997)

Catherine-Laurence Maire, *Les Possédées de Morzine 1857–1873* (Paris,
    1981)

Allen S. Weiss, 'Narcissistic Machines and Erotic Prostheses', in Richard
    Allen and Malcolm Turvey (eds), *Camera Obscura, Camera Lucida*
    (Amsterdam, 2003)

DERMATILLOMANIA

Michael B. Brodin, 'Neurotic Excoriations', *Journal of the American
    Academy of Dermatology*, Vol. 63, No. 2 (2010)

Celal Calikusu and Ozlem Tecer, 'Skin Picking: Clinical Aspects', in Elias
    Aboujaoude and Lorrin M. Koran (eds), *Impulse Control Disorders*
    (Cambridge, 2010)

Jon E. Grant and Marc N. Potenza, *The Oxford Handbook of Impulse
    Control Disorders* (Oxford, 2011)

Jon E. Grant and Samuel R. Chamberlain, 'Prevalence of Skin Picking
    (Excoriation) Disorder', *Journal of Psychiatric Research*, Vol. 130
    (2020)

G. E. Jagger and W. R. Sterner, 'Excoriation: What Counsellors Need to
    Know about Skin Picking Disorder', *Journal of Mental Health
    Counseling*, Vol. 38, No. 4 (2016)

G. M. Mackee, 'Neurotic Excoriations', *Archives of Dermatology and
    Syphilology*, Vol. 1, No. 256 (1920)

DIPSOMANIA

Jean-Étienne Esquirol, *Mental Maladies: A Treatise on Insanity*, trans.
E. K. Hunt (London, 1845)

Friedrich-Wilhelm Kielhorn, 'The History of Alcoholism: Brühl-
Cramer's Concepts and Observations', *Addiction*, Vol. 91, No. 1
(1996)

Pierre Janet, 'On the Pathogenesis of Some Impulsions', *Journal of
Abnormal Psychology*, Vol. 1, No. 1 (1906)

Daniel Hack Tuke, *A Dictionary of Psychological Medicine*
(Philadelphia, 1892)

Mariana Valverde, *Diseases of the Will: Alcohol and the Dilemmas of
Freedom* (Cambridge, 1998)

DORAPHOBIA

G. Stanley Hall, 'A Study of Fears', *American Journal of Psychology*,
Vol. 8, No. 2 (1897)

Helen Thomson, 'Baby Used in Notorious Fear Experiment is Lost No
More', *New Scientist*, 1 October 2014

John B. Watson and Rosalie Rayner, 'Conditioned Emotional Reactions',
Journal of Experimental Psychology, Vol. 3, No. 1 (1920)

DROMOMANIA

Charlotte Brontë, *Jane Eyre* (London, 1847)

Ian Hacking, *Mad Travellers: Reflections on the Reality of Transient
Mental Illness* (Charlottesville, Virginia, 1998)

Sabrina Imbler, 'When Doctors Thought "Wanderlust" was a
Psychological Condition', *Atlas Obscura*, 15 April 2019

Pierre Janet, 'On the Pathogenesis of Some Impulsions', *Journal of
Abnormal Psychology*, Vol. 1, No. 1 (1906)

Sarah Mombert, 'Writing Dromomania in the Romantic Era: Nerval,
Collins and Charlotte Brontë', in Klaus Benesch and François Specq
(eds), *Walking and the Aesthetics of Modernity: Pedestrian Mobility
in Literature and the Arts* (New York, 2016)

G. Nicholson, *The Lost Art of Walking: The History, Science,
Philosophy, Literature, Theory and Practice of Pedestrianism*
(Chelmsford, Essex, 2011)

Emmanuel Régis, *A Practical Manual of Mental Medicine*, trans.
H. M. Bannister (New York, 1894)

Rebecca Solnit, *Wanderlust: A History of Walking* (New York, 2000)

Wilhelm Stekel, *Peculiarities of Behaviour: Wandering Mania,
Dipsomania, Cleptomania, Pyromania and Allied Impulsive Acts*,
trans. James S. Van Teslaar (New York, 1924)

EGOMANIA

Max Nordau, *Degeneration*, trans. Howard Fertig (London, 1895)

W. S. Walker, *Poetical Works* (London, 1852)

EMETOPHOBIA

Marcel A. van den Hout and Iris M. Engelhard, 'How Does EMDR
Work?', *Journal of Experimental Psychopathology*, Vol. 3, No. 5
(2012)

Ad de Jongh, 'Treatment of a Woman with Emetophobia: A Trauma
Focused Approach', *Mental Illness*, Vol. 4, No. 1 (2012)

Alexandra Keyes, Helen R. Gilpin and David Veale, 'Phenomenology,
Epidemiology, Co-Morbidity and Treatment of a Specific Phobia of
Vomiting: A Systematic Review of an Understudied Disorder',
Clinical Psychology Review, Vol. 60, Nos 15–31 (2018)

David Veale, Philip Murphy, Neil Ellison, Natalie Kanakam and Ana
Costa, 'Autobiographical Memories of Vomiting in People with a
Specific Phobia of Vomiting (Emetophobia)', *Journal of Behavior
Therapy and Experimental Psychiatry*, Vol. 44, No. 1 (2013)

ENTOMOPHOBIA

Anon., 'Celebrities' Secret Phobias Revealed', *Economic Times*,
7 July 2008

Steve Coll, 'The Spy Who Said Too Much', *New Yorker*, 1 April 2013

Millais Culpin, 'Phobias: With the History of a Typical Case', *The
Lancet*, 23 September 1922

Dani Fitzgerald, 'New Castle Native Who Served Prison Time for
Blowing Whistle on "Enhanced Interrogation Techniques" Shares
Story with Slippery Rock Crowd', *Beaver County Times*,
1 March 2018

Aurel Kolnai, *On Disgust*, edited by Carolyn Korsmeyer and Barry Smith (Chicago, 2004)

Julia Kristeva, *Powers of Horror: An Essay on Abjection*, trans. Leon Roudiez (New York, 1982)

Jeffrey A. Lockwood, *The Infested Mind: Why Humans Fear, Love and Loathe Insects* (Oxford, 2013)

William I. Miller, *The Anatomy of Disgust* (Cambridge, Massachusetts, 1997)

M. Schaller and L. A. Duncan, 'The Behavioral Immune System: Its Evolution and Social Psychological Implications', in J. P. Forgas, M. G. Haselton and W. von Hippel (eds), *Evolution and the Social Mind: Evolutionary Psychology and Social Cognition* (New York, 2007)

Mick Smith and Joyce Davidson, '"It Makes My Skin Crawl ..." The Embodiment of Disgust in Phobias of "Nature"', *Body & Society*, Vol. 12, No. 1 (2006)

US Senate Select Committee on Intelligence, *Committee Study of the Central Intelligence Agency's Detention and Interrogation Program* (Washington DC, 9 December 2014)

ERGOPHOBIA

Anon., 'Ergophobia: A Diagnosis', *The Bystander*, Vol. 6, No. 79 (1905)

Anon., 'New Name for Laziness', *Baltimore Sun*, 27 February 1905

W. D. Spanton, 'An Address on Ergophobia', *British Medical Journal*, 11 February 1905

EROTOMANIA

G. E. Berrios and N. Kennedy, 'Erotomania: A Conceptual History', *History of Psychiatry*, Vol. 52, No. 4 (2002)

Jean-Étienne Esquirol, *Mental Maladies: A Treatise on Insanity*, trans. E. K. Hunt (London, 1845)

Ian McEwan, *Enduring Love* (London, 1997)

Maria Teresa Tavares Rodriguez, Tomaz Valadas and Lucilla Eduarda Abrantes Bravo, 'De Clérambault's Syndrome Revisited: A Case Report of Erotomania in a Male', *BMC Psychiatry*, Vol. 20, No. 516 (2020)

Kate Summerscale, *Mrs Robinson's Disgrace: The Private Diary of a Victorian Lady* (London, 2012)

ERYTHROPHOBIA

Mark Axelrod, *Notions of the Feminine: Literary Essays from Dostoevsky to Lacan* (New York, 2015)

Edmund Bergler, 'A New Approach to the Therapy of Erythrophobia', *Psychoanalytic Quarterly*, Vol. 13, No. 1 (1944)

http://chronicblushinghelp.com (Q&A with Enrique Jadresic)

W. Ray Crozier, *Blushing and the Social Emotions: The Self Unmasked* (London, 2006)

—'The Puzzle of Blushing', *Psychologist*, Vol. 23 (2010)

Charles Darwin, *The Expression of the Emotions in Man and Animals* (London, 1872)

Alexander L. Gerlach, Karin Gruber, Frank H. Wilhelm and Walton T. Roth, 'Blushing and Physiological Arousability in Social Phobia', *Journal of Abnormal Psychology*, Vol. 2, Nos. 247–58 (2001)

G. Stanley Hall, 'A Synthetic Genetic Study of Fear: Part 1', *American Journal of Psychology*, Vol. 25, No. 2 (1914)

Leo Tolstoy, *Anna Karenina*, trans. Louise and Aylmer Maude (Oxford, 1980)

FYKIAPHOBIA

Otto Renik, 'Cognitive Ego Function in the Phobic Symptom', *Psychoanalytic Quarterly*, Vol. 41 (1972)

Charles A. Sarnoff, 'Symbols and Symptoms: Phytophobia in a Two-Year-Old Girl', *Psychoanalytic Quarterly*, Vol. 39 (1970)

GELOTOPHOBIA

Neelam Arjan Hiranandani and Xiao Dong Yue, 'Humour Styles, Gelotophobia and Self-Esteem Among Chinese and Indian University Students', *Asian Journal of Social Psychology*, Vol. 17, No. 4 (2014)

Graham Keeley, 'Britain has a Bad Case of Paranoia, Humour and Laughter Symposium is Told', *The Times*, 8 July 2009

R. Proyer, W. Ruch et al., 'Breaking Ground in Cross-Cultural Research on the Fear of Being Laughed At: A Multi-National Study Involving 73 Countries', *International Journal of Humor Research*, Vol. 22, Nos 1–2 (2009)

Willibald Ruch, 'Fearing Humor? Gelotophobia: The Fear of Being Laughed at, Introduction and Overview', *International Journal of Humor Research*, Vol. 22, Nos 1–2 (2009)

Grace Sanders, 'Fearing Laughter', *Psychologist*, 9 April 2021

Michael Titze, 'Gelotophobia: The Fear of Being Laughed At', *International Journal of Humor Research*, Vol. 22, Nos. 1–2 (2009)

GERASCOPHOBIA

J. M. Barrie, *Peter Pan, or The Boy Who Wouldn't Grow Up* (London, 1904)

Laurencia Perales-Blum, Myrthala Juárez-Treviño and Daniela Escobedo-Belloc, 'Severe Growing-Up Phobia, a Condition Explained in a 14-Year-Old Boy', *Case Reports in Psychiatry* (2014)

Oscar Wilde, *The Picture of Dorian Gray* (London, 1891)

GIFTOMANIA

Anon., 'Suffering from "Giftomania"', *Daily News* (London), 22 January 1897

GLOBOPHOBIA

Anon., '7 Korean Celebrities Terrifying Fears with Super Uncommon Phobias', koreaboo.com, 27 January 2018

Ken Lombardi, 'Oprah Winfrey Reveals Her Phobia of Balloons', *CBS News*, 10 September 2013

GLOSSOPHOBIA

Cicero, 'De Oratore', in *Cicero on Oratory and Orators*, trans. and ed. J. S. Watson (Carbondale, Illinois, 1970)

Karen Kangas Dwyer and Marlina M. Davidson, 'Is Public Speaking Really More Feared Than Death?' *Communication Research Reports*, Vol. 29, No. 2 (2012)

John Lahr, 'Petrified: The Horrors of Stage Fright', *New Yorker*, 28 August 2006

D. L. Rowland and J. J. D. M. van Lankveld, 'Anxiety and Performance in Sex, Sport, and Stage: Identifying Common Ground', *Frontiers in Psychology*, Vol. 10 (2019)

Kenneth Savitsky and Thomas Gilovich, 'The Illusion of Transparency and the Alleviation of Speech Anxiety', *Journal of Experimental Social Psychology*, Vol. 39, No. 6 (2003)

Jerry Seinfeld, *I'm Telling You for the Last Time*, HBO, 9 August 1998

GRAPHOMANIA

Lennard J. Davis, *Obsession: A History* (Chicago, 2008)

Tillie Elkins, 'Hypergraphia: A Two-Sided Affliction', *Doctor's Review*, September 2016

Max Nordau, *Degeneration*, trans. Howard Fertig (London, 1895)

Helen Thomson, 'Epilepsy Gives Woman Compulsion to Write Poems', *New Scientist*, 19 September 2014

HAPHEMANIA

Fred Penzel, 'Compulsion to Touch Things in OCD Cases', https://beyondocd.org/expert-perspectives/articles/a-touching-story\

Melissa C. Water, 'Reach Out and Touch It – Haphemania – OCD', Tourette Canada, 20 July 2019, https://tourette.ca/reach-out-and-touch-it-haphemania-ocd/

HAPHEPHOBIA

E. Weill and M. Lannois, *Note Sur un Cas D'Haphéphobie* (Lyon, 1892)

HIPPOPHOBIA

Harold P. Blum, 'Little Hans: A Centennial Review and Reconsideration', *Journal of the American Psychoanalytic Association*, 1 September 2007

Franco Borgogno, 'An "Invisible Man"? Little Hans Updated', *American Imago*, Vol. 65, No. 1 (Spring 2008)

Sigmund Freud, 'Analysis of a Phobia of a Five-Year-Old Boy', *Standard Edition of the Complete Psychological Works of Sigmund Freud, Vol X: The Cases of 'Little Hans' and the Rat Man (1909)*, trans. James Strachey (London, 1953–74)

Julia Kristeva, *Powers of Horror: An Essay on Abjection*, trans. Leon Roudiez (New York, 1982)

Francis Rizzo, 'Memoirs of an Invisible Man', *Opera News*, 5 February 1972

Jerome C. Wakefield, 'Max Graf's 'Reminiscences of Professor Sigmund Freud' Revisited: New Evidence from the Freud Archives', *Psychoanalytic Quarterly*, Vol. 76, No. 1 (2007)

HIPPOPOTOMONSTROSESQUIPEDIOPHOBIA
Dennis Coon and John O. Mitterer, *Introduction to Psychology: Exploration and Application* (Eagan, Minnesota, 1980)

HOMICIDAL MONOMANIA
J. P. Eigen, 'Delusion in the Courtroom: The Role of Partial Insanity in Early Forensic Testimony', *Medical History*, Vol. 35 (1991)

Jean-Étienne Esquirol, *Mental Maladies: A Treatise on Insanity*, trans. E. K. Hunt (London, 1845)

Michel Foucault, *Madness and Civilisation: A History of Insanity in the Age of Reason* (London, 1967)

Jan Goldstein, 'Professional Knowledge and Professional Self-Interest: The Rise and Fall of Monomania in 19th-Century France', *International Journal of Law and Psychiatry*, Vol. 21, No. 4 (1998)

David W. Jones, 'Moral Insanity and Psychological Disorder: The Hybrid Roots of Psychiatry', *History of Psychiatry*, Vol. 28, No. 3 (2017)

R. Smith, *Trial by Medicine: Insanity and Responsibility in Victorian Trials* (Edinburgh, 1981)

Kate Summerscale, *The Wicked Boy: The Mystery of a Victorian Child Murderer* (London, 2016)

HOMOPHOBIA
Lige Clarke and Jack Nichols, 'He-Man Horse-Shit', *Screw*, 23 May 1969

William Grimes, 'George Weinberg Dies at 86', *New York Times*, 22 March 2017

Gregory M. Herek, 'Beyond "Homophobia": Thinking About Sexual Prejudice and Stigma in the Twenty-First Century', *Sexuality Research and Social Policy*, Vol. 1, No. 2 (2004)

Amanda Hess, 'How "-Phobic" Became a Weapon in the Identity Wars', *New York Times*, 20 January 2016

Celia Kitzinger, 'Heteropatriarchal Language: the Case against "Homophobia"', *Gossip*, Vol. 5 (*c.*1986–88)

George Weinberg, 'Homophobia: Don't Ban the Word – Put it in the
    Index of Mental Disorders', *Huffington Post*, 12 June 2012
—*Society and the Healthy Homosexual* (New York, 1972)
Daniel Wickberg, 'Homophobia: On the Cultural History of an Idea',
    Critical Inquiry, Vol. 27, No. 1 (Autumn 2000)

HYDROPHOBIA

James Joyce, *Ulysses* (Paris, 1922)
Don James McLaughlin, 'Infectious Affect: The Phobic Imagination in
    American Literature', PhD dissertation, University of Pennsylvania,
    Philadelphia (2017)
Benjamin Rush, *Medical Inquiries and Observations*, Vol. 4
    (Philadelphia, 1798)

HYPNOPHOBIA

R. G. Mayne, *An Expository Lexicon of the Terms, Ancient and
    Modern, of Medical and General Science* (London, 1853)
Wilfred R. Pigeon and Jason C. DeViva, 'Is Fear of Sleep a Valid
    Construct and Clinical Entity?', *Sleep Medicines Review*, Vol. 55
    (2021)

HYPOPHOBIA

G. Stanley Hall, 'A Study of Fears', *American Journal of Psychology*,
    Vol. 8, No. 2 (1897)
Isaac M. Marks and Randolph M. Nesse, 'Fear and Fitness: An
    Evolutionary Analysis of Anxiety Disorders', *Ethology and
    Sociobiology*, Vol. 15, No. 5 (1994)

KAYAK PHOBIA

Ivan Lind Christensen and Søren Rud, 'Arctic Neurasthenia – the Case of
    Greenlandic Kayak Fear 1864–1940', *Social History of Medicine*, Vol.
    26, No. 3 (2013)
Zachary Gussow, 'A Preliminary Report of Kayak-Angst Among the
    Eskimo of West Greenland: A Study in Sensory Deprivation',
    International Journal of Social Psychiatry, Vol. 9 (1963)

Klaus Georg Hansen, 'Kayak Dizziness: Historical Reflections About a
  Greenlandic Predicament', *I FOLK, Journal of the Danish
  Ethnographic Society*, Vol. 37 (1996)

KLAZOMANIA

G. D. L. Bates, I. Lampert, M. Prendergast and A. E. Van Woerkom,
  'Klazomania: the Screaming Tic', *Neurocase*, Vol. 2, No. 1 (1996)
A. Hategan and J.A. Bourgeois, 'Compulsive Shouting (Klazomania)
  Responsive to Electroconvulsive Therapy', *Psychosomatics*, Vol. 54,
  No. 4 (2013)
William Pryse-Phillips, *Companion to Clinical Neurology* (Oxford,
  2009)

KLEPTOMANIA

Elaine A. Abelson, 'The Invention of Kleptomania', *Signs*, Vol. 15, No. 1
  (1989)
Anon., 'Homicidal Monomania', *Journal of Psychological Medicine and
  Mental Pathology*, Vol. 5, No. 20, 1 October 1852
Anon., 'Kleptomania', *The Lancet*, 16 November 1861
Clara Bewick Colby, 'Kleptomania and the Wife's Income', *Woman's
  Signal*, 31 December 1896
Jenny Diski, 'The Secret Shopper', *London Review of Books*, 26
  September 2011
Paul Dubuisson, *Les Voleuses de Grands Magasins* (Paris, 1902)
Ronald A. Fullerton and Girish N. Punj, 'Shoplifting as Moral Insanity:
  Historical Perspectives on Kleptomania', *Journal of Macromarketing*,
  Vol. 24, No. 1 (2004)
Carolynn S. Kohn, 'Conceptualisation and Treatment of Kleptomania
  Behaviors Using Cognitive and Behavioral Strategies', *International
  Journal of Behavioral Consultation and Therapy*, Vol. 2, No. 4 (2006)
Thomas Lenz and Rachel MagShamhráin, 'Inventing Diseases:
  Kleptomania, Agoraphobia and Resistance to Modernity', *Society*,
  Vol. 49 (2012)
Wilhelm Stekel, *Peculiarities of Behaviour: Wandering Mania,
  Dipsomania, Cleptomania, Pyromania and Allied Impulsive Acts*,
  trans. James S. Van Teslaar (New York, 1924)

—'The Sexual Root of Kleptomania', *Journal of Criminal Law and Criminology*, Vol. 2, No. 2 (1911)

Émile Zola, *The Ladies' Paradise*, trans. Brian Nelson (Oxford, 1995)

KOUMPOUNOPHOBIA

Anon., 'Button Phobia is Ruining My Life', *Metro* (London), 20 April 2008

Chris Hall, 'Can Anything Cure My Lifelong Fear of Cotton Wool?', *Guardian*, 10 November 2019

Anne Jolis, 'Steve Jobs's Button Phobia Has Shaped the World', *Spectator*, 22 November 2014

Kateri McRae, Bethany G. Ciesielski, Sean C. Pereira and James J. Gross, 'Case Study: A Quantitative Report of Early Attention, Fear, Disgust, and Avoidance in Specific Phobia for Buttons', *Cognitive and Behavioral Practice*, 18 September 2021

Lissette M. Saavedra and Wendy K. Silverman, 'Case Study: Disgust and a Specific Phobia of Buttons', *Journal of the American Academy of Child and Adolescent Psychiatry*, Vol. 41 (2002)

LAUGHING MANIA

Robert E. Bartholomew and Bob Rickard, *Mass Hysteria in Schools: A Worldwide History Since 1566* (McFarland, California, 2014)

Hilary Evans and Robert Bartholomew, *Outbreak! The Encyclopedia of Extraordinary Social Behavior* (San Antonio, Texas, 2009)

Suzanne O'Sullivan, 'The Healthy Child Who Wouldn't Wake Up: The Strange Truth of "Mystery" Illnesses', *Guardian*, 12 April 2021

—*The Sleeping Beauties: And Other Stories of Mystery Illness* (London, 2021)

LYPEMANIA

G. E. Berrios, 'The Psychopathology of Affectivity: Conceptual and Historical Aspects', *Psychological Medicine*, Vol. 15, No. 4 (1985)

Jean-Étienne Esquirol, *Mental Maladies: A Treatise on Insanity*, trans. E. K. Hunt (London, 1845)

MEGALOMANIA

Horatio Clare, *Heavy Light: A Journey Through Madness, Mania and Healing* (London, 2021)

Rebecca Knowles, Simon McCarthy-Jones and Georgina Rowse, 'Grandiose Delusions: A Review and Theoretical Integration of Cognitive and Affective Perspectives', *Clinical Psychology Review*, Vol. 31, No. 4 (2011)

MICROMANIA

Anon., 'Micromania', *Yorkshire Evening Post*, 22 September 1920

Lewis Carroll, *Alice's Adventures in Wonderland* (London, 1865)

Osman Farooq and Edward J. Fine, 'Alice in Wonderland Syndrome: A Historical and Medical Review', *Pediatric Neurology*, Vol. 77 (2017)

Caro W. Lippman, 'Certain Hallucinations Peculiar to Migraine', *Journal of Nervous and Mental Disease*, Vol. 116, No. 4 (1952)

H. Power, Leonard William Sedgwick and Robert Gray Mayne, *The New Sydenham Society Lexicon of Medicine and the Allied Sciences* (London, 1879)

MONOMANIA

Mary Elizabeth Braddon, *Lady Audley's Secret* (London, 1864)

Emily Brontë, *Wuthering Heights* (London, 1847)

Lennard J. Davis, *Obsession: A History* (Chicago, 2008)

Jean-Étienne Esquirol, *Mental Maladies: A Treatise on Insanity*, trans. E. K. Hunt (London, 1845)

Jean-Pierre Falret, *De la Nonexistence de la Monomanie* (Paris, 1854)

Jan Goldstein, 'Professional Knowledge and Professional Self-Interest: The Rise and Fall of Monomania in 19th-Century France', *International Journal of Law and Psychiatry*, Vol. 21, No. 4 (1998)

Herbert Melville, *Moby-Dick* (New York, 1851)

Edgar Allan Poe, 'Berenice', *Southern Literary Messenger*, March 1835

Lindsey Stewart, 'Monomania: The Life and Death of a Psychiatric Idea in Nineteenth-Century Fiction 1836–1860', PhD thesis, Open University (2018)

Kate Summerscale, *The Suspicions of Mr Whicher; or, The Murder at Road Hill House* (London, 2008)

Anthony Trollope, *He Knew He Was Right* (London, 1869)

MONOPHOBIA

George Miller Beard, *A Practical Treatise on Nervous Exhaustion (Neurasthenia): Its Symptoms, Nature, Sequences, Treatment* (New York, 1880)

G. Stanley Hall, 'A Study of Fears', *American Journal of Psychology*, Vol. 8, No. 2 (1897)

MUSOPHOBIA

Sigmund Freud, 'Notes Upon a Case of Obsessional Neurosis', *The Standard Edition of the Complete Psychological Works of Sigmund Freud, Vol X: The Cases of 'Little Hans' and the Rat Man (1909)*, trans. James Strachey (London, 1953–74)

George Orwell, *Nineteen Eighty-Four* (London, 1949)

D. J. Taylor, *Orwell: The Life* (London, 2003)

MYSOPHOBIA

Frederick Aardema, 'Covid-19, Obsessive-Compulsive Disorder and Invisible Life Forms that Threaten the Self', *Journal of Obsessive-Compulsive and Related Disorders*, Vol. 26 (2020)

Josh M. Cisler, Bunmi O. Olatunji and Jeffrey M. Lohr, 'Disgust, Fear, and the Anxiety Disorders: A Critical Review', *Clinical Psychological Review*, Vol. 29, No. 1 (2009)

Valerie Curtis, 'Why Disgust Matters', *Philosophical Transactions of the Royal Society of Biological Sciences*, Vol. 366, No. 1583 (2011)

Jean-Étienne Esquirol, *Mental Maladies: A Treatise on Insanity*, trans. E. K. Hunt (London, 1845)

Sigmund Freud, 'Fear and Anxiety', *A General Introduction to Psychoanalysis, Part 3: General Theory of the Neuroses*, trans. G. Stanley Hall (New York, 1920)

Cassandre Greenberg, 'Self-Exposure: Therapy and a Pandemic', *White Review*, August 2020

William A. Hammond, *Neurological Contributions* (New York, 1879)

Don James McLaughlin, 'Infectious Affect: The Phobic Imagination in American Literature', PhD dissertation, University of Pennsylvania, Philadelphia (2017)

Isaac Marks, 'Behavioral Treatments of Phobic and Obsessive-Compulsive Disorders: A Critical Appraisal', in (eds) Michel Hersen, Richard M. Eisler and Peter M. Miller, *Progress in Behavior Modification, Vol. 1* (Amsterdam, 1975)

Ira Russell, 'Mysophobia', *The Alienist and Neurologist*, Vol. 1, October 1880

MYTHOMANIA

Michèle Bertrand, 'Pathological Lying and Splitting of the Ego', *Revue Française de Psychanalyse*, Vol. 79, No. 1 (2015)

Emmanuel Carrère, *The Adversary: A True Story of Monstrous Deception* (London, 2001)

Helene Deutsch, 'On the Pathological Lie (Pseudologia Phantastica)', in *The Therapeutic Process, the Self, and Female Psychology* (New York, 1999)

Charles C. Dike, Madelson Baranoski and Ezra E.H. Griffith, 'Pathological Lying Revisited', *Journal of the American Academy of Psychiatry and Law*, Vol. 33 (2005)

William Healy and Mary Tenney Healy, 'Pathological Lying, Accusation, and Swindling', *Criminal Science Monographs No. 1* (1915)

Stephen Grosz, *The Examined Life: How We Lose and Find Ourselves* (London, 2013)

Andrew Hull, 'Pseudologia Fantastica: What is Known and What Needs To Be Known', *Forensic Scholars Today*, Vol. 3, No. 4 (2018)

Ranit Mishori, Hope Ferdowsian, Karen Naimer, Muriel Volpellier and Thomas McHale, 'The Little Tissue that Couldn't – Dispelling Myths about the Hymen's Role in Determining Sexual History and Assault', *Reproductive Health*, Vol. 16 (2019)

Kate Summerscale, *The Haunting of Alma Fielding* (London, 2020)

NOMOPHOBIA

Nicola Luigi Bragazzi and Giovanni del Puente, 'A Proposal for Including Nomophobia in the New DSM-V', *Psychology Research and Behavior Management*, Vol. 16, No. 7 (2014)

Amber Case, 'The Cell Phone and its Technosocial Sites of Engagement', PhD dissertation, Lewis and Clark College, 2007

Russell B. Clayton, Glenn Leshner and Anthony Almond, 'The Extended iSelf: The Impact of iPhone Cognition, Emotion, and Physiology', *Journal of Computer-Mediated Communication*, Vol. 20, No. 2 (2015)

Charlie D'Agata, 'Nomophobia: Fear of Being Without Your Cell Phone', *CBS News*, 3 April 2008

Keith Griffith, 'Cambridge Dictionary Reveals Its Word of the Year: Nomophobia', *Daily Mail*, 30 December 2018

Chuong Hock Ting and Yoke Yong Chen, 'Smartphone Addiction', in Ceclia A. Essau and Paul H. Delfabbro (eds), *Adolescent Addiction: Epidemiology, Assessment, and Treatment, 2nd Edition* (Cambridge, Massachusetts, 2020)

NYCTOPHOBIA

David Cohen, *J. B. Watson: The Founder of Behaviourism* (London, 1979)

George Devereux, 'A Note on Nyctophobia and Peripheral Vision', *Bulletin of the Menninger Clinic*, Vol. 13, No. 3 (1949)

Tim Edensor, *From Light to Dark: Daylight, Illumination, and Gloom* (Minnesota, 2017)

Sigmund Freud, 'Fear and Anxiety', *A General Introduction to Psychoanalysis, Part 3: General Theory of the Neuroses*, trans. G. Stanley Hall (New York, 1920)

Jocelynne Gordon, Neville J. King, Eleonora Gullone, Peter Muris and Thomas H. Ollendick, 'Treatment of Children's Nighttime Fears: The Need for a Modern Randomised Controlled Trial', *Clinical Psychology Review*, Vol. 27, No. 1 (2007)

G. Stanley Hall, 'A Study of Fears', *American Journal of Psychology*, Vol. 8, No. 2 (1897)

David A. Kipper, 'In Vivo Desensitization of Nyctophobia: Two Case Reports', *Psychotherapy*, Vol. 17, No. 1 (1980)

Peter Muris, Harald Merckelbach, Thomas Hollendick, Neville J. King and Nicole Bogie, 'Children's Nighttime Fears: Parent–Child Ratings of Frequency, Content, Origins, Coping Behaviors and Severity', *Behaviour Research and Therapy*, Vol. 39, No. 1 (2001)

NYMPHOMANIA

Lilybeth Fontanesi et al., 'Hypersexuality and Trauma: A Mediation and Moderation Model From Psychopathology to Problematic Sexual Behavior', *Journal of Affective Disorders*, Vol. 281 (2021)

R. B. Gartner, *Betrayed as Boys: Psychodynamic Treatment of Sexually Abused Men* (New York, 1999)

J. R. Giugliano, 'Sex Addiction as a Mental Health Diagnosis: Coming Together or Coming Apart?', *Sexologies*, Vol. 22, No. 3 (2013)

Carol Groneman, *Nymphomania: A History* (New York, 2001)

—'Nymphomania: The Historical Construction of Female Sexuality', *Signs*, Vol. 19, No. 2 (1994)

Barry Reay, Nina Attwood and Claire Gooder, *Sex Addiction: A Critical History* (Cambridge, England, 2015)

Sarah W. Rodriguez, 'Rethinking the History of Female Circumcision and Clitoridectomy: American Medicine and Female Sexuality in the Late Nineteenth Century', *Journal of the History of Medicine and Allied Sciences*, Vol. 63, No. 3 (2008)

Keren Skegg, Shyamala Nada-Raja, Nigel Dickson and Charlotte Paul, 'Perceived "Out of Control" Sexual Behavior in a Cohort of Young Adults from the Dunedin Multidisciplinary Health and Development Study', *Archives of Sexual Behavior*, Vol. 39, No. 4 (2009)

ODONTOPHOBIA

Dina Gordon, Richard G. Heimberg, Marison I. Tellez and Amid I. Ismail, 'A Critical Review of Approaches to the Treatment of Dental Anxiety in Adults', *Journal of Anxiety Disorders*, Vol. 27, No. 4 (2013)

Isaac M. Marks and Randolph M. Nesse, 'Fear and Fitness: An Evolutionary Analysis of Anxiety Disorders', *Ethology and Sociobiology*, Vol. 15, No. 5 (1994)

Rosa de Stefano, 'Psychological Factors in Dental Patient Care: Odontophobia', *Medicina*, Vol. 55, No. 10 (2019)

ONIOMANIA

Jean Harvey Baker, *Mary Todd Lincoln: A Biography* (New York, 1987)

Bernardo Dell'Osso, Andrea Allen and A. Carlo Altamura, 'Impulsive-Compulsive Buying Disorder: Clinical Overview', *Australian and New Zealand Journal of Psychiatry*, Vol. 42, No. 4 (2008)

Darian Leader, *Strictly Bipolar* (London, 2013)

ONOMATOMANIA

Daniel Hack Tuke, 'Imperative Ideas', *Brain*, Vol. 17 (1894)

ONYCHOTILLOMANIA

Evan A. Rieder and Antonella Tosti, 'Onychotillomania: An Underrecognized Disorder', *Journal of the American Academy of Dermatology*, Vol. 75, No. 6 (2016)

Ivar Snorrason and Douglas W. Woods, 'Nail Picking Disorder (Onychotillomania): A Case Report', *Journal of Anxiety Disorders*, Vol. 28, No. 2 (2014)

OPHIDIOPHOBIA

Stephen T. Asma, 'Monsters on the Brain: An Evolutionary Epistemology of Horror', *Social Research*, Vol. 81, No. 4 (2014)

Charles Darwin, *The Expression of the Emotions in Man and Animals* (London, 1872)

G. Stanley Hall, 'A Synthetic Genetic Study of Fear: Part 2', *American Journal of Psychology*, Vol. 25, No. 3 (1914)

Lynne A. Isbell, 'Snakes as Agents of Evolutionary Change in Primate Brains', *Journal of Human Evolution*, Vol. 51 (2006)

—*The Fruit, the Tree, and the Serpent: Why We See So Well* (Harvard, Massachusetts, 2009)

Arne Öhman and Susan Mineka, 'Fears, Phobias, and Preparedness: Towards an Evolved Module of Fear and Fear Learning', *Psychological Review*, Vol. 108, No. 3 (2001)

—'The Malicious Serpent: Snakes as a Prototypical Stimulus for an Evolved Module of Fear', *Current Directions in Psychology*, Vol. 12, No. 1 (2003)

Arne Öhman, 'Phobia and Human Evolution', in Larry R. Squire (ed.), *Encyclopedia of Neuroscience* (London, 2009)

ORNITHOPHOBIA

Dell Catherall, 'Birdwoman: Or My Fear of Feathers', *Globe and Mail*, 20 March 2015

Adam Phillips, *On Kissing, Tickling, and Being Bored: Psychoanalytic Essays on the Unexamined Life* (London, 1998)

S. Pink, '1D Crisis as Birds Flock to US Gigs: Exclusive Niall Pigeon Phobia Flap', *Sun*, 30 March 2012

OSMOPHOBIA

Duika L. Burges Watson, Miglena Campbell, Claire Hopkins, Barry Smith, Chris Kelly and Vincent Deary, 'Altered Smell and Taste: Anosmia, Parosmia and the Impact of Long Covid-19', *PLOS ONE*, 24 September 2021

Ahmad Chitsaz, Abbas Ghorbani, Masoumed Dashti, Mohsen Khosravi and Mohammedreza Kianmehr, 'The Prevalence of Osmophobia in Migrainous and Episodic Tension Type Headaches', *Advanced Biomedical Research*, Vol. 6, No. 44 (2017)

OVOPHOBIA

Oriana Fallaci, *The Egotists: Sixteen Surprising Interviews* (Chicago, 1963)

Casey McCittrick, *Hitchcock's Appetites: The Corpulent Plots of Desire and Dread* (London, 2016)

PANTOPHOBIA

Wilhelm Stekel, *Peculiarities of Behaviour: Wandering Mania, Dipsomania, Cleptomania, Pyromania and Allied Impulsive Acts*, trans. James S. Van Teslaar (New York, 1924)

PEDIOPHOBIA

Ernst Jentsch, 'On the Psychology of the Uncanny', (1906), trans. Roy Sellars, in Jo Collins and John Jervis (eds), *Uncanny Modernity* (London, 2008)

Rachana Pole and G. K. Vankar, 'Doll Phobia – Single Session Therapy', *Archives of Indian Psychiatry*, Vol. 13 (2013)

Leo Rangell, 'The Analysis of a Doll Phobia', *International Journal of Psycho-Analysis*, Vol. 33 (1952)

Laura Spinney, 'Spooked? Locating the Uncanny Valley', *New Scientist*, 29 October 2016

Kate Summerscale, *The Queen of Whale Cay: The Extraordinary Life of 'Joe' Carstairs, the Fastest Woman on Water* (London, 1997)

PHONOPHOBIA

Zamzil Amin Asha'ari, Nora Mat Zain and Ailin Razali, 'Phonophobia and Hyperacusis: Practical Points from a Case Report', *Malaysian Journal of Medical Science*, Vol. 17, No. 1 (2010)

Jody Doherty-Cove, 'Fight in Sussex over Person "Eating Too Loudly",' *Brighton Argus*, 27 July 2021

Sukhbinder Kumar et al., 'The Brain Basis for Misophonia', *Current Biology*, 2 February 2017

PLUTOMANIA

Nick D'Alton, 'The American Planet', *American History*, Vol. 40, No. 4 (2005)

Edwin Lawrence Godkin, 'Who Will Pay the Bills of Socialism?' *The Forum*, Vol. 17 (1894)

Thomas Urquhart, 'Ekskybalauron' (1652), *Tracts of the Learned and Celebrated Antiquarian Sir Thomas Urquhart of Cromarty* (Edinburgh, 1774)

PNIGNOPHOBIA

Richard J. McNally, 'Choking Phobia: A Review of the Literature', *Comprehensive Psychiatry*, Vol. 35, No. 1 (1994)

Lars-Göran Öst, 'Cognitive Therapy in the Case of Choking Phobia', *Behavioural Psychotherapy*, Vol. 20 (1992)

POGONOPHOBIA

Valerie A. Curtis, 'Dirt, Disgust and Disease: A Natural History of Hygiene', *Journal of Epidemiological Community Health*, Vol. 61, No. 8 (2007)

Roald Dahl, *The Twits* (London, 1980)

Sam Jones, 'Disney Lifts Beard Ban for Workers', *Guardian*, 24 January 2012

Ed Lowther, 'A History of Beards in the Workplace', *BBC News*,
14 August 2013

Danielle Sheridan, 'Why Roald Dahl Bristled at the Sight of Beards',
The Times (London), 12 September 2015

David A. Smith and James M. Willson, 'Affairs Abroad', *Covenanter*,
Vol. 7 (1851)

Alun Withey, *Concerning Beards: Facial Hair, Health and Practice in
England 1650–1900* (London, 2021)

POPCORN PHOBIA

College of Curiosity, 'Popcorn (Maizophobia)', *Pantophobia*, Episode 5,
28 March 2016

Mary Douglas, *Purity and Danger: An Analysis of the Concept of
Pollution and Taboo* (London, 1966)

PTERONOPHOBIA

G. Stanley Hall, 'A Study of Fears', *American Journal of Psychology*,
Vol. 8, No. 2 (1897)

PUBLIC URINATION PHOBIA

Mark Hay, 'How People Deal with Having Shy Bladder Syndrome', *Vice*,
31 May 2018

Kenley L. J. Kuoch, Denny Meyer, David W. Austin and Simon R.
Knowles, 'A Systematic Review of Paruresis: Clinical Implications and
Future Directions', *Journal of Psychosomatic Research*, Vol. 98 (2017)

PYROMANIA

American Psychiatric Association, *Diagnostic and Statistical Manual 5*
(Washington DC, 2013)

Jonathan Andrews, 'From Stack-Firing to Pyromania: Medico-Legal
Concepts of Insane Arson in British, US and European Contexts,
*c.*1800–1913', *History of Psychiatry*, Vol. 21 (2010)

Lydia Dalhuisen, 'Pyromania in Court: Legal Insanity versus Culpability
in Western Europe and the Netherlands (1800–1950)', *International
Journal of Law and Psychiatry*, Vol. 58 (2008)

Jean-Étienne Esquirol, *Mental Maladies: A Treatise on Insanity*, trans.
E. K. Hunt (London, 1845)

Sigmund Freud, 'The Acquisition of Power over Fire', *International Journal of Psychoanalysis*, Vol. 13 (1932)

Jeffrey L. Geller, Jonathon Eden and Rosa Lynn Pinkus, 'A Historical Appraisal of America's Experience with "Pyromania" – a Diagnosis in Search of a Disorder', *International Journal of Law and Psychiatry*, Vol. 9 (1986)

J. E. Grant, N. Thomarios and B. L. Odlaug, 'Pyromania', in George Koob (ed.), *Encyclopedia of Behavioural Neuroscience* (Vancouver, 2010)

Nolan D. C. Lewis and Helen Yarnell, *Pathological Fire-Setting (Pyromania)* (New York, 1951)

Wilhelm Stekel, *Peculiarities of Behaviour: Wandering Mania, Dipsomania, Cleptomania, Pyromania and Allied Impulsive Acts*, trans. James S. Van Teslaar (New York, 1924)

Sarah Wheaton, 'Memoirs of a Compulsive Firesetter', published online on 1 August 2001 at ps.psychiatryonline.org/doi/full/10.1176/appi.ps.52.8.1035

SEDATEPHOBIA

Bruce Fell, 'Bring the Noise: Has Technology Made Us Scared of Silence?' *The Conversation*, 30 December 2012

Imke Kirste, Zeina Nicola, Golo Kronenberg and Tara L. Walker, 'Is Silence Golden? Effects of Auditory Stimuli and their Absence on Adult Hippocampal Neurogenesis', *Brain Structure and Function*, Vol. 220 (2015)

SIDERODROMOPHOBIA

George Miller Beard, *A Practical Treatise on Nervous Exhaustion (Neurasthenia): Its Symptoms, Nature, Sequences, Treatment* (New York, 1880)

Sigmund Freud, *Three Essays on the Theory of Sexuality*, trans. James Strachey (London, 1949)

Laura Marcus, *Dreams of Modernity: Psychoanalysis, Literature, Cinema* (Cambridge, England, 2014)

Malcolm Alexander Morris, *The Book of Health* (London, 1884)

Peter L. Rudnytsky, *Reading Psychoanalysis: Freud, Rank, Ferenczi, Groddeck* (Cornell, Ithaca, 2002)

SOCIAL PHOBIA

George Miller Beard, *A Practical Treatise on Nervous Exhaustion (Neurasthenia): Its Symptoms, Nature, Sequences, Treatment* (New York, 1880)

Xinyin Chen, Kenneth H. Rubin and Boshu Li, 'Social and School Adjustment of Shy and Aggressive Children in China', *Development and Psychopathology*, Vol. 7, No. 2 (1995)

Pierre Janet, *Obsessions and Psychasthenia* (Paris, 1903)

Christopher Lane, *Shyness: How Normal Behavior Became a Sickness* (New Haven, 2007)

Helen Saul, *Phobias: Fighting the Fear* (London, 2001)

SYLLOGOMANIA

Charles Dickens, *Bleak House* (London, 1853)

E. L. Doctorow, *Homer and Langley* (London, 2009)

Erich Fromm, *Man for Himself: An Inquiry into the Psychology of Ethics* (New York, 1947)

Randy O. Frost and Gail Steketee, *Stuff: Compulsive Hoarding and the Meaning of Things* (New York, 2010)

Nikolai Gogol, *Dead Souls*, trans. Richard Pevear (London, 1997)

Scott Herring, *The Hoarders: Material Deviance in Modern American Culture* (Chicago, 2014)

Allan V. Horwitz, *Creating Mental Illness* (Chicago, 2002)

Janet Malcolm, *The Silent Woman: Sylvia Plath and Ted Hughes* (New York, 1993)

Kenneth J. Weiss, 'Hoarding, Hermitage, and the Law: Why We Love the Collyer Brothers', *Journal of the American Academy of Psychiatry and the Law*, Vol. 38, No. 2 (2010)

TAPHEPHOBIA

Jan Bondeson, *Buried Alive: The Terrifying History of Our Most Primal Fear* (New York, 2001)

Matt Moffett, 'A Man Called Freud Can't Keep His Phobia Buried', *Wall Street Journal*, 31 October 2008

Enrico Morselli, 'Dysmorphophobia and Taphephobia: Two Hitherto Undescribed Forms of Insanity with Fixed Ideas' [English translation of a paper of 1891], *History of Psychiatry*, Vol. 12, No. 45 (2001)

Edgar Allan Poe, 'The Premature Burial', *Philadelphia Dollar Newspaper*, July 1844

TELEPHONOPHOBIA
Anon., 'Gossip', *Merthyr Express*, 8 November 1913
Australian Associated Press, 'Queen Mary Fears Phones', *Sun* (Sydney), 12 March 1953
Daisy Buchanan, 'Wondering Why That Millennial Won't Take Your Phone Call? Here's Why', *Guardian*, 26 August 2016
Sigmund Freud, *Civilisation and its Discontents* (London, 1930)
Robert Graves, *Goodbye to All That* (London, 1929)
Rob Stott, 'Telephonophobia: It's a Real Thing', *Now Associations,* 11 October 2013
David Trotter, *The Uses of Phobia: Essays on Literature and Film* (Malden, Massachusetts, 2010)
John Zilcosky, *Kafka's Travels: Exoticism, Colonialism and the Traffic of Writing* (London, 2004)

TETRAPHOBIA
Anon., 'Nothing to Fear … But Four Itself', *Economist*, 5 December 2015
Anon., 'Tetraphobia and Doing Business in Asia', *Acclaro*, 4 April 2012
Jo Chim, 'Tetraphobia: Overcoming My Fear of Four', 24 August 2020, medium.com/@jochim/tetraphobia-15778da79bd1
David P. Philips, George C. Liu, Kennon Kwok, Jason R. Jarvinen, Wei Zhang and Ian S. Abramson, 'The *Hound of the Baskervilles* Effect: A Natural Experiment on the Influence of Psychological Stress on the Timing of Stress', *British Medical Journal*, 22 December 2001

THALASSOPHOBIA
Seán J. Harrington, 'The Depths of Our Experience: Thalassophobia and the Oceanic Horror', in Jon Hackett, and Seán Harrington (eds), *Beasts of the Deep: Sea Creatures and Popular Culture* (London, 2018)
Alan J. Jamieson, Glenn Singleman, Thomas D. Linley and Susan Casey, 'Fear and Loathing of the Deep Ocean: Why Don't People Care About the Deep Sea?', *ICES Journal of Marine Science*, 21 December 2020

H. P. Lovecraft, 'Dagon', *The Vagrant*, No. 11 (1919)

Kate Lyons, 'Mining's New Frontier: Pacific Nations Caught in the Rush for Deep-Sea Riches', *Guardian*, 23 June 2021

TOKOPHOBIA

Kristina Hofberg and Ian Brockington, 'Tokophobia: An Unreasoning Dread of Childbirth', *British Journal of Psychiatry*, Vol. 176, No. 1 (2000)

Laura Jacobs, 'The Devil Inside: Watching *Rosemary's Baby* in the Age of #MeToo', *Vanity Fair*, 31 May 2018

Ashley Lauretta, 'Too Afraid to Have a Baby', *The Atlantic*, 29 June 2016

Maeve A. O'Connell, Patricia Leahy-Warren, Ali S. Khashan, Louise C. Kenny and Sinéad M. O'Neill, 'Worldwide Prevalence of Tocophobia in Pregnant Women: Systematic Review and Meta-Analysis', *Acta Obstetricia et Gynecologica Scandinavica*, 30 March 2017

P. Slade, K. Balling, K. Sheen and G. Houghton, 'Establishing a Valid Construct of Fear of Childbirth: Findings from In-Depth Interviews with Women and Midwives', *BMC Pregnancy and Childbirth*, Vol. 19 (2019)

TRICHOMANIA

Charles Baudelaire, *Le Spleen de Paris*, trans. Cat Nilan (Paris, 1999)

Robert Graves, *The Common Asphodel* (London, 1949)

Richard von Krafft-Ebing, *Psychopathia Sexualis: A Clinical-Forensic Study*, trans. Charles Gilbert Chaddock (London, 1894)

TRICHOTILLOMANIA

Bridget Bradley, and Stefan Ecks, 'Disentangling Family Life and Hair Pulling', *Medical Anthropology*, Vol. 10 (2018)

Hemali Chhapia, 'Ordinary Jains into Extreme Penance: Every Hair Pulled Out', *Times of India*, 19 August 2012

François Henri Hallopeau, 'Alopecia par Grattage (Trichomania ou Trichotillomania)', *Annales de Dermatologie et Syphilologie*, Vol. 10 (1889)

Pierre Janet, 'On the Pathogenesis of Some Impulsions', *Journal of Abnormal Psychology*, Vol. 1, No. 1 (1906)

Miri Keren, Adi Ron-Miara, Ruth Feldman and Samuel Tyano, 'Some Reflections on Infancy-Onset Trichotillomania', *Psychoanalytic Study of Childhood*, Vol. 61 (2006)

Jemima Khan, 'Beautiful Women Who Tear Out Their Hair', *The Times* (London), 22 February 2009

Daniela G. Sampaio and Jon E. Grant, 'Body-Focused Repetitive Behaviors and the Dermatology Patient', *Clinical Dermatology*, Vol. 36, No. 6 (2018)

S. Swedo and J. Rapoport, 'Trichotillomania', *Journal of Child Psychology and Psychiatry and Allied Disciplines*, Vol. 32 (1991)

TRISKAIDEKAPHOBIA

Melissa Chan, 'Why Friday the 13th Is a Real Nightmare for Some People', *Time*, 13 October 2017

Scott Grier and Alex R. Manara, 'Admission to Bed 13 in the ICU Does Not Reduce the Chance of Survival', *Journal of Critical Care*, Vol. 48 (2018)

Brian Handwerk and John Roach, 'Where Our Fear of Friday the 13th Came From', *National Geographic*, 13 November 2015

TULIPOMANIA

Hilary Evans and Robert Bartholomew, *Outbreak! The Encyclopedia of Extraordinary Social Behavior* (San Antonio, Texas, 2009)

Anne Goldgar, *Tulipmania: Money, Honor, and Knowledge in the Dutch Golden Age* (Chicago, 2007)

Charles Mackay, *Extraordinary Popular Delusions and the Madness of Crowds* (London, 1841)

TRYPOPHOBIA

Jennifer Abbasi, 'Is Trypophobia a Real Phobia?', *Popular Science*, 25 July 2011

Anon., 'Living with Trypophobia: a Fear of Honeycomb-Like Patterns', *USNews.com*, 30 October 2017

Chrissie Giles, 'Why Do Holes Horrify Me?', *Mosaic*, Wellcome, 12 November 2019

Tom R. Kupfer and An T. D. Le, 'Disgusting Clusters: Trypophobia as an Overgeneralised Disease Avoidance Response', *Cognition and Emotion*, Vol. 32, No. 4 (2018)

Juan Carlos Martinez-Aguayo et al., 'Trypophobia: What Do We Know So Far? A Case Report and Comprehensive Review of the Literature', *Frontiers in Psychiatry*, Vol. 9 (2018)

Ali Szubiak, 'Kendall Jenner Suffers From "Really Bad" Trypophobia', *Popcrush*, 18 August 2016

XENOPHOBIA

David M. Amodio, 'The Neuroscience of Prejudice and Stereotyping', *Neuroscience*, Vol. 15 (2014)

Joanna Bourke, *Fear: A Cultural History* (London, 2005)

Amanda Hess, 'How "-Phobic" Became a Weapon in the Identity Wars', *New York Times*, 20 January 2016

Joost Abraham Mauritis Meerloo, *Aftermath of Peace: Psychological Essays* (New York, 1946)

Mark Schaller, 'The Behavioural Immune System and the Psychology of Human Sociality', *Philosophical Transactions of the Royal Society of Biological Sciences*, 12 December 2011

XYLOPHOBIA

David Alegre Lorenz, 'Fear and Loathing on the Eastern Front: Soviet Forests and the Memory of Western Europeans in the German Military Forces, 1941–1944', *Journal of Modern European History*, Vol. 19, No. 1 (2021)

ZOOPHOBIA

Graham C. L. Davey et al., 'A Cross-Cultural Study of Animal Fears', *Behaviour Research and Therapy*, Vol. 36 (1998)

Jakub Polák, Silvie Rádlová et al., 'Scary and Nasty Beasts: Self-Reported Fear and Disgust of Common Phobic Animals', *British Journal of Psychology*, 11 June 2019

Vincent Taschereau-Dumouchel et al., 'Towards an Unconscious Neural Reinforcement Intervention for Common Fears', *Proceedings of the National Academy of Sciences of the United States of America*, Vol. 114, No. 13 (2018)

ACKNOWLEDGEMENTS

I am so grateful to everyone who talked to me about this book or read parts of it – especially through the long stretches of lockdown – among them Anjana Ahuja, Hal Currey, Graham Davey, Rose Dempsey, Shomit Dutta, Miranda Fricker, Victoria Lane, Sinclair McKay, Ruth Metzstein, Robert Randall, John Ridding, Laurence Scott, Sophie Scott, Wycliffe Stutchbury, Ben Summerscale, Juliet Summerscale and Frances Wilson. My thanks to the staff at the Wellcome Collection and the British Library, and to Martha Stutchbury for her wonderful research.

Thank you to all those who helped produce the book, most of all my brilliant editor Francesca Barrie at Wellcome Collection, and also Alex Elam, Andrew Franklin, Graeme Hall, Pete Dyer, Hannah Ross, Rosie Parnham, Jack Murphy, Claire Beaumont and Ellen Johl at Profile Books, and Ann Godoff, Virginia Smith Younce and Caroline Sydney at Penguin Press. Thank you to Kate Johnson for her superb copy-editing, and to Nathan Burton and James Alexander for design. Huge thanks as ever to my literary agents Georgia Garrett and Melanie Jackson, and to Honor Spreckley. This book is dedicated with love to my son Sam.

PHOBIAS

MANIAS